Model-Driven Ar

Oscar Pastor · Juan Carlos Molina

Model-Driven Architecture in Practice

A Software Production Environment Based on Conceptual Modeling

With 48 Figures and 35 Tables

Springer

Authors

Oscar Pastor
DSIC, Universitad Politécnica de Valencia
Camino de Vera s/n
46022 Valencia, Spain
opastor@dsic.upv.es

Juan Carlos Molina
CARE Technologies, S.A.
Pda. Madrigueres Sud, 44
03700 Denia, Spain

ISBN 978-3-642-09094-3   e-ISBN 978-3-540-71868-0

ACM Computing Classification (1998): D.2, I.6, H.1, J.6

Springer is a part of Springer Science+Business Media

springer.com

© Springer-Verlag Berlin Heidelberg 2010

Cover design: KünkelLopka Werbeagentur, Heidelberg

Printed on acid-free paper   45/3100/YL - 5 4 3 2 1 0

To Carmen, Oscar and Daniel, Regina and Oscar...
Past, Present and Futur, all together making me easy
to face the fascinating challenge of life

Oscar Pastor

To Belén, for everything. You enlighten my life.
To my parents, sisters and brother, for being so wonderful and supportive.

Juan Carlos Molina

To everybody, past and present, at CARE Technologies and Integranova.
You have turned the ideas in this book into a solid working reality.

To José Miguel Barberá, for his guidance and comradeship.

To Siegfried Borho, for his enduring vision and spirit.

Juan Carlos Molina and Oscar Pastor

Contents

Part I The OO-Method and Software Production from Models

1 Let's Get Philosophical 3

2 The Purpose of this Work 7

3 The Need for New Development Environments 13
   3.1 Software Development Today 14
        3.1.1 Current Tools Are Inadequate 14
        3.1.2 Development Processes Are Negatively Affected 15
   3.2 Better Development Environments Are Needed 16

4 Object-Oriented Modelling as the Starting Point 19
   4.1 The Chosen Model 19
   4.2 Key Aspects of the Desired Method 21
        4.2.1 Cataloguing of Conceptual Patterns 22
        4.2.2 Enriching the Object Model 28
        4.2.3 Software Architecture: Architectural Patterns 32

5 The OO-Method 39
   5.1 Historical Background 39
   5.2 General Features of the OO-Method 42
   5.3 Other Approaches 43

Part II Conceptual Modelling: About the Problem Space

6 Conceptual Modelling Primitives 49
   6.1 Conceptual Modelling. The Four Models 52

7   Object Model.. 55
     7.1   Classes 55
           7.1.1   Attributes 58
           7.1.2   Services 62
           7.1.3   Integrity Constraints 73
     7.2   Relationships Between Classes 75
           7.2.1   Agents and Agent Relationships 76
           7.2.2   Association, Aggregation, and Composition 80
           7.2.3   Specialisation 95
           7.2.4   Parallel Composition 104
           7.2.5   Visibility Between Related Classes 106
     7.3   Complexity Management 111

8   Dynamic Model 115
     8.1   State Transition Diagram 116
           8.1.1   States 117
           8.1.2   Transitions 118
           8.1.3   Basic Statechart Diagram 120
           8.1.4   Managing Complexity in State Transition Diagrams 121
           8.1.5   Operations and State Transition Diagrams 122
           8.1.6   Specialisation and State Transition Diagrams 123
     8.2   Object Interaction Diagram 124
           8.2.1   Triggers 125
           8.2.2   Global Transactions and Global Operations 131

9   Functional Model 137
     9.1   Event Effect Specification Using Evaluations 139
     9.2   Evaluation Conditions 139
     9.3   Categorization of Evaluations 141
     9.4   Creation Events and the Functional Model 142
     9.5   Destruction Events and the Functional Model 144
     9.6   Specialisation and the Functional Model 144
     9.7   Transactions, Operations, and the Functional Model 145

10   Presentation Model 147
     10.1 General Structure 148
     10.2 Basic Elements 151
           10.2.1 Entry 151
           10.2.2 Defined Selection 153
           10.2.3 Argument Grouping 155
           10.2.4 Argument Dependency 157
           10.2.5 Filter 159
           10.2.6 Order Criterion 163
           10.2.7 Display Set 165
           10.2.8 Navigation 167

            10.2.9 Actions.. 169
      10.3 Interaction Units 171
            10.3.1 Service Interaction Units 172
            10.3.2 Instance Interaction Unit..................................... 175
            10.3.3 Population Interaction Unit 178
            10.3.4 Master/Detail Interaction Unit 181
      10.4 Action Hierarchy Tree 184
            10.4.1 Agents and Action Hierarchy Trees 187
      10.5 Constructing a Presentation Model 188

11 Conceptual Modelling of Legacy Systems 191
      11.1 Introduction to the Concept of Legacy View 191
      11.2 Object Model 192
            11.2.1 Legacy Views.. 192
            11.2.2 Relationships 201
      11.3 Dynamic Model 207
            11.3.1 State Transition Diagrams................................... 207
            11.3.2 Object Interaction Diagrams 208
      11.4 Functional Model 208
      11.5 Presentation Model 209
            11.5.1 Basic Elements 209
            11.5.2 Interaction Units 213
            11.5.3 Action Hierarchy Tree 213

12 Conceptual Model Validation 215
      12.1 Introduction.. 215
      12.2 Object Model 217
            12.2.1 Classes 217
            12.2.2 Relationships Between Classes 221
      12.3 Dynamic Model 223
            12.3.1 State Transition Diagram................................... 223
            12.3.2 Object Interaction Diagram 224
      12.4 Functional Model 224
            12.4.1 Evaluations 224
      12.5 Presentation Model 225
            12.5.1 Basic Elements 225
            12.5.2 Interaction Units 229
            12.5.3 Action Hierarchy Tree 231

Part III Conceptual Model Compilation: from the Problem Space to the Solution
Space

13 Transforming Models into Applications 235

14 Requirements for the Compilation of Conceptual Models 239

15 Application Execution Strategy 241
    15.1 System Access 242
    15.2 System View 242
    15.3 System Interaction 243
         15.3.1 Service Execution 244
         15.3.2 Query Execution 255
         15.3.3 Interaction Units 257

16 Application Architecture 261

17 Transformation Strategy 265
    17.1 Mappings 265
    17.2 Transformations 266

18 Building a Conceptual Model Compiler 269

19 Issues with Other Approaches 271
    19.1 Issues with Modelling Languages 271
         19.1.1 Lack of Adequacy 271
         19.1.2 Imprecise Semantics 274
         19.1.3 Strong Versus Weak Formalisms 274
         19.1.4 Low Abstraction Level 275
         19.1.5 Action Semantics 276
         19.1.6 Formulae 277
         19.1.7 Overspecification and Redundancy 277
    19.2 Issues with Model Compilation 278
         19.2.1 Lack of an Application Execution Strategy 278
         19.2.2 Issues with Application Architectures 279
         19.2.3 Insufficient Transformations 279
    19.3 State of the Art 280

20 Analogies Between OO-Method and MDA 281
    20.1 OO-Method and MDA 281
    20.2 Properties of OO-Method Absent from MDA 282

21 The OO-Method Development Process 285

22 OO-Method Implementations 289
    22.1 OLIVANOVA Modeler 289
    22.2 OLIVANOVA Transformation Engines 290

Conclusions 293

References 295

Index 301

How this Book Is Organized

Programming technologies have improved continuously during the last decades but, from an Information Systems perspective, some well known problems associated with the design and implementation of an Information Systems persist: Object-Oriented Methods, Formal Specification Languages, Component-Based Software Production, Aspect-Oriented Approaches. This is only a very short list of technologies proposed to solve a very old and, at the same time, very well-known problem: how to produce software of quality. Programming has been the key task during the last 40 years, and the results have not been successful yet. This book will explore the need of facing a sound software production process from a different perspective: conceptual model-based software production. There are several ways to refer to that strategy. There are people dealing with the non-programming perspective where, by non-programming, we mean mainly modelling. Rather than Extreme Programming, the issue is that an Extreme Non-Programming (Extreme Modelling-Oriented) approach should be taken.

Other people focus on Conceptual Schema-Centred Software Production, based on the assumption that, to develop an Information System (IS), it is necessary and sufficient to define its Conceptual Schema. This is presented in (Olivé 2005) as a grand challenge for Information Systems Research. This book is oriented to face this challenge, providing concrete solutions. In particular, we will show how to achieve the objective of generating code from a higher-level system specification, normally represented as an Object-Oriented Conceptual Schema. Nowadays, the interest in MDA has provided a new impetus for all these strategies. New methods propose different types of model transformations that cover all the different steps of a sound software production process from an Information Systems Engineering point of view. This must include Organizational Modelling, Requirements Engineering, Conceptual Modelling and Model-Based Code Generation techniques. In this context, it seems that the time of Model-Transformation Technologies is finally here.

Under the push of this technological wave, and taking advantage of our years of experience working on Model-Driven Development, we will defend the main idea that, to have a software product of quality, the key skill is modelling; the issue is that "the model is the code" (rather than "the code being the model"). Considering this hypothesis, a sound Software Production Process should provide a precise set of models (representing the different levels of abstraction of a system domain description), together with the corresponding transformations from a higher level of abstraction to the subsequent abstraction level. For instance, a Requirements Model should be properly transformed into its associated Conceptual Schema, and this Conceptual Schema should be converted into the corresponding Software Representation (final program).

Assuming that, behind any programmer decision, there is always a concept, the problem to be properly faced by any Model-Transformation Technology is that of accurately identifying those concepts, together with their associated software representations. A precise definition of the set of mappings between conceptual primitives or conceptual patterns and their corresponding software representations provides a solid basis for building Conceptual Model Compilers.

This is what we wish to do in this book. Our precise objective is to show how an MDA-based Software Production Environment based on Conceptual Modelling can be put into practice. To do this, three main goals need to be fulfilled. First, the main concepts involved in such a method must be properly introduced. Second, how to construct an adequate Conceptual Model has to be explained in detail. Third, the process of transforming the source Conceptual Model into its corresponding Software Product must be explained. In accordance with these goals, the structure of this book is divided into three parts:

- The OO-Method and Software Production from Models
- Conceptual Modelling: About the Problem Space
- Conceptual Model Compilation: from the Problem Space to the Solution Space

Now it is time for the reader to explore how to put all these ideas into practice, making Conceptual Model-Driven Development an affordable dream.

Foreword

Not another OO methodology book, I hear you say. But you are wrong. This is the first of a new trend that makes MDD (model-driven development) a reality. Written collaboratively by the inventor of OO-Method and OASIS (Pastor) and a leading industry spokesman who has put Pastor's ideas into practice (Molina), this offers both a rigorous academic treatment of conceptual modelling as a precursor to full code generation and a practitioner's insights into realizing this dream.

The book commences with philosophy, argues that existing modelling languages are not formal enough to create anything more than code skeletons and then describes in detail the necessary semantics that a conceptual modelling language needs for MDD. This means that, for an industry development team, the abstraction level is now raised. No longer do they need to worry about technicalities (and "features") of programming languages but can devote themselves to the less mechanistic and more creative parts of software engineering: analysis and design.

There are a number of models (strictly viewpoints) presented: a structural model, a behavioural model, a functional model and a presentation model. These emphasize different aspects of the (single) underlying reality and the conceptual schema that characterizes it in the software modelling domain. It is stressed how these must be a single whole, integrated in such a way that the final transformation to code is accomplished as a single coherent action.

Of critical importance from an industry perspective is the Presentation Model. Many authors would assume that this should not be part of a theoretical development or a conceptual modelling language – tools do that, don't they? However, the success or failure of any particular software application depends on the user's view of it. If it is difficult or clumsy to use, then it won't be used. Thus these sections on presentation modelling will be critical to any tool's success, including the OlivaNova tool described here in the last section of the book.

Of course, there are many other research and industry efforts to create high quality MDD tools. Some of these are discussed and, although the authors are clearly promoting their own way, the analysis of the alternatives is rational and unemotional.

Nor is this just a greenfield discussion – legacy systems are also discussed in the MDD context.

The book also has a running example of a car rental system. Not only is this easy to comprehend but, as it happens, I have seen the generated system running successfully.

So beware. If you are a UML addict, don't be blinded by the bits of OASIS and OO-Method that look somewhat like UML. Read the details that make this approach really viable for full code generation. See what can be done by a real collaboration between academe and industry. Enjoy.

Geneva,   Brian Henderson-Sellers
February 2007

Part I

The OO-Method and Software Production from Models

1. Let's Get Philosophical
2. The Purpose of this Work
3. The Need for New Development Environments
4. Object-Oriented Modelling as the Starting Point
5. The OO-Method

1

Let's Get Philosophical

It certainly is not common to begin a book on Software Engineering with a philo-sophical perspective; however, this book is not intended to be "just another software engineering book". Therefore, an original way of introducing the results that are going to be presented is to remind the reader of some problems that philosophers have been focused on for centuries.

The methods used in Software Engineering aim to represent models of the real world with computational models used by computers. To do so, the notion of abstraction becomes the cornerstone: the goal is to abstract key concepts, represent them appropriately, and transform them correctly.

From a philosophical point of view, the problem of universals is associated with the concept of abstraction. The problem of universals and abstraction was ad-dressed by the ancient Greeks (Plato and Aristotle); however, it is in the Middle Ages that the controversy reached its height and thinkers defined their positions. The philosophical tradition distinguishes between *universals* (*abstract*) and *particulars* (*concrete*).

"A universal can be defined as an abstract object or term that ranges over particular things".

Examples of universals are "man" and "triangle". A major problem that is related to universals and that was thoroughly examined in the Middle Ages is that of their form of "existence": what kind of entities are they? In other words, the problem involves whether abstract objects exist in a realm that is independent of human thought. What appears to be an ontological question has had its repercussions in logic, in knowledge theory, and even in theology. Although this is not the place to discuss it, later in this book, we will see how this problem is reflected also in Software Engineering.

The main questions raised by the problem of *universals* are:

1. The question of concept (the nature and functions of the concept, the nature of particulars and their relations with universals)

2. The question of trueness (the truth criteria and the connection of universals with particulars; in other words, the correspondence of specification with implementation)
3. The question of language (the nature of signs and their relation with signified entities)

In brief, some of the principal philosophical perspectives that appeared in the Middle Ages with respect to these questions are the following:

- *Realism*, which argues that universals really exist and their existence is prior to that of things. It would be impossible to grasp particulars if it were not for their connection to universals. This does not mean that universals exist as physical entities. If that were so, then universals would be restricted to the same contingencies as for empirical beings and, as such, they would not be universals.
- *Nominalism*, which in discussions on universals, argues that species and genres (and universals in general) are not realities that exist prior to things (in contrast to *Realism*), nor are they realities in things (as stated in *Conceptualism*); they are rather names or words that we apply to a collection of things. According to *Nominalism*, there are only individual entities, and universals are nonexistent entities; they are simply terms of a language. Realists could not agree on a universal being a voice because it would then be a "physical" reality, and so names would be something.
- *Moderate realism*, which argues that universals really exist, though only as the form of particular things, that is, they are based on those things.

What do we want all this philosophy for? We are not going to discuss who is right and who is not. However, it is significant that, in the field of Software Engineering, the mental models from which a Conceptual Schema is built must represent precisely those universals that participate in the analysed system.

Every software product that results from a transformation process will constitute a world formed by particulars that will be instances of the corresponding universals. Therefore, independently of whether you consider yourself to be a realist, a nominalist or a conceptualist, virtual worlds that are built from a Conceptual Schema will always be the representation of the universals considered to be relevant. In these virtual worlds, there will never be a particular that is not an instance of its corresponding universal. This sets the starting point for the philosophical interpretation of the ideas that are presented in this book.

Reliable implementations can be generated only by correctly specifying universals. In other words, to correctly build Software Systems, it is necessary to precisely and non-ambiguously specify the universals and their relationships that are considered to be relevant. This will result in a useful Conceptual Schema. In order to do so, we need to define an ontology in which the relevant concepts for specifying universals are perfectly defined.

The correct representation of this Conceptual Schema in the computational world in which all particulars will live is the essential challenge to every software production method. To achieve this goal, new software development environments must be created. The goal of this book is to provide a concrete and effective solution to this problem. No matter how stimulating it is to participate in philosophical discourse, we must eventually come back to the crude reality of today's Software Engineering.

The Purpose of this Work

The main goal of Software Engineering is to obtain quality products that offer high productivity. The way to achieve this goal with adequate software production methods is, nevertheless, always a problem. To date, it has not been solved satisfactorily, even though the multiple solutions that have appeared in the last decade have always presented themselves as being the ultimate solution to the problem.

We could talk about the dozens of third- and fourth-generation programming languages that have been proposed, or about the multitude of software production methods, for a start the structured languages, then the object-oriented ones. We could also discuss the most advanced programming techniques based on the use of components (Component-Based Development, CBD), or the more recent Extreme Programming proposals, the introduction of Agent-Oriented Programming and Aspect-Oriented Programming.

We could talk about Agile Software Development Methods proposals, or about techniques that are linked to Requirements Engineering. There is a true universe of technologies that have repeatedly claimed to have found the Philosopher's Stone for developing an automated process to develop quality software. However, these same technologies have taken us back to the starting point not long after their introduction.

All the evidence shows that the development of software products (commonly referred to as applications) has always been and still is a complex task, especially in management environments (which are linked to Organizational Systems). What is worse is that their complexity, rather than decreasing, continues to increase. This has become a constant factor in Software Engineering and is due mainly to the fact that the customers' needs for products are always more sophisticated. Also, the resulting applications are developed using highly dynamic, constantly changing technologies, which are usually presented with a facade of simplicity.

Complexity also increases because development technologies must structure the final software product according to protocols that are associated to different architectures, which are usually based on object-oriented models and on the development of distributed components and their associated software architectures (DCOM, CORBA, multi-tiered architectures as an evolution of the traditional client/server architectures, internet/intranet environments, etc.)

In most situations, the technological complexity ends with the software engineer devoting more effort to getting to know the technical aspects of a particular solution, rather than focusing on understanding the problem to be solved by the application. This raises the following questions to pursue: modelling vs. programming; understanding and representing the problem vs. implementing the solution; focusing on the modelling (the problem space) and temporarily ignoring the technical aspects (the solution space).

We must bear in mind that only after we have a thorough understanding of what the software product must do, will we be able to define how it should be built. It is absolutely necessary to have production methods that allow us to specify and represent the Conceptual Schema of an Information System and to then transition to the implementation phase, which is responsible for producing a software product that is functionally equivalent to the specification created in the conceptual modelling phase.

Therefore, the question arises as to why this "family of methods" is not common practice in Software Engineering. Perhaps the answer is simply that we do not possess methods and development environments that are advanced enough to allow the construction of software applications from conceptual models, methods that are advanced enough to allow the engineer to focus on *what* the system is, and not on *how* the system will be represented in a given programming environment, methods that are advanced enough to allow the use of notations that are close to the problem space, and not the solution space.

These goals have guided the history of Software Engineering for years. In order to obtain a quality software product in an effective manner, we have witnessed how the level of abstraction in programming languages, tools and environments has evolved, coming ever closer to the user space. This is only natural, if we take into account that any analysis of an information system is characterized by the existence of two fundamental actors:

1. The stakeholders, who know the problem to be automated by a software product. They are the final users of this software product.
2. The software engineers, who must build a coherent model from the knowledge of the stakeholders. The resulting Conceptual Schema must represent (in the Problem Space) the concepts comprehended and captured during the interaction with the stakeholders. Naturally, the next step is to correctly represent this Conceptual Schema by using the specific set of software representations provided by a given programming environment, in what we have denoted the Solution Space.

From the times of the first assembler languages to the modern conceptual modelling environments and the production of software products driven by conceptual models, Software Engineering has tried to provide engineers with production methods that are closer to the Problem Space with the twofold goal of:

1. Easing the specification of Information Systems to make it feasible in terms that are close to the knowledge of the stakeholders.
2. Easing the conversion to the notation of the Solution Space in an organized and precise manner by defining the corresponding transformation mechanisms (the ideal case being the use of model compilation techniques).

As a result of this, one of the critical tasks in modern Software Engineering is Requirements Specification, and the Conceptual Modelling tasks associated with it that lead to building a Conceptual Schema where these requirements are adequately represented. This phase of Conceptual Modelling is strongly related to the final quality of the software product and to the productivity of the corresponding software process because the requirements describe the goals of the effort to develop the software, provide guidelines for the design of the software architecture, and set the basis for measuring the quality of the final product.

In the late 1990s, several studies on software development in Client/Server and Object-Oriented environments (Douglas et al. 1996) supported the thesis that the most critical tasks in the software production process are still the specification and analysis of requirements. They also recognized that errors produced in this phase of the software development process could have a huge impact on the reliability, cost and robustness of the system. These errors are commonly attributed to the lack of tools that offer integral support to the development process and that are closely linked to the subsequent phases of the development process.

An immediate conclusion is that 21st century developers require new development tools that provide them with higher-level constructs, so that they can specify applications using concepts that are closer to the ones used by humans in our cognitive and communicative processes. The "programs" that are built with these conceptual primitives or conceptual patterns of a higher level should then be transformed into the equivalent software product through a translation process that associates each conceptual primitive to its corresponding software representation. Under this hypothesis, the automatic generation of programs from Conceptual Schemas is no longer an unreachable dream but a solid reality.

In accordance with what has so far been discussed, it is useful to analyse the development methods that are currently being used in the software industry. This analysis shows that these methods propose development processes that consider software construction to be the completion of a high number of tasks in several phases. In most of the cases, the resulting process is extremely complex and of little use in day-to-day practice.

Another problem that is commonly observed in current approaches is that some of the effort put into the completion of some of the tasks and in the production of documentation has little or no effect at all on the final product. That is, in the line of what we could refer to as "traditional CASE" methods, much of the effort required to set up the model of a system is often nothing more than an elegant (in the best of cases) documentation of it, but this then has to be manually transformed into a software product by using a notation and concepts that are totally different from those used to build the model.

This "semantic gap" between the model notation and the programming language usually makes the use of a CASE tool a problem because engineers not only have to obtain the software product but they have to model it as well. This explains the problems that have historically prevented the universal use of CASE. In addition to this, when maintenance problems arise and there are changes to the specification of the systems, it is almost impossible to avoid the temptation of performing the modifications directly to the software product, so that the model and its implementation usually are not synchronized.

To avoid this situation, the construction of information systems of a certain size and complexity requires the use of methods to carry out the development process in a rigorous and systematic way. These methods must perform the phases that are strictly needed to obtain a quality software product in a practical and productive manner. Experience shows that in Software Engineering, as in any other discipline where the goal is to obtain a certain quality product, simplicity and effectiveness are the two quality attributes that must be co-guaranteed. Software production methods that are based on an exaggerated and unjustified number of tasks and phases will simply not be used in day-to-day practice and will inevitably be discarded by developers.

The goal of this book is to present a development method that provides a solution to these challenges. This introductory chapter will present some of the problems that application development faces today in an attempt to find a functional and practical solution to these. To do so, we will focus on the most relevant features that any advanced development method or environment should provide for the software development process to be viewed as an iterative process of constructing and refining conceptual schemas.

With such a process, the traditional implementation phase will play a secondary role because the traditional role of the programmer is played by the higher-level role of the modeller. That is, the level of abstraction of the artefact used as the programming language is raised, following an evolution that is similar to the one that took us from assembler languages to third-generation programming languages. This evolution attempted to provide the programmer with languages of which the notation was closer to the problem space and less linked to the solution space.

Within this context, the subsequent sections of this chapter will present three fundamental ideas:

1. A justification of the need for new development environments that provide a solution to the endemic problems that for the last two decades have typically been associated with the term "Software Crisis".
2. The use of a precise ontology of concepts that act as the foundations of our proposal. Specifically, we will analyse why the Object-Oriented approach is the candidate that is best suited to characterize our proposal.
3. The advantages of using patterns at three different levels:
   - Conceptual primitives or conceptual patterns, which are appropriately catalogued and have a formal support.
   - Architectural and design patterns, which are in charge of the definition of the Software Architecture that is best suited for the resulting software product.

- Design patterns, which associate every conceptual pattern with the software representation that is best suited in the solution space.

This book presents a software production method that has been created as a response to all of these problems, the OO-Method. The OO-Method provides an environment for object-oriented conceptual modelling and automatic generation of the software product, which allows engineers to build applications from conceptual models in an automated fashion. This introductory chapter is structured in accordance with the three points stated above. It includes the introduction to the most relevant features of the OO-Method, and also includes the analysis of other approaches that share the goals of OO-Method in order to highlight the main contributions of our approach.

3

The Need for New Development Environments

Software products that are associated with an Organizational Information System usually share the following common features:

- Huge volumes of data are stored in databases that act as repositories of persistent information and represent the structured data architecture of the system under analysis;
- Great amounts of lines of code are programmed to build user interfaces to provide the different users of the resulting application with different ways of accessing data and services;
- Every user must be provided with the correct implementation of the functionality available, so that the business rules are adequately represented and there is a customized functional appearance;
- The aforementioned levels of presentation (or user interface), functional and persistence (or database) must be conveniently interrelated so that it is possible to: set up the execution of a service by collecting the values of all arguments needed to enable execution; send the appropriate message with these data from the presentation layer to the functional layer; and retrieve the data involved in the execution of the service from the persistence layer and store the data result of this execution;
- A large number of users must be able to use the application from different environments, which are usually distributed over a network.

To incorporate these features, the construction of this type of software products requires technical knowledge about matters that differ as strongly as database design and construction, conceptual modelling, user-interface design, middleware technologies, programming languages, operating systems, prototyping tools, test tools, etc. – and these are only the elementary ones. With such a volume of knowledge and technology required, and with the need for the integration of all these disciplines so that the resulting software product is correct, the greatest hurdle in the path to successfully delivering a new project is the ability to integrate all the tools involved into a single development environment and to incorporate all the knowledge required to implement these huge applications in a single team.

3.1 Software Development Today

We are witnessing a continuous evolution in the context of Software Engineering due to the fact that the required levels of software product quality are becoming ever higher for both the applied technologies and the stakeholders' requirements. New disciplines (Requirements Engineering, Web Engineering, MDA, Business Process Modelling, etc.) continue to be developed in an effort to provide correct and complete solutions. These disciplines must be:

- *correct* because, intuitively, both functional and non-functional requirements of stakeholders must be satisfied according to their specification.
- *complete* because, again from an intuitive perspective, every requirement must be adequately represented in the solution. Any lack at this level decreases the quality of the final product.

However, the root cause of the problem of today's development of large software products is that technology is constantly changing and becoming more complex, without helping to increase the quality of the software process nor the software product. All of this is happening in a context in which the dominant factor is the lack of adequate tools to hide all of this technological complexity from the developer, and thereby ease the process of obtaining the complete and correct software product that is desired.

3.1.1 Current Tools Are Inadequate

Current development tools share two generic problems:

- They do not provide developers with high-level constructs in a well-defined methodological framework. Therefore, applications are typically constructed from code fragments that are at a level lower than that of the problem specification. The semantic gap between the Problem Space and the Solution Space, between modelling and programming, usually causes the system specification that is created in the scope of the Problem Space to be incorrectly represented in the scope of the Solution Space. This happens because the constructors that are common in the programming environments are not suited to represent the real-world models produced in the conceptual modelling phase in a direct and easy way. Additionally, the existence of two different processes and notations (which must be kept consistent) does nothing but introduce an unavoidable level of complexity and noise into the software production process.
- They do not adequately hide the technological complexity, and often do exactly the opposite: technology and its inherent complexity are sometimes promoted as a feature of the development environment, rather than being kept as low-level implementation details. Most market tools are too specialised and focused on only some part of the development process, so that many of these have to be integrated with others in order to have a cohesive development environment that covers all the phases in the development of a software product. However, this

too has a clear impact on the ever-increasing complexity of the development environment.

Applications development with current development tools becomes an intensive programming task, which is always working at an abstraction level that is too low and, in the context of the Solution Space: moving data in the database, manipulating the user interface to capture user actions that are then sent to the functional part of the application, etc. Most of the produced code is tightly coupled to the underlying technology: it necessarily relies on operating systems, databases, middleware products, etc.

3.1.2 Development Processes Are Negatively Affected

Current development processes are focused on the codification (the "how", or the Solution Space), rather than on modelling (the "what", or the Problem Space), which negatively affects productivity and the quality of the final software product. Curiously enough, this situation does not occur in other engineering guilds: no engineer ever thinks about beginning the construction of anything without having the "blueprints" where the stakeholders and technical requirements are clearly specified. Needless to say, these blueprints continuously guide the development process of the subject under construction (the equivalent in Software Engineering would be the software product). The current situation brings about some remarkable negative effects, as discussed below.

- The analysis and design documents produced to specify the problem and the application architecture are seldom used in a straightforward manner to obtain the implementation. In the best cases, they are used to specify the basic system architecture; however, from that point on, a huge "manual" programming effort is required to convert these models into a finished product. Most of the time, these system models are used as mere documentation that becomes obsolete as the products evolve, so that the effort put into creating the models is useless.
- Communication problems arise between developers because of the differences in the process and notation used in the Problem Space (where analysts and modellers work) and the Solution Space (where designers and programmers work). In organizations where different groups coexist and cooperate to carry out each of the development tasks, the chances are high that errors will appear and communication problems will occur. This results in long iterations in the specification-design-implementation-test lifecycle.
- Due to the ever-increasing complexity of technology, large development teams that consist of members with great amounts of technical knowledge and great programming skills are needed. As a consequence of technological complexity, large team sizes create communication problems and bureaucratic overload that negatively affect productivity.
- It takes a lot of time and effort to obtain a prototype that is functionally equivalent to the system requirements specification and that can be delivered to the user, and so user feedback usually takes place at later stages of the lifecycle. This delay

in feedback raises the cost of introducing changes because the product will be in an advanced state of implementation when the changes are requested.

3.2 Better Development Environments Are Needed

Summarizing, in terms of stating the problem, we face a problem that is both simple to state and complicated to solve. The issue is that producing an Information System today is costly (because expensive resources have to be used over extended periods of time), much too slow for modern business conditions, very risky (in the sense that it is hard to control and has a high failure rate), and highly unsafe (because it introduces hidden failure points).

The main problem is that – from a high-level, software process-oriented perspective – the development process has not changed much over the past 40 years; that is, the task of programming is still the "essential" task. Programming is the key activity associated with the fact of creating a software product. We are not claiming that programming technologies have not improved year after year, with new proposals and their associated tools. However, the issue here is that, considering the very bad results the programming-oriented techniques are historically obtaining, a simple question arises: is it worth searching for a better way of producing software?

We should ask ourselves why so many software systems historically fail to meet the needs of their customers. For decades, the "silver bullet" has apparently been provided to the community in the form of some new, advanced software technology, but always unsuccessfully. We have a large list of technologies that were intended to solve the problem: we could set down in this list Assembler, Third-Generation Languages, Relational Databases, Declarative Programming, Methodologies and CASE tools (Structured Analysis and Design initially, Object-Oriented extensions for Analysis and Design, UML-based, subsequently), Component-based Programming, Aspect-based, Agent-Oriented, Extreme Programming, Agile Methods, Requirements Engineering, Organizational Modelling, etc. Nevertheless, the same "phantom of the opera" is always present: the unsolved Crisis of Software notion.

What we now need are new techniques, methods and development environments that enable us to take the software development process to a higher abstraction level by using an expressiveness that is much closer to the Problem Space, thereby increasing the productivity and quality of the application development process.

Current approaches for this goal are modelling tools with code generation capabilities, or complex prototyping tools that attempt to help developers by providing them with a way of rapidly iterating the production process. The common problem is that applications produced by such tools are used only once and then discarded, and so the effort put into the construction of the prototype seldom pays off.

Another remarkable fact is that the term "code generation" has traditionally been misused. Most modelling environments use the "code generation" tag as a marketing claim. Nevertheless, the term is used in a deceptive way because it never applies to tools that produce code from conceptual schemas, as a conceptual schema compiler would do. At best, such tools partially transform the conceptual specification of the system into general-purpose code templates, which are often of little or no use from the point of view of the final software product.

If these templates are to be reused, something that is feasible from the architectural point of view of the final real product, then they must be adapted in a nontrivial way, and manually completed according to the technological features of the development environment in use. This adds to the problem of the unavoidable desynchronization (lack of synchronization) between the conceptual schema and the resulting software product, when the modifications and changes are applied to the latter but not to the former.

Having said this, we can now introduce the desirable features that should exist in the advanced, "ideal" development environment we are aiming for.

1. It must provide us with facilities to rapidly construct quality applications, quality being the functional equivalence between user requirements, the conceptual schema, and the resulting software product.
2. It must also allow team development, and cover the entire software production lifecycle in an iterative and incremental way. To do so, it must provide a clearly specified and structured software production process.
3. It must effectively hide all the technical complexity, focus on the specification of the problem to be developed, and provide a complete and correct set of conceptual primitives to act as basic constructors in the elaboration of a correct and complete conceptual schema.
4. Such basic constructors (conceptual patterns or conceptual primitives) must have an underlying formal support to ensure syntactic and semantic consistency. An interesting alternative is the use of information system formal specification languages as a high-level data repository. This hides the complexity that is historically associated to such languages from the developer, and allows the introduction of relevant information by means of graphical editors, using graphical notations that are compliant with widely used standards such as UML (UML 2004). Thus, the best features of formal and conventional modelling techniques can be combined in a practical and effective way.
5. All of this must also allow the specification of a system regardless of the technological and programming aspects. The work of software engineers should be focused on the scope of the Problem Space, where the main goal is to specify the "what", regardless of the "how" that is typically associated with the low-level considerations of a concrete representation in the Solution Space, and with the inherent complexity of any software technology.

The best way to ensure this functionality is to allow the real, automatic generation of code for the full application from models built by analysts. The term "real" is important in this context. The goal is that the Conceptual Schema can be compiled directly by applying a transformation mechanism based on the definition, design and implementation of a finite set of mappings between conceptual patterns and their associated software representations. This will constitute the core of the model compiler that, in turn, will be the core of this new breed of development environments.

By turning the existence of software production tools with these desired features into reality, we will be able to definitively leave behind all the traditional CASE tools that, as we have mentioned above, try to offer solutions to the needs of developers but only manage to provide environments with very limited code generation capabilities. Such environments have never delivered on their promises to solve the problems associated with the well-known "software crisis". If you closely examine the results of the traditionally promised "code generation", you will find that it never leads to a complete software product that is functionally equivalent to the description captured by the conceptual schema. Moreover, it never fulfils the list of features presented above. In the context of an object-oriented development environment – which is commonplace – what developers really get is nothing but a set of templates for the declaration of classes where no method is implemented and no software architecture aspects are reflected, and so there is still a great need for tedious, manual programming tasks.

Some tools of this kind allow code to be written together with modelling constructs, thereby offering a false impression of code generation from conceptual models. The problem in this case is that there is a mixture of the expressiveness of the Problem Space (based on the use of these modelling constructs) with the expressiveness of the Solution Space (based on the use of constructs of a programming language). This results in hybrid solutions that, far from being effective for the problem of producing quality software, turn out to be development environments that inherit all the problems that arise when the *what* and the *how* are not adequately separated, as we have stated in this section.

4

Object-Oriented Modelling as the Starting Point

Generally speaking, the goal is to answer the question of how to define a development method that solves the selection of the conceptual framework that will support both the methodological proposal and its associated development environments. We need to introduce an ontology that characterizes the basic concepts upon which we will build the desired method in a precise way. To do so, we must select the most appropriate model as the referential conceptual framework. We will then justify why we have chosen Object-Oriented Modelling for the definition of this framework.

4.1 The Chosen Model

A method is a systematic way of working that obtains a desired result. This desired result might be the requirements specification for a product, the specification of a system decomposition, the implementation of a product, its deployment, etc. At this point, it is interesting to highlight the confusion in terminology that usually occurs when using the terms "method" and "methodology". In the Software Engineering literature, the term "methodology" is frequently applied to what is in fact a "method". In this book, we will use the term "method" with its correct meaning, leaving the term "methodology" to refer to the "study of methods". For instance, the methodology of mathematics is the study of methods to find and prove mathematical truths. In a similar way, the methodology of engineering is the study of the methods used to obtain quality products. Having established this, let us now present a software production method that answers the problems described above.

In the recent and short history of Software Engineering, there are two approaches to the study of traditional methods for the analysis and design of information systems:

- *The process-oriented methods*, which are focused on the description of events that occur in the system under consideration.
- *The data-oriented methods*, which are focused on the description of the architecture of entities within the system under consideration.

Structured Analysis and Design techniques have been using these two differentiated abstractions for some time now: the former for the dynamic perspective or process architecture, and the latter for the static perspective or data architectures. Each of these has had its own notation, techniques and associated development process. The use of Semantic Models (of which the Entity-Relationship Model (Chen 1976) is the paradigmatic example) as data modelling techniques is commonplace, as is the use of Data Flow Diagrams (DFDs; Gane and Sarson 1979) as an example of process modelling techniques. Of course, consistency analysis techniques have always been used to guarantee that the static and dynamic perspectives complement each other correctly in the specification of the information system under study, thereby avoiding contradictory (and thus, inconsistent) specifications of data and processes. A classical example of this is the verification that every entity of an E-R Model is used in a process of a DFD.

These methods have always had the handicap of performing the development of systems through these two different abstractions. Reality, which these Universals are made up of and that we introduced above, does not consist simply of data or processes treated separately. Therefore, it seems a logical conclusion that static and dynamic – data view and process view – should be viewed together, as the heads and tails of the same coin, and as the reality under study indeed is. We perceive them in a homogeneous way. Therefore, the problem is how to manage a method that is expressive enough to respect this principle of homogeneity when treating data and processes. This goal will not be achieved with methods using concepts and notations that are different for data and processes, or methods that necessarily capture only partial views of reality that are different from how we perceive reality.

In this context, the object-oriented paradigm seems to be the ideal approach, because it attempts to capture reality as it is, composed of objects that are data and processes that altogether result in a synergic whole. No data or process exist independently. The main contribution of the object paradigm in this context is that, unlike what has just been described, it introduces a single abstraction – that of the object – which adequately encapsulates both the static and dynamic perspectives that characterize the analysis and design of information systems.

Since the focus required is such that it helps perceive the properties of a system under a single abstraction of object, the conceptual framework we have chosen is the object-oriented one. This framework achieves the following goals:

- It facilitates the conceptual modelling of a system by interpreting reality as it is, in a way that is closer to human cognitive mechanisms through the notion of object.
- It reduces the complexity of the system under specification, especially if the notion of object is maintained throughout the production process and is refined as the implementation phase is approached: objects are modelled in the Problem Space; objects are implemented in the Solution Space.
- It improves the communication with stakeholders during the conceptual modelling phase, under the hypothesis that an Object-Oriented Conceptual Schema can be presented to them and discussed, because it uses an abstraction – the object – that can be shared by both engineers and stakeholders.

- It represents the relationships between the constituent elements in a natural way because the system is seen as a society of interacting objects.
- It equally emphasizes data and processes by specifying objects as self-contained execution units.

4.2 Key Aspects of the Desired Method

In the following, we will enumerate some of the key aspects that must be taken into account prior to the construction of advanced, object-oriented software production methods as well as the development environments that will support the proposed production process, so that they satisfy our requirements in an effective and practical way.

- To start with, we need to define and document the structural and behavioural patterns that are present in most information system specification in order to detect what components and expressiveness must be provided by the modelling method to then capture and represent these patterns. These conceptual patterns or conceptual primitives will act as the basic units in the construction of conceptual schemas. We will refer to the process of defining and representing these as *cataloguing of conceptual patterns*.
- In accordance with the above, we must enrich the object model used to specify an information system. The conceptual patterns or conceptual primitives considered to be relevant must be characterized in a precise and unambiguous way. To do so, a reasonable approach would be to use a widespread notation such as the standard UML notation, which has been conveniently enriched to represent the patterns needed to completely specify organizational systems. The textual format of such a specification must be performed by means of a *formal specification language*, so that we have a precise characterization of the ontology associated to the chosen object-oriented model. This will ease the rapid and correct construction of a final software product that is functionally equivalent to the specification, because the precise correspondences between conceptual patterns (and their formal support) and their corresponding software representations can be defined. The implementation of these correspondences constitutes the core of a powerful conceptual schema compiler.
- One of the most important problems concerning UML today is associated with its complexity, due to the amount of concepts in each of its diagrams. This claim has been constantly present together with any new UML extension (France et al. 2006). In practice, the percentage of UML concepts used in the resolution of real problems is significantly low. From the point of view of the UML proposal, we must point out that the proposed formal definition of the conceptual patterns has a double positive effect:
  1. It allows the characterization of an expressively complete core of UML that, far from including the hundreds of concepts proposed by recent versions of the standard, rationalizes its use, reducing it to those concepts that are really needed to specify information systems.

2. It benefits from the advantages of the standard where its usefulness is undeniable: as a unified notation, it avoids the effect of "reinventing the wheel" when assigning graphical representations to the concepts of a methodological proposal. The relevant conceptual patterns will be specified by means of the most convenient UML diagram, and those concepts that are not present in the standard will be documented as stereotypes, using the expressive power provided by UML.

• To obtain a quality software product, this process of generating the final product must be performed by using an adequate set of *architectural patterns* that provide a software architecture that is suited for the final product we wish to obtain, as well as an adequate set of design patterns that favours the reuse of designs of which the efficiency has been proven in the resolution of similar problems. Additionally, the development process must be organized by defining the guidelines that transform the system specification into this resulting software architecture using the most convenient design patterns in accordance with the context. In this way, we can ensure that the quality levels for the final software product will be met from both the architectural point of view and from the particular software components point of view.

In the following sections, we will explain each of these aspects in more detail.

4.2.1 Cataloguing of Conceptual Patterns

In order to correctly describe something, there must be an adequate set of concepts of which the semantics are defined unambiguously. This set must have the necessary number of concepts, no more and no less. Having a surplus of concepts results in overspecification and semantic ambiguity, which negatively affects the correctness of the conceptual model. Missing concepts will result in a lack of expressiveness in terms of conceptual patterns, which negatively affects completeness.

In the field of Software Engineering, this translates into the fact that the requirements expressed by the stakeholders of an information system under consideration must be correctly represented in the corresponding conceptual schema. The basic constructors used to create such conceptual schemas must be part of a finite and precise set of conceptual patterns, which will make the task of specifying the relevant abstractions and their relationships a precise, clear and easy one. We will refer to this set of detailed patterns as the *catalogue of conceptual patterns*, and it will be one of the foundations of the desired software production method.

If those basic building blocks for specifying Organizational Systems that we call conceptual patterns and that are needed to create a complete Conceptual Schema are clearly identified, then it will be possible to specify a precise set of mappings between these and their corresponding software representations. A model compiler will then be constructed, by implementing all these mappings. This is the only strategy to make this possible. Providing as much expressiveness as possible in a model-based code generation context is not the right approach. If the input is unpredictable due to the amount of modelling elements that are provided, then no precise model-transformation process will be feasible, because there will exist primitives with no concrete software representation counterpart. This has been accepted even by many UML researchers who recognize that UML will properly support MDA only by tailoring the language and defining precise subsets of it with clear semantics. An excessively large and complex modelling language presents a problem not only for MDA tool developers but also for the working groups responsible for evolving a given standard.

The best way to explain what the features of these conceptual patterns are is through an easy example that will allow us to analyse the relevant abstractions that are used to build the conceptual schema of the system under study. In the following section, we will identify abstractions that will constitute the object-oriented ontology that is correctly and completely characterized by an object-oriented formal specification language.

The proposed example refers to "a simple management system in which a firm has a portfolio of customers who issue orders that must be served. Each order consists of several lines, each of which references a product. Customers can be notified if they fail to pay the invoices that the firm sends them within 90 days". Figure 4.1 shows a UML class diagram that represents a possible architecture of classes and relationships as a solution for this example system.

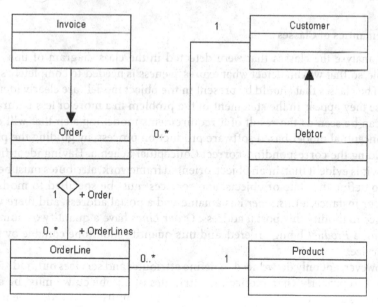

Fig. 4.1 Object model for the example system.

Let us analyse the example system in detail to obtain all the relevant information. This abstraction process must take us to an architecture of classes represented in the corresponding Conceptual Schema. In this architecture, the structure of the solution proposed for the example system must be specified to include classes such as the basic modelling components, the relationships between these basic components, and the behaviour associated with both the components and their relationships. All of this will be presented from the perspective introduced in this book: the precise definition of the conceptual patterns required to adequately represent the abstractions considered to be relevant.

The goal is to understand why most of the object-oriented models in use today fail to totally and adequately capture the semantics of an information system. We will justify the need for enriching the expressiveness of the object-oriented model to convert it into a correct and complete model that represents all the concepts that are semantically needed. This will be done by defining the corresponding conceptual patterns or conceptual primitives as basic units in the construction of conceptual schemas.

This book will show that the only way to build a transformation engine that is capable of establishing a correspondence to the most suitable software representation for each conceptual pattern is to have a precise specification of the modelling primitives, together with their associated formal environment. In this way, the implementation of a conceptual schema compiler will be more than a reachable dream; it will become the reality that will guide the systematic development of a final software product that is functionally equivalent to the original conceptual schema.

The Semantics of Classes

Let us analyse the classes that were detected in the class diagram of this simple example, so that we can detect what expressiveness is needed to completely specify these. The classes that should be present in the object model[1] are clearly identified because they appear in the statement of the problem in a more or less natural way. They can be seen as the result of a requirements modelling step that will enrich any conceptual model-based software production process, by guiding the process of building the corresponding, correct Conceptual Schema. Having identified the classes, it is evident that, in an object-oriented framework, attributes must be specified to define the state of objects, and services must be specified to modify the state. For instance, a *Customer* has a name and a postal address, and there will be a service to modify this postal address; *Order Lines* have a quantity or number of items for a *Product* being ordered, and this quantity should be editable by means of a service.

However, not only do we need to define attributes and services but, additionally, we need to properly characterize the attributes of an object; we must be able to define constraints over their values, such as "the quantity in an order line must be equal to or less than the stock of the related product". In the specification, we may need to express conditions on the state of objects to prevent services from executing.

---

[1] Following the user guidelines of well-known software production methods such as OMT, which use the term Object Model to refer to the representation of an architecture of classes of a system represented by a UML Class Diagram, we will use the terms Object Model and Class Diagram interchangeably. The Class Diagram is used as a representation of the Object Model of the system under study.

This happens when, for instance, we wish to prevent the purchase of products unless the minimum stock is reached. Alternatively, there can be situations where objects react by issuing service requests to objects when some conditions on their state are met: for instance, when the minimum stock for a product is reached, a purchase order is automatically issued.

To be able to completely describe the functionality associated to objects of a system, an essential task is the specification of how services modify the value of attributes. A clear example of this functionality are services that allow the modification of one or more attributes of an object. In this case, the value of the attribute in the final state will be characterized by the value of an argument of the service in charge of performing the modification.

It is also common to specify derived attributes of which the values are calculated from the values of other attributes; therefore, it is also necessary to specify how those values are calculated. For instance, the total amount of an order will be calculated as the sum of the prices of each order line (quantity*product price) of that order.

Finally, all the objects in a system follow behavioural patterns that define the valid sequences of services, which characterize their valid lives; for instance, we cannot sell products unless we first purchase them; if the customer does not place an order, he/she does not have to pay any bill. In these terms, an object can be defined as an observable process, and the specification of this process allows the characterization of its valid lives as stated above.

All the situations that we have introduced so far show that the correct and complete specification of an information system requires having a precise set of primitives that act as building blocks or basic constructors of the specification of the classes of the system. Examples of constructors of this kind have been presented above: declaration of attributes and services, constraints on attributes, preconditions of services, post-conditions for the execution of a service, derivation formulas for derived attributes, specification of triggers. Each one denotes a particular type of expressiveness that a specification method should provide as basic constructors (conceptual primitives, conceptual patterns) in the scope of the class.

Therefore, it will be possible to generate correct conceptual schemas only if the software production method that is used has all the conceptual primitives or conceptual patterns that will eventually allow us to perform such specifications correctly, with no ambiguity and without expressive deficiencies. Thus far, we have analysed this problem in the scope of a class, without taking into account the fact that classes are related to one another. In the following, we also examine the problem at the level of relationships between classes, characterizing which relationships must be defined, and determining their associated semantics.

The Semantics of Class Relationships

One of the most important factors in evaluating the power of an object-oriented software development method is the analysis of relationships between classes that it provides as well as the preciseness of the associated semantics. Many UML-based methods provide ambiguous semantics and, consequently, these are too imprecise for constructors as elementary as generalisation, or association and aggregation. If the semantic interpretation of these relationships depends on the designer, then the result in terms of the software product will always be unpredictable. The truth is that class relationships have more semantics than those proposed by most methods, and the conceptual schema will be precise only if these relationships are clearly defined. In this section, we will analyse some examples of conceptual patterns that are typical of class relationships in order to clearly state what expressiveness should be provided by any effective object-oriented modelling method. According to the strategy followed, the final goal is to set the foundations for what should be a rigorous process of cataloguing conceptual patterns, which includes the basic primitives to build conceptual schemas.

In the example at hand, there are two interesting relationships: a customer *places* one or several orders, and each order *has* a set of order lines. The semantics of each relationship are determined by the behaviour of these business objects in the universe under study. The relationship between order and order lines is a typical example of aggregation; this also has the master/detail pattern associated to it and is quite common in management applications. With the aid of the expressiveness provided by the concept of cardinality, we know that when an order is created, it may not have order lines initially (a minimum cardinality of 0 in the sense order – order line). The user of the application will be able to dynamically add as many order lines as needed. Here, there are two important features:

1. The multi-valued cardinality in the sense order–order line.
2. The dynamic character of the aggregation, which implies the existence of insertion and deletion of order lines from the corresponding order. If this aggregation were static, its components would be determined by the creation service of the requested object, which clearly represents a different situation.

We also know that an order line belongs to a single order (a maximum cardinality of 1 in the sense order line–order). An order line must also be associated to some order. When an order is deleted, its order lines have to be deleted as well. A stricter type of aggregation then appears. Logically, not being able to specify any of these characteristics results in a lack of expressiveness and negatively affects the efficacy of a modelling method.

Therefore, the *has* relationship clearly implies semantics of inclusion because order lines cannot exist without being related to an order. Since this is an associative relationship between two classes, it also possesses a cardinality, which in this case, implies that an order can have zero or more order lines, and an order line belongs to one and only one order. The semantics of inclusion imply a clearly determined behaviour, which is the deletion of all order lines when deleting the order. All of this can be specified by creating a conceptual pattern specific to aggregation that groups all the characteristics mentioned above. It could also be reused for specification purposes every time a similar situation exists.

The behaviour associated with the relationship between customer and order (*places*) is that an order must necessarily be placed by a customer. A customer can place several orders, so the order must know which customer placed it, whereas a customer must know which orders were placed by him/her. If we compare this with the previous case, the relationship between customer and order does not imply inclusion because a customer is not composed of his/her orders. The *places* relationship is not as strong, and it is bidirectional because, in this case, it is not relevant to know which object is part of which other object. Nevertheless, note the dynamic character of this association, because the orders that a customer places vary through time (customers usually place orders as needed!), and so we need services to allow the correct representation of that behaviour.

In addition to these association/aggregation relationships, there is another one that is considered to be relevant: the agent (active object) relationship, which will determine which objects are authorised to execute which services of which classes. Some objects in the system can request services of other objects, as we saw in the case of customers who can place orders (in this case, customers would be active objects, acting as agents of the system). Orders, however, cannot request services from other objects, so they are regarded as passive objects of which the only responsibility is that of offering services to the system that will be activated by the corresponding agents. This client–server perspective proves to be useful when building a conceptual schema that represents service activations that occur in the interacting object society being modelled.

And, of course, we need to correctly specify specialisation relationships that benefit from the notion of inheritance in the context of an object-oriented conceptual schema. Let us consider the customer and debtor classes. There is an inheritance relationship between them that also has interesting emerging features. From the statement of the problem, we can see that a customer can become a debtor from the moment that something happens (the customer is declared to be a debtor) or some conditions are met (for instance, that the amount of debt is greater than a certain limit). A customer can also cease to be a debtor after satisfying his/her debts or by returning the goods from the unpaid orders. It is important to emphasize that this inheritance relationship is more expressive than the typical *is–a* relationship; it is a temporal or dynamic specialisation because the customer can "become" or "cease to be" a debtor at any time. In addition, this specialisation takes place because some service of the customer is activated or some condition on the state of the customer is met, and the same applies when a customer ceases to be a debtor.

Logically, this simple example is not intended to show all the elements needed to correctly specify the basic conceptual primitives of the system, but it is useful in emphasizing the importance of having a set of precise conceptual patterns that a high-quality specification method must provide. The main goal is to capture the semantics as fully as possible by specifying all possible situations when modelling an organizational system. The correct completion of this task involves cataloguing the set of conceptual patterns that act as basic units for the construction of a conceptual schema, both for defining classes and for defining class relationships. The precise determination of that set of conceptual primitives or conceptual patterns is therefore a must for a software production software to be effective.

4.2.2 Enriching the Object Model

The conclusion so far is that in order to correctly specify a system, we need the expressiveness to adequately represent the semantics of this system. Moreover, if the catalogue of conceptual patterns is defined in a precise way with a formal support, it will be possible to establish a correspondence between each of these conceptual primitives and a suitable software representation in a given development environment. In this way, we will have eased the construction of methods and improved development tools that will eventually allow application development by working exclusively at the conceptual level and providing automatic code generation.

Next, we will see how to combine desirable properties of the object-oriented formal languages (as support for the precise definition of conceptual primitives) with a commonly used standard notation in industrial contexts of software production (such as UML), which allows the representation of each modelling pattern with the most suitable graphical constructors available.

Object Model and Formal Specification Languages

If our goal is the definition of an object model that has the required expressiveness and precision (not ambiguous), then the best way to define a systems specification method that satisfies that goal is by basing it on the use of formal techniques. With these, we will be able to correctly define the semantics of the constructs to be used in modelling by determining in a clear and unambiguous way what the classes, objects and class relationships are, and how objects behave and interact. The reasonable approach in this context is the definition of an object-oriented formal specification language with well-defined semantics. The use of such a language will allow us to specify the notions considered to be relevant for the correct specification of an information system.

Methods based on formal specification languages possess a solid mathematical base that is usually founded on logic, algebra, set theory or theory of categories, which provide a rigorous framework for the specification of systems. That is the only way to avoid the concepts on which an object-oriented software production method is based from being imprecise. The main example of such an undesirable situation can be found in current object-oriented methods that are based to a certain degree on the standard UML. They inherit the semantic impreciseness derived from the different interpretations of the same concepts – depending on the context of use, or depending on the person using them.

Historically, and particularly in the 1990s, formal methods have contributed significant advantages to the software development process because they have used precise and verifiable notations that eased the automatic generation of executable prototypes. Among such proposals, we can highlight OBLOG (Sernadas et al. 1987) and TROLL (Jungclaus et al. 1991; Hartmann et al. 1994), which were developed in the scope of the European project ESPRIT IS-CORE (Wieringa and Feenstra 1994). OBLOG formalizes its semantics by means of a theory of categories, and offers a supporting method with several graphical models to express different properties of a system. OBLOG once had a commercial tool called OBLOG/CASE (Esdi 1993).

TROLL has an expressiveness that is based on first-order predicate logic, temporal logic (dynamic constraints, pre/post-conditions) and process algebra (lifecycle specifications). It provides a methodological support called OMTroll (Wieringa et al. 1993), which is based on OMT and has elemental CASE support called TBench.

LCM ("Language for Conceptual Modeling"; Wieringa 1990, 1991) was also developed by this time, and has a similar syntax but with semantics of initial algebra and dynamic logic. LCM provided a development method called MCM ("Method for Conceptual Modeling") that combined LCM specifications with ER diagrams, DFDs and JSP. There is CASE support for MCM (also an academic product like TBench, as well as freeware) called TCM ("Toolkit for Conceptual Modeling"). Another interesting formal specification language in this context is Albert II (Dubois 1995), which is based on real-time temporal logic and is used in the scope of the European project ESPRIT CREWS (CREWS 1996) for requirements validation. It shares the view of considering a basic issue to provide a formal framework to characterize the concepts that constitute the core of any system specification language.

All these proposals are interesting approaches, though none have resulted in a relevant automatic software production environment. It is evident that their use in an industrial context has always been limited. This is essentially due to the fact that formal specifications have a complex syntax because of their mathematical basis, which requires much organization and planning by the software engineer in order to obtain modular and legible specifications. Moreover, even small changes in the requirements often result in a tedious reorganization of the specification, which is itself complex enough. None of the environments associated with these proposals have ever produced a tool that generates a complete software product from formal specifications. In practice, neither these languages nor other formal specification languages – though not object-oriented, such as VDM (Bjorner et al. 1990) and Z (Spivey 1992) – have ever reached a significant maturity level.

In summary, different proposals have followed one another, especially in the academic world. Although none have led to a successful industrial software production environment, they have made an important contribution to the world of Software Engineering: the need to formally define the basic concepts comprising the ontology of a given approach. For instance, in our case, the best way to characterize the set of conceptual primitives that we propose as elementary components for modelling organizational systems is to define a formal, object-oriented language in which these basic notions are clearly defined. Another remarkable piece of evidence that concepts need to be formalized to have correct and complete software production methods are the efforts made in the context of P-UML (Precise-UML; pUML 2004; Astesiano et Reggio 2004) to determine which subset of UML concepts are truly relevant when specifying systems, and then try to formalize this "precise subset" of UML so that the basic concepts included in that subset are defined in a precise way.

It is in these circumstances that, in the early 1990s, the Technical University of Valencia defined the OASIS language ("Open and Active Specification of Information Systems"; Pastor 1992; Pastor et al. 1992; Pastor and Ramos 1995; Letelier et al. 1998) as a formal, object-oriented specification language based on dynamic logic and process algebra. OASIS is the language that formally character-izes the ontology of an Automatic Software Production Method from Conceptual Schemas called the OO-Method. This is the method described in this book, and is an operational implementation of all the ideas discussed here, properly adapted to the MDA approach.

Providing an Intuitive Graphical Notation

Once the set of basic modelling constructs has been determined, a graphical nota-tion that allows for its representation in the process of creating a conceptual schema must be chosen. In order to have an easy, intuitive and effective modelling phase, notationally speaking, we have to avoid the "reinvent the wheel effect". The 1990s saw the advent of some well-known object-oriented software production methods – we could mention proposals such as OMT (Rumbaugh et al. 1991), OOSE (Ja-cobson et al. 1992), Wirfs-Brock (Wirfs-Brock et al. 1990), Booch (Booch 1994) and Fusion (Coleman et al. 1994) – of which the notations usually proposed different representations for analogous concepts. This proliferation of methods with similar foundations but different notations justified the need for a notational standard that provided a unified graphical notation.

In terms of modern Software Engineering, and particularly in the scope of the object paradigm, this problem already has a satisfactory solution. Nowadays, there is a standard that is widely known and used: UML, the Unified Modeling Language (Booch et al. 1997; UML 2004). UML is "a language to specify, visualize, and construct artefacts of software systems ..." (Booch et al. 1997) and that, besides having been accepted as a standard by the OMG (http://www.omg.org) in 1997, has also been acknowledged "de facto" by the industry.

As such, a reasonable alternative is to adopt a well-defined subset of UML with the required extensions as the notation. This is feasible due to the extension mecha-nisms that UML itself provides, which are essentially stereotypes, tags and profiles. Furthermore, the use of UML as an environment for the graphical representation of a finite and precise set of conceptual primitives provides additional value: it limits the complexity resulting from the excess of concepts provided by the standard UML, and it also unambiguously determines the semantics of the corresponding model elements. Its value as a standard is thus improved, because we can characterize a precise subset of UML that contains the primitives considered to be relevant in the formal framework that we introduced in the previous section.

Integrating Formal and Semi-Formal Techniques

On the one hand, we have introduced the idea that the most suitable way to define an expressive object model is by means of a formal specification language that will precisely determine the concepts that comprise the ontology of the model. On the other hand, we have argued on the convenience of selecting semi-formal graphical notations to construct conceptual models. These notations are traditionally linked to the conventional object-oriented software production methods mentioned above

(OMT, OOSE, etc.), which have resulted in the UML notational standard. In this group, we can distinguish conventional and semi-formal approaches:

- Conventional approaches are those that follow the CASE tradition of Structured Analysis and Design Methods of the 1980s, extending these with the particularities of the object model. However, there is still a wide semantic gap between the problem space (the conceptual schema) and the solution space (the final software product).
- Semi-formal approaches are those that, even though their modelling primitives are not formally based from a mathematical point of view, introduce a set of concepts of which the semantics are clarified by means of informal definitions or by the use of meta-modelling techniques. These at least allow the graphical representation and structuring of their elements and their relations.

Of course, both approaches (formal specification languages and conventional object-oriented methods) have their pros and cons. Therefore, a reasonable approach would be to try to combine the desirable properties of both perspectives, in an effort to take advantage of the positive aspects and to omit the negative ones. This "rational" line of work aims to overcome the "old" dichotomy between formal and semi-formal methods in an attempt to integrate the best of both proposals to model and develop software systems. Obviously, such an approach will be able to reuse the following positive aspects:

- The fact that formal specification languages can be used to detect and eliminate ambiguities and elements of questionable utility from the early stages in software development. They also provide a formal and rigorous framework as part of a "true" engineering process.
- The use of formalisms for the construction of conceptual models makes engineers define what has to be implemented independently of design decisions to be taken at later stages.
- The use of formal specification languages, which are generally coupled with a system of logic inference combined with analysis methods, enables the existence of CASE tools that verify the formal properties of correctness and completeness of the conceptual models created in the modelling phase.
- The use of graphical notations that intuitively and precisely capture the aspects that are related to the structure and behaviour of objects, which are closely linked to an internal formal representation, enables the automatic generation of formal specifications by using well-defined translation mechanisms.
- The fact that textual, formal specifications resulting from the graphical diagrams that comprise the conceptual schema are constructed as a combination of conceptual patterns or basic conceptual primitive allows this specification to be converted into the corresponding final software product, transforming each primitive into the corresponding software representation. This final product will be functionally equivalent to the original specification, because of its construction method.

The question to be posed now is whether this unifying strategy is possible or not. In other words, how can we combine a notation *without* a well-defined semantics (the one provided by the UML) with a specification language *with* well-defined semantics (such as OASIS). This question has an immediate affirmative answer. It is a matter of defining a correspondence between the grammar that represents the graphical notation and the grammar of the selected specification language. This grammar must match the conceptual patterns detected in the problem space (which is conveniently expressed with the graphical notation) with the elements of the specification language they represent. This results in a visual modelling technique that is perfectly integrated with the semantics of the object model underlying the specification language.

To define such a correspondence, the essential idea is to build (if we lack the notation) or simply to adapt (the standard UML notation that already exists) the graphical notation. The notation can express every concept (conceptual primitives or conceptual patterns) defined in the specification language in an effort to make the graphical modelling a visual and intuitive task. When the use of a graphical notation is not applicable to all primitives, the syntax of the specification language can be used contextually, meaning by contextually that these primitives have to be properly associated to the corresponding graphical elements. If, however, the standard provides a language for specifying constraints, then such a language could be used, as happens with UML and OCL. It is important to note that we will exclude the elements that are not needed to model the problem according to the expressiveness provided by the object model determined by the formal framework from the graphical notation. By doing so, we will avoid the semantic overload that is associated to notations such as UML, which allows the same concept to be defined in different ways.

Thus far, we have discussed how to correctly construct the specification of a system that, in the scope of the Problem Space, produces the corresponding Conceptual Schema that reflects the architecture of the system classes and their dynamic and functional behaviour. The effort to obtain this Conceptual Schema is aimed at a very specific goal: to obtain the *system blueprint* that will guide the process to obtain the final software product. Next, we will see how to transition from the Problem Space (Conceptual Schema) to the Solution Space (software product), and we will discuss how to set the foundations to enable the automation of this transition process. The first step will necessarily be to determine the Software Architecture to structure the components of the final software product.

4.2.3 Software Architecture: Architectural Patterns

The work done in the conceptual modelling phase to obtain the Conceptual Schema that correctly and completely represents the requirements of the stakeholders for a software system is not free, and we have not put so much effort into it simply for academic etiquette (prestige). This modelling effort has a primary goal: to ensure the construction of a software product that adequately represents every aspect specified in the Conceptual Schema. As we discussed above, the construction of the resulting software product will have the required quality only if we precisely define the blueprints that will be the reference and guide to the process of constructing the product.

From the conceptual patterns used to build the original Conceptual Schema in the Problem Space, it is now important to determine which software components are going to be constructed in the Solution Space in order to correctly represent these in a given programming technology, and to determine which architecture should be selected in order to structure these components in an effective way. In this context, a basic task is to select the software architecture that will determine which software components will comprise the final software product, and how these components will relate to one another.

Selecting a software architecture is not a trivial task. Moreover, the decision affects the production process. Fortunately, there is a widespread trend to consider three-layered architectures as suitable to structure software applications and, as such, to structure the production process that is related to their elaboration. The architectural patterns of this three-layer (three-tiered) architecture structure the software product in three, clearly differentiated and interconnected parts:

- *The presentation layer*: this contains the software components responsible for presenting the user with an application interface, which reasonably facilitates interaction of the user with the software product.
- *The application layer*: this provides the services that implement the functionality offered by the application.
- *The persistence layer*: this provides the services required to ensure the persistence of the data involved in the execution of the application.

Figure 4.2 shows a graphical representation of the software architecture discussed above.

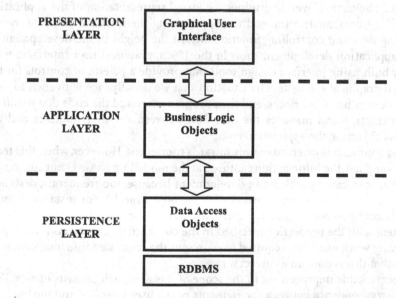

Fig. 4.2 A three-layered software architecture.

To obtain a correct and complete software production process, we first need to determine how the objects detected in the modelling phase should be represented in each layer. Basically, in the presentation layer, we will place the components that implement the graphical user interface (user interaction), which is the visual representation of data and services offered by the components in the application layer. In the application layer, we will place the components that fully implement the behaviour of the classes (which in commercial environments are usually referred to as "business classes") that are specified in the conceptual modelling phase. Following this architectural approach, the presentation layer will construct the messages that represent services of which the implementation resides in the application layer. The communication between these two levels produces the sending of messages from components in the presentation layer to components in the application layer.

The components in the application layer will, in turn, use the persistence services offered by the next layer. This persistence layer will comprise a set of database classes and relationships and act as a data warehouse for the modelled objects. Any commercial database management system (be it relational, object-relational or even purely object-oriented) can be used as a means of support and persistence service for the software components required in this layer.

In this way, we will have an execution strategy that, depending on the software architecture selected, will allow us to correctly structure the software components of the final software product. We will now discuss the relevant features of each layer in more detail.

The Presentation Layer

As stated above, this layer determines the visual representation of the application that will be presented to the end users, providing them with a concrete way of accessing data and controlling functionality. At the height of the development of rapid application development tools in the 1990s, graphical user interfaces were usually built using interface design tools that provide a palette of controls for the required graphical elements. The situation that we usually face with such tools is that designers build interfaces, and then programmers add the code that monitors user interaction and manages the data flow between the user interface and the business objects in the application layer.

This approach is oriented mainly towards user needs. However, when this technique is applied, the information captured at the modelling phase is not adequately used. This can cause problems in development because, too frequently, designers build interfaces that are inconsistent with the object model. For instance, a set of controls could be selected to represent an attribute or a relationship that is not consistent with the properties specified in the conceptual schema; additional programming work would be required to represent the requested information and to ensure that this is done in a correct way.

A remarkable improvement in the scope of this approach consists of establishing a correspondence between the elements of the user interface and the business objects that are represented in the conceptual schema. Such an approach would allow the construction of the user interface directly from the object model, limiting the use of a design tool and reducing design to essentially aesthetic aspects. This strategy would be feasible if the Conceptual Schema containing the static and dynamic properties of the system also included Presentation Patterns that are adequately embedded in the joint system specification. Philosophically speaking, this approach is an attractive interpretation because it implies that considering "how" a user of the software product will perceive the reality represented by this product must be part of the conceptual schema of the system.

It is remarkable to realise that, even if the design and the implementation of User Interfaces (UIs) are recognized to be the most time-consuming step of any software production process, its modelling has rarely been considered at the same level of data and function modelling when specifying a system. A whole community emerged to face that problem: the Human–Computer Interaction community (HCI). To face and solve this dichotomy, one challenging goal in the context of both Software Engineering and HCI is to provide proper bridges between their best-known software production methods and techniques. To face this problem, Interaction Modelling has to be properly considered in any modelling-based approach, with the same importance as that of the more conventional and commonly used data and process modelling.

As we discuss below, to provide a solution to this problem, another essential component of an Object-Oriented Conceptual Schema is the Presentation Model, where all the aspects of Human–Computer Interaction will be specified. To build correct and complete Conceptual Schemas, the conceptual patterns corresponding to this presentation layer will be as important and necessary as the ones used to specify the static structure and the behaviour of system classes.

Easy as it may appear, the problem gets more complicated. For user interfaces constructed this way to be useful and to follow certain functionality and graphical standards, the tool must allow us to change the location of the controls generated and also to provide mechanisms for designers to customize interface styles. This approach may be of interest if we examine studies of real development projects (Lauesen 1998). In these studies, users have pointed out two main aspects:

- First, they consider that having a small number of windows (only those strictly needed) to perform frequent tasks is desirable.
- Second, they wish to see the structure of the problem in these windows.

These requirements are easily achieved with this approach. From information that is associated to the object model, the relationships between classes have a clear representation in windows, which reflect the architectural features of the system in the interface. Moreover, these relationships also group functionalities that, in conventional environments, are usually scattered among the different related components in an imprecise way. By avoiding this, the resulting interface for the software product becomes more solid (from the conceptual point of view), more ergonomic (functionally speaking), and easier (under the usability criteria) to use.

The Application Layer

Once we have determined the location of the components that are associated with the aspects of the user interaction with the software product at the level we refer to as the presentation layer, we need to determine where to place those components that ensure the functionality of the system is what we specified in the original Conceptual Schema.

Therefore, in this layer (which we will refer to as the application layer), we will place this set of software components in charge of explicitly, correctly and completely implementing the behaviour of the classes specified during the conceptual modelling phase. In this context, we commonly refer to these classes as "business classes" because they represent objects of which the existence in the discourse universe is directly perceived.

The implementation of these components will be performed so that the functional equivalence between the description of the system and its reification in a given programming language is preserved. The problem adequately represents the functional properties that have been captured in the system specification in the corresponding language. To ensure that the software product verifies the properties of correctness and completeness, we must guarantee that all the specified properties are reflected in the resulting software product through the software components in this application layer. We must also ensure that the behaviour they manifest is the one that we defined in the conceptual schema.

In practice, this implies that every service specified in the modelling phase for each class must be available in the application layer. The execution of these services must also modify the state of objects in a correct way, thereby satisfying the constraints defined on the state of objects, triggering the corresponding services when some conditions are met after the change of state takes place, etc. In summary, the implementation must guarantee that the behaviour of any object in response to a service request will be the one defined in the specification of the problem according to an abstract execution model that will establish the steps and checks to be performed when executing a service. The abstract execution model will depend on the semantics of the adopted object model. This will be defined to precisely determine the behaviour of the object society specified according to the object model underlying the method.

The Persistence Layer

Once the components in charge of the interface (presentation layer), and the components in charge of the system functionality specified in the original conceptual schema (application layer) are determined, all that remains to be done is to determine which software components will be in charge of managing the persistence of objects in the data storing device selected. These are the software components we refer to as persistence layer.

In this layer, we will place the software components that encapsulate the access to data servers and are essentially going to manage the creation of the database that supports the persistence of application data and the operation of the database at execution time. In management applications, data persistence means Data Base Management Systems (DBMS). Therefore, the common implementation mechanism will be to produce a database schema from the object model created in the modelling phase. If, for instance, the DBMS is a relational one, then classes should be represented as database tables, and class attributes should be represented as database table fields. If it is object-oriented, or it is an object-relational extension to Relational DBMSs, then the conversion will be even easier because the semantic gap will be narrower: there will be classes in the Conceptual Schema and classes in the DBMS.

Class relationships can be a little more complex in the case of conversion but, in the end, every type of relationship will have its specific representation by adequately using the expressiveness provided by the target database environment. The generation of the relational schema can become quite a complicated task if the constructions available at the object model level are sophisticated and complex from the semantic point of view (especially in the case of class relationships). In any case, in accordance with what we have discussed so far, the conceptual patterns that capture the information in the Problem Space must allow the specification of the properties that are relevant for the generation of a correct database schema. This schema will be the representation of the static architecture of the system in the Solution Space.

With the system in execution, the activation of services will require recovering the state of the objects involved in the execution of these services. These data will be transferred from the persistence layer to the application layer, where they will be conveniently modified according to the semantics of the service before being updated in the persistence layer. To conclude our discussion on the software architecture proposed for the final software product, we describe the communication between the different layers in the next section.

Communication Between Layers

The components associated to the three layers that we have introduced are not independent. The communication between layers and, hence, between components in different layers is a basic feature of the resulting software product. Not surprisingly, its complexity can be greater than that of the individual components in each layer, due to the difficulty associated to the connection between potentially different technological platforms.

We must also point out that the communication between layers is a fundamental part of the final software product. It is responsible for ensuring that each layer is properly linked to the others. To do so, there must be a middleware that, for instance, ensures that a service request message created in the presentation layer is sent to the functional component associated with the object involved in the execution of this service. In turn, this component will have to interact with the database in the persistence layer through a given communications protocol in order to retrieve the data corresponding to the state of the object; it must modify these data and persist these again by storing them in the database. The software associated to these communication processes must be implemented according to certain protocols that have been specially created to standardize the transit of information from one layer to another as much as possible. The dynamism of the involved technologies commonly makes this part of the product an expensive and complex one, because it usually involves the interconnection of different technological platforms.

In summary, this set of software components, along with its interrelation-communication mechanisms, constitutes the resulting software product that can accurately represent in the Solution Space the properties that are specified in the Problem Space. In what follows, we introduce the methodological proposal presented in this book to ensure that this software production process is correctly implemented. The method is called OO-Method, and its distinctive feature is the definition of a set of conceptual patterns or conceptual primitives that are needed to specify Conceptual Models; it then associates each of these conceptual patterns to its corresponding software representation in a given programming environment. The implementation of this set of correspondences between conceptual patterns and software representations is the foundation that enables the implementation of a fully operational Conceptual Schemas Compiler. The final objective of such a software process is to make true the challenge of what the conceptual model itself becoming the program.

5
The OO-Method

In this section, we will review the most relevant historical proposals that, from the methodological point of view, have attempted to provide specific solutions to the problem of producing quality software. Then, we will briefly introduce the method presented in this book as an operational solution for the problems discussed.

5.1 Historical Background

As we have stated, in the last few decades, different approaches have been proposed in an attempt to provide a methodological solution to the problem of building quality software; these have followed the disciplines that are typical of any engineering field.

Everybody takes for granted that the Problem Space seriously constrains any software production method. This forces us to make the first decision: which model should be used for conceptual modelling? Historically, in an effort to provide a suitable and practical response, a variety of methods for the conceptual modelling of information systems have been proposed. All of these have tried to structure the space of software requirements by means of a set of components with well-defined semantics.

We have already explained that such approaches fall into two main categories:

- Structured Analysis and Design
- Object-Oriented Analysis and Design

Structured Analysis and Structured Design (SA/SD) methods, which appeared towards the end of the 1970s, take classical concepts of procedural programming to the modelling level, and introduce several diagrams as modelling languages of the structure of the system. Structured models are based on the notion of functional decomposition, and information flows are represented by hierarchical Data Flow Diagrams (DFDs).

Many methodologists put into practice the ideas behind the structured paradigm, using and developing the notion of functional decomposition and the DFDs framework. Among these are the proposals by Tom DeMarco (DeMarco 1979) and Larry Constantine and Ed Yourdon (Yourdon and Constantine 1979). Also relevant was the contribution by David Parnas (Parnas 1972). By the mid-1980s, some authors (Hatley and Pirbhai 1987; Ward and Mellor 1991) had enriched the structural framework with State Diagrams. Also, Harel proposed the use of the richer language of *statecharts* (Harel 1984; Harel et al. 1987), which added behaviour specification. The idea was to associate a state diagram or *statechart* to each function or activity, thereby characterizing its behaviour. Nevertheless, as we mentioned in previous sections, many nontrivial aspects had to be taken into account in order to connect structure and behaviour so that the modelling constructs used by software engineers could be regarded as semantically rigorous and precise.

Statemate (Harel and Naamad 1996) can be regarded as the first commercial tool to execute models and generate code from conceptual models at a higher abstraction level. In this sense, it is a pioneer tool that, despite its limited generation capabilities, can be considered as the precursor of much more generic and ambitious methods from the point of view of code generation (such as the one we introduce in this book).

Other formalisms that were used to specify behaviour at that time were Petri nets and more algebraic methods that had been proposed earlier, such as "Communicating Sequential Processes" (CSP; Hoare 1985) or "Calculus of Communicating Systems" (CCS; Milner 1980).

Object-Oriented Analysis and Design (OOAD) methods were born in the late 1980s. As in the case of SA/SD, we can state that, from the point of view of systems modelling, they represent an increase in the abstraction level of concepts from the world of programming to the world of modelling. However, in this case, the basic concept, the object, has features that will prove to be particularly useful for conceptual modelling, making these approaches a source of expressively powerful and operationally practical methods.

Inspired by the work of Peter Chen and his Entity-Relationship Diagrams (Chen 1976), several approaches produce different forms of Class and Object Diagrams to model the static structure of a system (Coad and Yourdon 1990; Rumbaugh et al. 1991; Booch 1994). To model behaviour, most of the object-oriented approaches at this time included some sort of State Transition Diagram (Harel 1987) that was associated to the notion of class to describe the behaviour or valid lives of any instance of a given class. This use of State Transition Diagrams is natural in an object-oriented framework, where the notion of change of state is central.

The connection between structure and behaviour is also more natural in an object-oriented framework because the concept of class encapsulates both static and dynamic properties. Behaviour modelling must, nevertheless, be precise in the specification of new aspects such as those of creation and destruction of objects, modification of class relationships, aggregation and inheritance.

Links between structure and behaviour require a detailed and rigorous definition in order to enable the implementation of tools that truly support model execution and full code generation. Some tools began to provide partial solutions, such as Object-Time, which is based on ROOM (Real Object-Oriented Modelling Method;

Selic et al. 1994). It is now included in Rational RealTime, or Rhapsody (Gery et al. 2002), which is based on the works of Eran Gery and David Harel on executable object modelling with statecharts (Harel and Gery 1997). These approaches focused on a set of carefully designed languages that included classes/objects diagrams that are adapted to the Booch (Booch 1994) and OMT (Rumbaugh et al. 1991) methods, which are driven by statecharts for specifying behaviour.

By the late 1990s, the acknowledged need for a common notation, which had been inspired in these two methods (OMT and Booch) and was used in the OOSE (Jacobson et al. 1992) method, became the basis for the definition of the Unified Modeling Language (Booch et al. 1997; UML 2004). The Object Management Group adopted this language as the standard modelling language in 1997.

The main problem of all the tools that attempt to provide an environment for the automatic generation of code from conceptual schemas is that the conceptual modelling primitives provided must have rigorous semantics to avoid ambiguity in their use. Formal support is key to characterizing the input of any hypothetical conceptual schema compiler. Additionally, each primitive must be associated to its corresponding software representation, so that a model compiler can be built as the implementation of all these precise correspondences between conceptual patterns and software representations.

All the tools discussed are *Model-Driven Code Generation* tools. They are normally based on the unrestrictive use of UML, a well-known representative being Rational (Rational 2006). They are *Model-Driven*, because the software production process clearly distinguishes two phases: modelling and programming. A programmer will have some code automatically generated that he/she will (hopefully) use for the implementation of the final software product. However, this still is the most expensive, tedious, manual and error-prone phase in the software production process.

Unlike the approaches above, the proposal that we present and defend in this book, the OO-METHOD, constitutes a *Model-Based Code Generation* method. The semantic difference between "Based" and "Driven" is crucial here. It is *Model-Based* because the software product will be obtained automatically from the source Conceptual Schema. Therefore, the produced implementation will be based on this Conceptual Schema, which will contain all the static, dynamic and presentation properties of the modelled system. It is here that we set a clear distinction from the other approaches. What underlies the OO-Method approach is the reality of a Conceptual Schemas Compiler that can be viewed as a kind of "Programming Machine" that will transform what until now have been source programming languages (Java, C#, VB, C++, ...) into assembly languages (in the classical sense of the term).

We will now provide an overview of the general features of the method, which will be explained in detail in the rest of the book.

5.2 General Features of the OO-Method

All the ideas introduced in this chapter make us realise that we need advanced software development environments that ensure agile and easy generation of reliable software products from Conceptual Schemas. If that generation process could also be automated, then this would represent a giant leap for the software production industry.

The goal of this book is to provide an operational solution in this context. To do so, we present the automatic software production method called OO-Method. This method is based on the ideas that we have introduced here, and provides a methodological approach for the construction of an object-oriented conceptual schema and its representation in a commercial development environment, thereby obtaining a quality software product.

In brief, the OO-Method proposal is based on the following principles:

• Supporting object-oriented conceptual modelling notions, in a framework where all the required conceptual primitives are defined in a precise way.
• Integrating formal and conventional methods of industrial acceptance.
• Providing an advanced software production environment that includes full code generation for the software architecture provided by the commercial development environment. By "full", we mean that the static, dynamic and presentation aspects that are specified in the Conceptual Schema are fully and correctly represented in the corresponding Software Product.

The development process suggested by OO-Method is related to the set of proposals that currently favour the notion of agility, thus emphasizing the creation of software processes that provide pragmatic solutions that are reasonably easy to use in industrial software production environments. It has two principal phases:

1. Conceptual Modelling (Problem Space) and
2. Generation of the Software Product (Solution Space) by applying an Abstract Execution Model.

The first phase of the conceptual model consists of eliciting and representing the set of essential properties of the information system under study, thereby creating the corresponding Conceptual Schema. Since the conceptual patterns or conceptual primitives used in its creation have a formal support, we can obtain the object-oriented formal specification (written in the OASIS language) at any time. In practice, this specification constitutes a high-level repository or data dictionary of the system. It is simply a matter of converting the graphical notation introduced in UML environments into the textual format of the formal syntax of the OASIS language. The process, as we described above, is reasonably easy, since each modelling primitive that is offered in the graphical environment exists because it represents a formal concept that is defined in the formal model associated to the object-oriented formal language (OASIS).

Moreover, from an industrial perspective, the textual format chosen to store OO-Method Conceptual Schemas (which is equivalent to OASIS specifications) can be based on the use of standards such as XML (or XMI) by defining a DTD to reflect the syntactic structure of an OASIS specification. This provides a textual representation with a well-known and widely used syntax that is easy to interpret.

In the second phase, we provide a precise execution model, which includes a strategy for code generation that determines which software representations correspond to each conceptual pattern of a Conceptual Schema. The implementation of these correspondences allows the creation of a Conceptual Schema Compiler that, for a given source Conceptual Schema, will automatically produce the corresponding software product. This software product will include all the static, dynamic and presentation aspects that are specified in the conceptual modelling phase. Therefore, we can conclude that the execution model determines how the concepts captured in the Conceptual Schema are represented in a computational environment.

The basic notion in this context is that of "functional equivalence". Previous works proved that a Conceptual Schema that corresponds to a formal specification written in OASIS is formally equivalent to a logic program that is obtained as a representation of this formal specification. (Pastor 1992) proves that an OASIS specification is equivalent to a first-order logic theory, along with its corresponding behaviour monitor. This formal equivalence property applies only to declarative programming environments.

However, in imperative environments, which are commonplace in the industry, we can introduce the alternative concept of functional equivalence to ensure consistency between the specification and the implementation of a system. If the resulting software product is the implementation of this set of precise correspondences between conceptual patterns and software representations, then the final product will always be functionally equivalent to the Conceptual Schema. This is because it will have been produced as a result of a deterministic reification that changes the abstraction level from the Problem Space to the Solution Space according to the code generation strategy defined in the execution model.

The OlivaNova Model Execution System (OlivaNova 2006) brands a set of tools that support the OO-Method and constitute an advanced environment for the automatic generation of software products from Conceptual Schemas. With the OlivaNova Model Execution System, we can say that true code generation ceases to be a dream and becomes a reality.

5.3 Other Approaches

Having introduced the general features of the OO-Method proposal, we will now analyse other approaches with similar aims in more detail to complete the general overview presented in the "Historical Background" section.

One of the problems faced by approaches based on Model-Based Code Generation (MBCG) is the widespread incorrect use of the term "code generation" in the last few decades. Any environment that offered some sort of assistance (no matter how small and irrelevant it was from the point of view of the final software product) has historically been called a "code generator".

A first important issue when discussing the State of the Art is to focus on a "serious" software generation environment. By "serious", we mean production methods that provide a generation environment that can prove with facts that the code that is produced as a result of the generation process represents a high percentage of the code of the final software product. This is the only way to unambiguously justify the benefits of using a given software production environment and its corresponding toolset.

There are two families of approaches within this perspective. The first are those approaches that are based on some sort of UML diagrams for modelling strategy, and provide automatic code generation capabilities among their features. The fact that these approaches lack formal support currently disqualifies them as potential generators of final applications. This is because any conceptual model compiler needs a source model built with modelling primitives that are precisely defined and that have precise semantics. The well-known modelling constructs such as specialisation / generalisation or association / aggregation / composition show that semantic ambiguity prevents the implementation of compilers that produce code that will be used as part of the final software product, as we discussed in the previous section.

The second family are those approaches that treat the problem by following the conceptual, two-phase strategy that consists of:

1. Determining the set of modelling primitives based on some formalism.
2. Providing a software production process based on specifications generated with these primitives of precise meaning.

In this area, Clyde et al. (1992), Jackson et al. (1994), Liddle et al. (1995), Liu et al. (1998) and Ceri and Fraternali (1996), among others, have developed proposals where the use of object-oriented formal languages in conjunction with conventional object-oriented methods facilitates the process of constructing prototypes from the specification created at the conceptual modelling phase.

Jackson and colleagues provide a tool called IPOST that automatically creates a prototype from a model that is obtained using his object-oriented analysis method (OSA). This proposal allows users to refine the model and generate a requirements specification. The generated prototype is used once and then discarded, and is used mainly for the validation and refinement of requirements.

Clyde and colleagues present the concept of *tunable formalism* in the context of the OSA model. This approach allows software engineers to work with different levels of formalism, from an informal level to a rigorous mathematical level. This allows both theory-oriented and practice-oriented individuals to work on the same model.

Liddle and colleagues show a new way of reducing the complexity of application specification and implementation by means of an implementation language that is equivalent to the model.

Liu and colleagues propose a language called SOFL and a method for this language. They attempt to introduce formal methods in the software production process at an industrial level by integrating formal methods, structured analysis and object-oriented methods.

The IDEA project led by S. Ceri focused on a deductive and active Object-Oriented DataBase Management System (OODBMS). It provides an object-oriented modelling environment to specify applications with the CHIMERA specification language. From these specifications, several software components that are common in database architectures (such as database triggers) can be generated and some of their formal properties validated (such as the confluence and completeness of triggers).

In summary, there are a large number of approaches that use concepts that are more or less analogous to those defined in this book. However, there is a fundamental difference that constitutes the main contribution of OO-Method: the fact that OO-Method makes the "compilation" of a Conceptual Schema to produce a final software product feasible. In other words, in the ideal case, the generated code does not need to be modified by the developer because the functionality of the system is already correctly represented in the implementation. In a way, this generated code could be viewed as a high-level assembly language (even though we are dealing with technological platforms such as NET, EJB, etc.).

In conclusion, the basic contributions of OO-Method with respect to existing proposals are the following:

- It uses of a graphical notation (similar to those used in conventional methods) that represents an abstraction of all the concepts in the underlying formal specification language (OASIS). Therefore, it uses a precise UML subset that is formally characterized.
- It provides automatic generation of software products that are functionally equivalent to the system specification in any language for which we define a transformation process. Therefore, it is not tied to any programming language or technological platform.
- It provides a different kind of tunable formalism because the expressiveness of OASIS is fully preserved and provides the analyst with a graphical, UML-based notation that is reified automatically on a given technological platform by means of the process of automatic generation that has already been introduced. It takes advantage of the desirable properties of a formal method while hiding its complexity. This produces an "illusion of simplicity", which makes it practical to use.

All that seen, it is time to enter into the particularities of the OO-Method. In Part II of this book, the focus will be placed on the Problem Space description, introducing the conceptual primitives proposed by the method to build correct and complete Conceptual Schemas. In Part III, the focus will be placed on how to proceed from the source Conceptual Schema (Problem Space) to its associated Software Product (Solution Space) through the corresponding process of model transformation.

Part II

Conceptual Modelling: About the Problem Space

6. Conceptual Modelling Primitives
7. Object Model
8. Dynamic Model
9. Functional Model
10. Presentation Model
11. Conceptual Modelling of Legacy Systems
12. Conceptual Model Validation

6

Conceptual Modelling Primitives

The objective of this chapter is to describe in detail all the modelling primitives (or conceptual patterns[1]) that are used by OO-Method to model Organizational Systems. Following from the previous section, OO-Method is an OO method for the automatic production of software that offers a framework for the construction of Organizational Information Systems. We must emphasize that FRISCO's (Falkenberg et al. 1998) proposed definition of Organizational System has been adopted. The first version of OO-Method was introduced in 1992, as one of the most relevant outcomes from the PhD thesis of Oscar Pastor (Pastor 1992), together with the Formal Language for Information System Specification OASIS. Since then, the method has incorporated a number of components until arriving at its current version, which is the one presented in this book.

OO-Method covers all the phases in the software development process, from the initial phases of requirements gathering and representation, to the development of the corresponding OO Conceptual Schema, plus the generation of the software product that represents it on a specific technological platform. The major contribution of the method resides in its ability to automatically generate a fully functional, final software product from a given Conceptual Schema. This is the part of the process analysed in this book. In MDA terms, the PIM *(Platform-Independent Model)* to PSM *(Platform-Specific Model)* transformation is performed automatically by a genuine Conceptual Model Compiler, which is responsible for the implementation of every single correspondence between conceptual constructors and their associated software representations.

In this section, we will introduce the complete range of conceptual constructors, leaving for the next part the explanation of the automatic source code generation process that takes place from these. OO-Method provides a collection of graphical elements, appropriately complemented by an optional precise textual specification, that represent those concepts supported by a formal specification – OASIS – and

---

[1] In this book, the terms "conceptual pattern", "modelling primitive" and "conceptual constructor" are used interchangeably to refer to the elements that compose the collection of basic units used to specify an information system.

that are used to gather the properties of a system and develop a conceptual schema (i.e. an abstract model of a given application domain). Afterwards, the definition of an execution model determines the details that will eventually guide the representation of the previously obtained conceptual schema in a specific development environment.

In summary, the major characteristics of OO-Method pertain to three different aspects:

- A graphical notation to help undertake the conceptual modelling phase. This notation is based on UML (UML 2004), a widespread and recognized standard, so that any experienced analyst will be familiar with its usage. The extension mechanisms of UML are used to introduce the necessary features not provided by UML itself.
- OASIS (Pastor 1992; Pastor et al. 1992; Pastor and Ramos 1995), an OO formal specification language that underpins the method and that determines the relevant conceptual patterns that are used to specify information systems. The graphical conceptual models that analysts create must deal only with those concepts from the detailed system specification that are provided by the OASIS language, which produce a repository or high-level data dictionary of the system being modelled. This repository can be represented, for any practical purpose, in well-known languages such as XML.
- An execution model that defines the process of representation of the conceptual schema in a particular software development environment.

OO-Method approaches software construction through the following two-phase process:

- Development of a *Conceptual Schema*, which is located in the problem space. A UML-based graphical language is provided to this effect. This language is expressive enough to represent the concepts of the OO model used as formal support. The Conceptual Schema allows us to gather and represent the static and dynamic properties of the system being developed. The major challenge at this stage is to obtain a precise definition of the system, independent of any implementation issue. Because of the mapping between the graphical elements and the underpinning specification language, an OASIS Formal Specification can be obtained at any time. This formal specification acts, as we have mentioned, as a high-level repository of the system being developed.
- Generation of an implementation according to a particular *Execution Model*, which is located in the solution space. The execution model determines the details necessary to obtain a specific implementation of the Conceptual Schema in a particular development environment, which will be dependent on the selected technological platform. Regardless of which platform is selected, the chosen code generation strategy dictates the way in which abstract OO-Method specifications can be executed.

The Conceptual Schema associated to a given Organizational System is not arbitrary, but must properly represent the set of requirements of the system being developed. OO-Method also provides mechanisms to build a Requirements Model from which a suitable Conceptual Schema can be obtained. The Requirements Model as well as its construction process can be found in Insfran (2003), and lie beyond the scope of this book.

The problem dealt with here is how to define a Conceptual Schema by characterizing the required conceptual primitives, and how to transform such a Conceptual Schema into the corresponding Software Product depending on the selected Software Architecture. Specifically, this book proposes as an example the use of a Software Architecture in which interface, functionality and persistence software components are appropriately differentiated (3-layer architecture). The widespread usage in industry of this kind of Software Architecture makes it generic enough for the associated Model Compiler to be immediately applicable.

Each element in the conceptual schema has its own representation within the chosen programming environment. This representation is made according to certain design and implementation patterns that are widely used and known, which deal with issues such as access control, user interface and object persistence. It is important to emphasize that these model-transformation principles are applicable to any other kind of Software Architecture, and therefore the results reported here can be exported to any other architecture. The process to follow must always be the same: once the conceptual patterns are fixed, each of them must have an associated software representation for any given Software Architecture. Once these correspondences between models are defined, the transformation process becomes the implementation of such a set of correspondences.

The interest in studying the transformation of specifications into implementations is not new in Software Engineering. In the realm of formal methods, and within declarative environments, it has been shown that the generated logic programs can be seen as first-order theories in a given logic (clausal, equational or dynamic in the most generic cases) where the three concepts of computation, logic deduction and satisfaction are equivalent. In the case of OO-Method, a software product that is formally equivalent to its OASIS specification can be obtained using declarative programming languages with well-defined operational and declarative semantics, with equivalence properties between both.

In imperative programming environments, the most widely used in the software production industry, the abovementioned formal declarative properties are lost. However, it is possible to obtain functionally equivalent programs by defining a set of correspondences between the elements of the conceptual model and their representation in the imperative programming environment. This is precisely what OO-Method does and what is presented in this book, in which only the imperative approach is examined. A similar work for declarative environments can be found in Pastor (1992). In either case, and as we have already said, the definition of the aforementioned set of correspondences enables the construction of Conceptual Schema Compilers, obtained as a result of the implementation of such sets of correspondences.

6.1 Conceptual Modelling. The Four Models

During the object-oriented conceptual modelling phase, the components of a society of objects (which represents the discourse domain) are described, avoiding any considerations about the implementation. The conceptual model of a system must specify all its properties (static and dynamic) and must not contain implementation details other than those already present in the requirements (Griethutsen 1982; Olivé 2004). A system is an assembly of different parts that constitute a unique whole with a specific purpose. The existence of this interaction between the components of a system is a very important fact, and such an interaction results in a system that, seen as a whole, has a function that is perceptible in the entities of its environment.

The Software Engineering discipline traditionally describes systems in three dimensions: data, control and process. Focusing on specification techniques, we can find the following types of techniques:

• Function specification techniques, which describe interactions (or parts thereof) that are relevant in the system domain.
• Behaviour specification techniques, which represent the order in which functions occur over time.
• Communication specification techniques, useful to specify how the system communicates with external entities, or how the system components interact with one another in order to carry out the functions.
• Decomposition specification techniques, which allow us to describe the components of the system, defined in terms of their meaning as far as their environment is concerned.

One of the major advantages that justify the use of the Object-Oriented modelling paradigm is that it treats the above-listed dimensions uniformly under the unifying concept of object. Seeing a System as an interacting society of objects is a reasonable way to approach the structuring of the system, comprising the identification and adequate representation of the objects and the relationships among objects for the system being analysed. Different OO methods provide a number of techniques and diagrams to cover the previously defined four areas. In order to capture all this information, OO-Method uses four models that describe a Society of Objects from four complementary viewpoints. In reality, each model in OO-Method represents a view on particular aspects of the Conceptual Schema (which is unique, seen as a whole). The goal is making system specification, of which the Conceptual Schema is the outcome, simpler and more functional. Each model, as we will describe, provides a series of techniques (together with their associated UML diagrams) to introduce the information considered relevant.

Specifically, OO-Method structures the development of a Conceptual Schema around the following models:

• *Object Model*, which defines the structure and static relationships between the classes that have been identified in the problem domain, as well as the service activator objects.

- *Dynamic Model*, which defines the possible sequences of services for the objects of a given class (possible valid lives) and the aspects related to the interaction amongst objects.
- *Functional Model*, which captures the semantics associated to object state changes, triggered by the occurrence of events.
- *Presentation Model*, which extends conventional conceptual modelling by incorporating a view responsible for capturing the information that defines the characteristics of the user interface and the way in which users will interact with the system.

The first three models capture the static and dynamic information necessary for the development of any OO Conceptual Schema. The presentation model contributes a fourth view that is necessary to specify how users will interact with the system. Consequently, how users interact with and perceive the system becomes a fundamental component of the modelling, very much like the specification of the static and dynamic aspects described above.

Detecting how the interaction between users and the system will be at the problem space level is very important. As we will detail, this information is captured by using interface patterns; once identified in the realm of conceptual modelling, these will allow us to determine the properties that each specific interface will have, independently of the particular implementation that will be eventually obtained as part of the final software product.

Below, we present the conceptual primitives associated with each of these four models, the aim being to detail the collection of constructors provided by OO-Method to develop Conceptual Schemas. The description of each primitive will be made according to a common structure, stating its name, its description, the set of characteristic properties, its graphical notation (if existing), and the list of related primitives, the specification of which will be done consecutively.

Example.   *We will use a simplified Rent-a-Car business management system as an example. We will use this example as we describe the different conceptual modelling primitives; a complete version of it can be found in Pastor and Molina (2006), which can be consulted for a better understanding of the problem domain.*

The following introduction is offered in order to familiarize the reader with the problem domain that will be solved in the book:

The major business activity of the company is renting cars without driver. Since the company is located in a main tourist area, most cars are acquired at the beginning of the high season (summer months) and are sold once it is over, although car sales can occur at any time if a price and delivery date are agreed upon with a buyer.

The company works with two kinds of customers: agencies and direct clients. Agencies are other companies (or divisions of the same company) that usually rent cars in order to re-rent them (keeping certain margins), whereas direct clients are individuals who directly rent cars. Direct clients can benefit from certain discounts.

Renting a car implies the creation of a contract between company and customer, which captures the rental details (car plate number, tariff, date, rental duration in days, place of return, etc.). The contract stays open until the car is returned, when the final computation of charges is performed and the bond is returned, if appropriate, and the amount due, if any, is paid. While the contract is open, some details such as the date or place of return can be altered, and extras (such as car phones or baby seats) can be added or removed.

The notation to be used in figures is that corresponding to the UML component that is selected in each occasion as a modelling element associated to the primitive.

7

Object Model

The Object Model of OO-Method consists of a Class Diagram that graphically describes the structure of the system in terms of its component classes plus their structural relationships, thereby giving a static view of the system architecture.

The major conceptual primitives or patterns are the class and the relationship between classes. The detailed characteristics of these primitives will be explored below. The accurate characterization of class properties and relationships between classes will define the collection of modelling elements that is necessary for the Class Diagram from the UML viewpoint. Only a relevant core of primitives is necessary. As we said before, this characterization comprises an important contribution of OO-Method, because it reduces complexity and removes the ambiguity often associated with the usage of UML in software production industrial environments.

The steps that must be followed in order to build a class diagram are:

- Identify which classes make up the System and define the structural relationships amongst them.
- Flesh out the internal structure of each class in terms of their properties: attributes, services and integrity constraints.
- Define the agents that are authorised to activate services as additional inter-class relationships.

Example. *From the description of our example, we can identify:*

- *Classes such as "Client", "Vehicle" or "Rental".*
- *Attributes such as "Name" (of "Client") or "Model" (of "Vehicle").*
- *Services such as "Rent" or "Return" (both of "Vehicle").*
- *Relationships such as that between the "Client" and the "Rent" service of the "Vehicle" class.*

7.1 Classes

The concept of class comprises the basic notion in the OO model associated to OO-Method. Its definition is the usual one in an object-oriented context: it denotes a structural and behavioural abstraction that is shared by a set of objects. Within the philosophical framework that we discussed in the Introduction, objects are the particulars whereas classes are the universals. In an OO-Method model, the conceptual schema represents the universals, and the computational model that implements it gives birth to a society of objects that comprise the particulars, seen as specific instances of the universals in the schema.

Class properties are organized in three large groups: attributes, services and integrity constraints. Each class holds a given internal structure that contains the features linked to attributes, services and integrity constraints.

Graphically, classes are represented by a rectangular box with three differentiated areas: Heading, Attributes and Services.

Example. *Figure 7.1 shows a graphical representation of a class named "Class" with two attributes named "Attribute1" and "Attribute2", and two services named "Service1" and "Service2".*

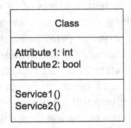

Fig. 7.1 Graphical notation of a class.

The attributes and services that can be seen in a class box correspond to those defined in the internal structure of the class. The heading area is the top part of the box, and contains the class name. Class names must be unique within a conceptual schema. Dashed lines can radiate from the box boundary towards services of other classes, representing, as we will describe below, agent relationships. In addition, solid lines (with an optional terminator) can also connect the boundary of a class box with other classes, representing structural relationships between these. As we will see, these structural relationships will be used to represent association/aggregation and inheritance.

Example. *The following classes can be identified in our car rental sample system:*

- *Client*
  - *Each actual client of the company will be a particular of this universal. Clients can book vehicles or rent them for a certain period of time.*
- *Vehicle*
  - *Each actual vehicle of the company's fleet will be a particular of this universal.*
- *WithdrawnVehicle*
  - *Every so often, vehicles are withdrawn from the fleet and offered on sale in order to keep the fleet current.*

- *VehicleKind*
  - *Instances of this class will allow us to classify the vehicles of the fleet.*
- *Tariff*
  - *Different tariffs are applicable, depending on the kind of vehicle and the rental season.*
- *Rental*
  - *Each instance of this class represents a contract by virtue of which a particular client rents a vehicle for a specific time.*
- *Invoice*
  - *Every time that a client returns a rented vehicle, an invoice is created that will reflect the charges derived from the rental.*
- *InvoiceItem*
  - *Each item in an invoice corresponds to a concept that results in a charge being made, such as the number of days of rental, the number of kilometres driven, extra devices included in the rental, or any penalties for delayed return or necessary repairs.*
- *IssuedInvoice*
  - *Once an invoice is complete, it is issued so it can be cashed. The actual charge can be made at the return time or later.*
- *Administrator*
  - *Administrators will manage the system, entering new vehicles, retiring existing ones, entering new clients, performing bookings and rentals, generating invoices and issuing them.*

Example. *Figure 7.2 graphically shows the "Vehicle" class. The attributes "PlateNumber", "CreationDate", "Make", "Model", "Fuel", "Kilometres", "Status" and "Notes" describe this class statically, "PlateNumber" serving also as a vehicle identifier. Class services include the basic "Create" and "Delete" as well as "Rent" and "Return".*

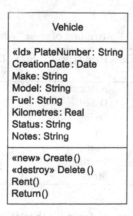

Fig. 7.2 The "Vehicle" class.

Later in the discussion, we will see how the "Vehicle" class will involve other services and attributes, but the description above is valid for the purpose of illustration.

The properties associated to attributes, services and integrity constraints are described now. Each property will be accompanied by its associated specification mechanism. Later figures will show sample representations.

7.1.1 Attributes

Attributes are the structural properties of a class. They are evaluated in the data domain, i.e. they are not object-valued. Object-valued attributes will be represented as a relationship between classes (association, aggregation or composition), as explained elsewhere. Each attribute takes a value for each instance of the class, which can be null if so specified. The well-known notion of state is characterized by the set of values assigned to the object attributes (those data-valued analysed in this section, together with those object-valued that will be introduced later).

An attribute's name must not be ambiguous within the context of the class (and, as explained below, must be unique within the specialisation network to which the class belongs). For identification purposes, object identifier attributes (one or many) can be determined for each class, in the appropriate order if there are several of these. In addition to the optional identifier declaration, every attribute has the following properties:

- A name
- A data type
- A size, for attributes of type "string"
- A default value
- A flag indicating whether the attribute value is required when an object of the class is created
- A flag indicating whether null values are accepted

Example.   *Table 7.1 shows the attributes of class "Vehicle".*

Table 7.1 Attributes of class "Vehicle".

Name	Type	Identifier	Data type	Size	Default value	Require on creation	Nulls allowed
PlateNumber	Constant	Yes	Autonumeric			Yes	No
CreationDate	Constant	No	Date			Yes	No
Make	Variable	No	String	10		Yes	No
Model	Variable	No	String	20		Yes	No
Kilometres	Variable	No	Real			Yes	No
Status	Variable	No	String	1		Yes	No
Notes	Variable	No	String	100		Yes	Yes

The default value is a well-formed formula that is type-compatible with the attribute, with the conventional meaning of associating the corresponding value to the attribute in case no value is provided for it at creation time.

If the value of the attribute is required on object creation, then the default value formula is optional. If the value of the attribute is not required on creation and the attribute does not allow null values, then a default value formula must be specified; otherwise, no value would be assigned to the attribute.

Example.   *It can be assumed that, when a new vehicle is acquired, the kilometre count is zero. Thus, requesting kilometre count information each time a vehicle is created would not be necessary, since this attribute would be assigned by default.*

The "Status" attribute stores the status of the vehicle in encoded form, following this convention:

A → *Available*
O → *Rented out*
S → *Being serviced*
B → *Retired*

Assuming that the initial status of a vehicle is always "Available", a default value can be specified for this attribute. Incorporating default values, Table 7.1 would be transformed into Table 7.2.

Table 7.2 Attributes of class "Vehicle".

Name	Type	Identifier	Data type	Size	Default value	Require on creation	Nulls allowed
PlateNumber	Constant	Yes	Autonumeric			Yes	No
CreationDate	Constant	No	Date			Yes	No
Make	Variable	No	String	10		Yes	No
Model	Variable	No	String	20		Yes	No
Kilometres	Variable	No	Real		0	No	No
Status	Variable	No	String	1	"A"	No	No
Notes	Variable	No	String	100		Yes	Yes

Additional and optional properties of attributes are:

- An alias
- Comments
- A help message

The alias, as its name suggests, is an alternative to the attribute name. An attribute's name is subject to some uniqueness, length and syntax restrictions, which are necessary in order to guarantee the integrity and validity of the conceptual model. The alias, however, is not subject to these restrictions, and therefore it can be used to better describe the attribute. Its usefulness is clear for presentation purposes, where the attribute is better referred to by its alias, which is more usable and understandable. For example, accented letters or spaces cannot be used for an attribute's name. The name cannot coincide with certain reserved words of the OASIS formal specification. Referencing the attribute by name would not be practical or correct if usability is considered a critical aspect of software quality – as it is. The issue is solved by using an alias as an alternative reference.

Example.   *The attribute name "PlateNumber" does not contain a space between the two words. The more readable "Plate Number" could be used as an alias of this attribute.*

Comments allow the analyst to document the attribute's purpose and usage, whereas the help message is useful to give some information about the attribute to the final users of the application.

Example.   *Comments for attribute "Status" could be as follows:*

"Possible vehicle states are:
A: Available
O: Rented out
S: Being serviced
R: Retired
The default status is Available."

The three properties described above (alias, comments and help message) are part of the definition of most conceptual modelling primitives. It is important to emphasize that a good usage of these properties and, in particular, of comments allows the analyst to keep excellent and up-to-date documentation of the conceptual schemas and, as a consequence, of the software applications that are automatically generated from these.

Example.   *Figure 7.3 shows classes "Client" and "Vehicle", including their attributes, as an example of the notation being used.*

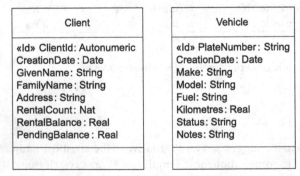

Client	Vehicle
«Id» ClientId: Autonumeric	«Id» PlateNumber: String
CreationDate : Date	CreationDate : Date
GivenName: String	Make: String
FamilyName : String	Model: String
Address: String	Fuel: String
RentalCount: Nat	Kilometres: Real
RentalBalance : Real	Status: String
PendingBalance : Real	Notes: String

Fig. 7.3 Classes "Client" and "Vehicle".

The second column of the tables shown earlier contains an attribute "type", which must not be confused with the attribute's data type. There are three types of attributes in OO-Method: constant, variable and derived. An attribute's type must be specified when it is created.

- *Constant.* The value of constant attributes remains unchanged once the object is created. It is common that one or more constant attributes act as instance identifiers.
- *Variable.* The value of variable attributes can change over time, depending on the occurrence of relevant services. Every variable attribute must have at least one relevant service, which is the one that causes the state change associated to the modification of the attribute's value.
- *Derived.* The value of derived attributes is computed from the value of other attributes of the class. Therefore, one or more derivations (derivation formulae) must be necessarily specified.

A derivation is a pair *<Condition, Effect>*. The *Condition* component is optional and consists of a well-formed Boolean formula. The *Effect* component is a required well-formed formula that establishes the value that the attribute would have if the associated condition evaluates to true. Understandably, the data type resulting from this formula must coincide with the declared data type of the derived attribute. It must be noted that a derived attribute cannot participate in any of the well-formed formulae that compose its derivations, since this would cause an infinite loop when computation of the attribute's value is attempted.

If only one derivation exists for a given derived attribute, then no derivation condition can exist. Since only one derivation exists, its value is unconditionally evaluated.

If multiple derivations exist for a given derived attribute, then all of them but one must necessarily have a derivation condition. The derivation without a condition plays the role of an "else", and acts as a default derivation, being applied whenever none of the conditions of the other derivations are satisfied.

Example.   *A good example of a derived attribute is found in class "Client", where the derived attribute "RentalCount" (of natural data type) represents the number of rentals that a particular client has completed. This is a derived attribute because its value is obtained by counting how many instances of the associated class Rentals refer to the desired type of rental.*

Table 7.3 shows the derivations for "RentalCount". The condition for the first derivation becomes true if no rentals exist for the client. The effect is 0, i.e. the value for the derived attribute will be set to zero. The second derivation, with no associated condition, sets the value of the attribute to the result of counting effective rentals (those for which "Status" is "E") of the client.

Table 7.3 Derivations of attribute "RentalCount".

Condition	Effect
EXIST(Rentals) = FALSE	0
	COUNT(Rentals)
	WHERE (Rentals.Status = "E")

Derivation conditions are verified in the same order as attribute derivations are defined. For this reason, ordering an attribute's derivations from the most specific to the most generic is considered a meaningful analysis practice.

Definition order is not relevant when derivation conditions are mutually exclusive. The only restriction imposed on the analyst is that the last derivation of any attribute must have no associated derivation condition.

For derived attributes, specifying a default value or whether it allows null values is meaningless. Similarly, stating whether the attribute value is required on object creation is also meaningless, since these properties depend on the attributes used for the derivation expression. Obviously, a default value can be specified for constant and variable attributes, as well as whether or not they allow null values.

Example.   *The class "Vehicle" has constant and variable attributes. Attributes "PlateNumber" and "CreationDate" are constant because their values do not change during the vehicle's lifetime. In addition, the plate number is used as a vehicle identifier, since its value is unique within the "Vehicle" class (it is impossible to have two or more vehicles with the same plate number). It is possible, on the other hand, to create multiple vehicles with the same date.*

The remaining attributes are variable, since their values can be modified during the object's lifetime. It is evident that kilometre count and vehicle status will change as different clients hire the vehicle. It is not so evident, however, that the make and model of a vehicle can change once the vehicle has been created. Still, these attributes are defined as variable in order to cater for typographical errors from the system administrator and to allow these data to be entered at a later time after the vehicle has been created. As we show elsewhere, services will be used to modify the values of these attributes.

Most of the time, the only constant attributes of a class are those that are employed to define its identification function (which, obviously, must be constant during the objects' lifetime), and the rest of the attributes are usually variable or derived.

7.1.2 Services

The local state of an object is modified when a service occurs. The services of a class therefore comprise the basic components associated with the specification of the behaviour of a class. The concept of service can be defined as a processing unit, which may be atomic (an event) or molecular (a local transaction or local operation).

Graphically, services are shown in the bottom part of the box used to represent a class. For each service, its name (which must be unique within the class) is shown, differentiating, as we explain below, those services that are used to create and destroy objects of the class (*new* and *destroy* respectively), and between own services and shared events.

Example.   *Figure 7.4 shows the graphical representation of classes "Client" and "Vehicle", already depicted in Fig. 7.3. This time, services are shown.*

Client
«Id» ClientId: Autonumeric CreationDate : Date GivenName : String FamilyName : String Address : String RentalCount : Nat RentalBalance : Real PendingBalance : Real
«new» NewClient () «destroy» DeleteClient () Edit()

Vehicle
«Id» PlateNumber : String CreationDate : Date Make: String Model: String Fuel: String Kilometres : Real Status: String Notes: String
«new» New () «destroy» Delete () Rent() Return ()

Fig. 7.4 Attributes and services of classes "Client" and "Vehicle".

As we have said, a service's name must be unique within the context of a class (i.e. there cannot be two services in a class with the same name). We will explain later that this characteristic must also hold in the context of the class' specialisation hierarchy.

In addition to the name, a service may also have an Alias, some Comments and a Help Message.

The following sections explain the details of events, local transactions and operations, which comprise the three kinds of services that can be specified within a class. This section will end with the introduction of service precondition specifications.

Events

Events are atomic processing units that represent the abstraction of a state change that occurs instantly. There exist different types of events.

1. *Creation (New).* The first event in any object's life is a creation event. Formally, this is a special event that is unique for each class. It can be seen as a meta-level service, associated to a meta-object that represents a class as an instance of a meta-class "Class" (which would contain all the properties that classes have). This event acts as an object-creating factory. In practice, such a *new* event is usually represented as an event of the class being specified, emphasizing the fact that it is the creation event in an intuitive and clear fashion.

In any case, creation events (as well as destruction events, which we discuss below) denote "strong" dynamics, since the object transitions from a state of non-existence to a state of existence (or vice versa, in the case of "destroy").

The activation of a creation event must provide values to all the attributes that have been marked as requiring a value on creation. Note that this applies to constant and variable attributes but not to derived ones, since the value of these is computed in terms of the values of other attributes of the class.

The proposed graphical representation is very simple, making use of the stereotype facility in UML. Creation events are marked with the "new" reserved word.

Example. *Creation events include the "New" event of class "Vehicle" and the "New-Client" event of class "Client". According to the properties defined for the attributes of class "Vehicle" shown in Table 7.2, the creation event of this class ("New") must provide a value for attributes "PlateNumber", "CreationDate", "Make", "Model" and "Notes".*

2. Destruction (Destroy). This event is in charge of destroying an object.

Example. *Destruction events include the "Delete" event of class "Vehicle" and the "DeleteClient" event of class "Client". The full declarations of these events, which include their arguments, are, respectively, "Delete(p_thisVehicle)" and "Delete-Client(p_thisClient)", where "p_thisVehicle" is the vehicle instance to delete and "p_thisClient" is the client instance to delete.*

The graphical representation of destruction events is similar to that of creation events, using the stereotype "destroy".

3. Own. These are events the occurrence of which affects the state of a single object. They are specified only in the signature of the class to which they belong. The state change caused by their occurrence is also specified within the class to which they belong, as we explain in the discussion on the Functional Model.

Example. *Own events include the "Edit" event of the "Client" class.*

4. Shared. These are events the occurrence of which affects the state of two or more objects. Graphically, they are depicted by solid lines connecting the involved events, as shown in Fig. 7.5.

Example. *The classes "Client" and "Vehicle" share the "Rent" and "Return" events.*

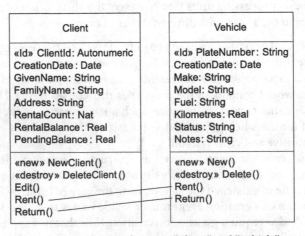

Fig. 7.5 Shared events between "Client" and "Vehicle".

Shared events are specified for each of the classes sharing them and, within each of these classes, the local effect of the occurrence of the event must be determined. The global effect of the event is obtained as the collection of its local effects.

Since an event is an abstraction of a state change, every own or shared event must generate a change of state and, consequently, modify the value of one or more attributes of the object associated to the event activation. Every variable attribute has at least one associated event that is responsible of its variability. The kind of state changes given by own and shared events characterizes the weak dynamics of the objects of a class. By weak dynamics, we mean those changes that occur during the active lifetime of an object, as opposed to strong dynamics, which imply a transition between existence and non-existence.

Arguments

A basic property of services is comprised by their arguments. Every service, except for creation ones, has an implicit argument that corresponds to the class to which the service belongs (if an own service) or the collection of classes that share the service (if a shared event). This implicit argument is, obviously, object-valued, since it refers to the class where the service is specified. Each additional argument of a service has an associated data type.

The properties of an argument are:

- A name
- A data type
- A size, for arguments of type "string"
- A default value (optional)
- A flag indicating whether null values are accepted
- An alias (optional)
- A help message (optional)
- Comments (optional)

The argument name must be unique within the context of the service. In order to make specification easier, it cannot coincide with the name of any property of the class. If it did, as explained elsewhere, then well-formed formulae used in the context of a class' services would not be able to distinguish between arguments of a service and properties of the class.

The default value is a well-formed formula of a type compatible with that of the argument, built from other arguments of the service and/or visible attributes[1] of the associated class. If a default value is given, then the system uses it as a suggested value, allowing the agent in charge of service activation to change it.

[1] In OO-Method, visible attributes of a class are those that are declared within the class, plus those declared within other classes related to the former via association, aggregation or composition.

In addition, there are two kinds of arguments:

- Input arguments. Their value must be determined for the service to execute. The agent in charge of activating the service is responsible for assigning a value to these.
- Output arguments. They take a value as a consequence of execution, once the service finishes successfully. Their value is expressed through a value expression (described below), which is a well-formed formula similar to that described for the default value. In addition, conditions can be incorporated into its specification, so that the value of an output argument can depend on their satisfaction.

Example.   *Tables 7.4 and 7.5 show, respectively, input and output arguments of the "Book" event of class "Rental".*

Table 7.4 Input arguments of event "Book".

Name	Data type	Size	Default value	Nulls allowed
p_agrClient	Client			No
p_agrVehicle	Vehicle			No

Table 7.5 Output arguments of event "Book".

Name	Data type	Size	Default value	Nulls allowed
ps_Message	String	100		No

The event has two object-valued input arguments: "p_agrClient", which identifies the client making the booking, and "p_agrVehicle", which refers to the vehicle being booked.

As output argument, "ps_Message" is used to return a message with information about the booking.

An output argument value expression is a pair <*Condition, Effect*>. The *Condition* component is optional and comprises a well-formed Boolean formula. The *Effect* component is also a well-formed formula[2], required in this case, which determines the value that the output argument will have if the condition evaluates to true, depending on class attributes and service arguments (both input and output) involved in the definition of the output argument being discussed. It must be noted that an output argument cannot be part of the well-formed formulae used for its value expressions, since this would cause an infinite loop.

If a unique value expression exists for a given output argument, then it must have no associate condition. Being the only one, its effect must be evaluated unconditionally in order to assign a value to the output argument.

---

[2] The syntax for this well-formed formula can be found in Pastor and Molina (2006).

If multiple value expressions exist for a given output argument, then all of them must have a condition except for one, which cannot have a condition. This latter value expression acts as a default value, and is applied whenever none of the conditions associated to the remaining value expressions are satisfied.

Example.   *Table 7.6 shows the value expressions that are defined for output argument "ps_Message" of event "Book" of class "Rental". As explained in the previous example, this event is used to make a vehicle booking, and the output argument is used to return information about the bookings.*

Specifically, the user making the booking must be informed of how many pending bookings they have (if more than one) or be reminded that the booking needs confirmation (if it is the first one).

Table 7.6 Value expressions for output argument "ps_Message".

Condition	Effect
COUNT(p_agrClient.Rentals) WHERE (p_agrClient.Rentals.Status = "R") > 1	"You still need to confirm " + IntToStr(COUNT(p_agrClient.Rentals) WHERE (p_agrClient.Rentals.Status = "R")) + " bookings."
	"Please remember confirming your booking."

Let us analyse these value expressions. The first one includes the condition:

COUNT(p_agrClient.Rentals) WHERE (p_agrClient.Rentals.Status = "R") > 1

This condition evaluates to true if the client has more than one booking (rentals with a status of "R"). In that case, and assuming, for the sake of exemplification, that the COUNT operator returned the value 3, the message would consist of the following text:

"You still need to confirm 3 bookings."

since "IntToStr"[3] is a predefined function that transforms an integer value into a character string, and the "+" operator, applied to character strings, means concatenation.

The second value expression has no condition, only an effect. This is therefore the default value expression, and results in the output argument having the value:

"Please remember confirming your booking."

---

[3] The usage of functions of an apparent low level such as "IntToStr" may lead to think that some aspects of the solution space are taken into the modelling realm, i.e. the problem space. This would go against the fundamental principles of OO-Method. It is not so. It is true that the existence of such low-level facilities is leveraged but this is done pragmatically, in order to facilitate the subsequent transition from model to program. A purely declarative style could be used, passing a more complex problem to the compiler. The usage of these facilities in such particular cases is done with the sole objective of making the transformation process somewhat more direct and efficient.

We have stated earlier that every service, except for creation services, receives an object-valued argument that represents the class (or classes, in the case of shared services) that owns the service.

What happens with creation services? Creation services and, specifically, creation events have the objective of giving values to the attributes (constant, variable and derived) that have been flagged as requiring a value (computing a value in the case of derived attributes) on object creation. This value is obtained via an argument in the creation event. Thus, every creation event has an argument for each attribute flagged to require a value on object creation. Logically, the argument's data type coincides with that of the corresponding attribute, and so happens with the data size and nulls allowed flag. In addition, the default value for the argument is the same as that defined for the attribute.

Example.   *Table 7.7 shows the arguments for the creation event "Create" of class "Vehicle". Note the correspondence between these and the attributes of the class, as shown in Table 7.2. For instance, the attribute "make" corresponds to the argument P_atrMake. Their properties must be – as, in fact, they are – compatible.*

Table 7.7 Arguments of creation event "Create" of "Vehicle".

Name	Data type	Size	Default value	Nulls allowed
P_atrPlateNumber	Autonumeric			No
P_atrCreationDate	Date			No
P_atrMake	String	10		No
P_atrModel	String	20		No
p_atrNotes	String	100		Yes

Example.   *Table 7.8 shows the arguments for event "Edit" of class "Client". This event has an object-valued argument that represents the client to edit. This is the first argument of the event, and its existence can be assumed implicitly, because any class event will have this first mandatory argument. In addition, it has three arguments that are used to modify the values of attributes "GivenName", "FamilyName" and "Address", each one with its corresponding data type, size, default value and null value acceptance.*

Table 7.8 Arguments of event "Edit" of "Client".

Name	Data type	Size	Default value	Nulls allowed
p_thisClient	Client			No
p_GivenName	String	20		No
p_FamilyName	String	30		No
p_Address	String	50		No

Transactions

The specification of the dynamics of a society of interacting objects cannot be fully achieved using only atomic units of execution. Events often appear grouped into execution units of a larger granularity, which we call transactions.

Intuitively, the concept of transaction can be defined as a molecular execution unit that is composed of services and has two fundamental properties:

- *No visibility of intermediate states.* A transaction is a composition of multiple services; the states realised between these services are not visible from the outside.
- *Execution "all or nothing".* Once a transaction has started, it necessarily continues until it is finished, or it aborts from the beginning (leaving the system in the same state as that immediately before the transaction started).

Formally, a transaction can be seen as a term of an elementary process algebra built over a basic alphabet composed of the class' services (events and other transactions), and using basic sequence and decision operators. The set of associated axioms includes the verification of the above-described properties.

From a practical point of view, every transaction is specified by a formula that uses other services in the class as well as sequencing, decision and iteration facilities:

- Sequencing, by using a basic operator in order to group services.
- Decision, by allowing each participating service to be preceded by a condition, or guard, so that the service is activated only if the condition is met.
- Iteration, by using operators such as "for all" to express iterative execution of a service over a collection of objects. This is particularly useful with multi-valued associations that affect the definition of a transaction, as explained later.

Transactions can also specify input arguments, which are used to initialize arguments of the component services, and output arguments, which have the same semantics as in the case of events.

Graphically, a service is defined as a transaction by using the stereotype "transaction"[4].

Example.   *The class "Vehicle" contains the local transaction "RETURN-VEHICLE", composed of two events of this class:*

- *"Return", which returns a rented vehicle, and*
- *"SendForMaintenance", which sends the vehicle to the garage for servicing before the next rental.*

This transaction has a single argument, representing the vehicle that is being returned. The events "Return" and "SendForMaintenance" also have a single argument that represents the vehicle in question.

---

[4] Syntactically, an "all caps" style will be used for transactions in order to differentiate these from events.

Thus, the transaction formula is:

$$RETURNVEHICLE(pt\_Vehicle) = Return(pt\_Vehicle) \, .$$
$$SendForMaintenance(pt\_Vehicle)$$

In this formula, "pt_Vehicle" is the name of the transaction's object-valued input argument, which is used to initialize the object-valued arguments of the events "Return" and "SendForMaintenance". Note that the dot (".") operator is used to indicate sequence.

Example.   *The previous example shows that a vehicle is always sent for maintenance when it is returned.*

Let us imagine that vehicles must be sent for maintenance only if their kilometre count is larger than 50,000. This means that the event "SendForMaintenance" must be executed only in such a case. The transaction formula would be changed as follows:

$$Return(pt\_Vehicle) \, . \, \{pt\_Vehicle.Kilometres > 50000\}$$
$$SendForMaintenance(pt\_Vehicle)$$

Note that the difference between this formula and the previous one is:

$$\{pt\_Vehicle.Kilometres > 50000\}$$

which is what has been called a guard, i.e. a well-formed Boolean formula that, depending on its value when evaluated, determines whether the service preceded by it is executed or not.

As we have said, and like in the case of events, local transactions can have output arguments with their corresponding value expressions. In the case of transactions, output arguments have additional functions. Firstly, they can be used in the transaction formula to initialize output arguments of the services that compose the transaction, so that they receive a computed value for the output argument that they initialize. Secondly, they can be part of a guard, so that it is possible to make the execution of a service depend on the value of some output arguments from services executed earlier.

Example.   *Let us imagine that the event "Return" has an output argument "ps_Km" that indicates the number of kilometres made by the vehicle during the rental. Let us also assume that returned vehicles must be sent for maintenance only if the number of kilometres made in the last rental is above 10,000. Let us describe how these changes would affect the transaction formula described in the previous example.*

First, an output argument in the transaction is necessary in order to capture the value of the output argument "ps_Km" of event "Return". If this new output argument of the transaction is called "pst_Km", then the call to the first event in the transaction formula would be changed into:

$$Return(pt\_Vehicle; pst\_Km).$$

Note that the declaration includes not one but two argument lists (input and output), each one with a single element, and separated by a semicolon (";") in order to differentiate this from the list separator, the comma (",").

With regard to the second service in the transaction, a guard was set on the value of the attribute "Kilometres" of the vehicle. This guard must be modified so that the "SendForMaintenance" event is executed only if the value of the output argument "ps_Km" of event "Return" is larger than 10,000. Since this value is captured into the transaction argument "pst_Km", as shown above, the guard will be changed into:

$\{pst\_Km > 10000\}$

The complete formula needs to be changed into the following:

$Return(pt\_Vehicle; pst\_Km) . \{pst\_Km > 10000\} SendForMaintenance(pt\_Vehicle)$

Example.   *In order to further illustrate the uses of output arguments, let us now show how to initialize an input argument of an event in a transaction with an output argument of another event previously specified in the corresponding transaction. To do that, let us imagine that the event "SendForMaintenance" has two input arguments: the object-valued argument that has already been discussed, which represents the vehicle, plus a new one, called "p_KmCount", which represents the number of kilometres made by the vehicle to be serviced. Looking at the transaction formula, it can be seen that the "p_KmCount" argument can be directly initialized to the value returned by the output argument "ps_Km" of event "Return", already captured by the output argument "pst_Km". The final transaction formula appears as follows:*

$Return(pt\_Vehicle; pst\_Km) . \{pst\_Km > 10000\}$
$SendForMaintenance(pt\_Vehicle, pst\_Km)$

Operations

Sometimes, the ordered grouping of services provided by transactions is needed in a system but without the need for the basic properties of invisibility of intermediate states and execution "all or nothing". In these cases, a failure that occurs during the execution of the component services does not require the cancellation of everything done up to that moment.

In order to contemplate these scenarios, OO-Method introduces the concept of operations as non-transactional molecular execution units. The method's expressive power is thus enhanced by this concept.

Given the similarity between operations and transactions, everything stated about the specification of transactions also applies to the specification of operations. The relevant semantic difference is that already mentioned: operations do not satisfy the two basic transactional requirements. This difference understandably results in a different behaviour in the software product that results from the specification.

Preconditions

We have described how services (events, transactions and operations) can be defined within a class. These services can be assigned preconditions, i.e. conditions that must hold before the service can be executed.

A precondition is a well-formed Boolean formula that can be defined using constants, functions, attributes and arguments of the service that owns the precondition.

Although preconditions are said to be associated to services at this point, it will become clear when agents relationships are discussed that they are actually associated to actions (combinations of a service plus a list of authorised agents), rather than services.

In addition to the formula that defines the condition that must be satisfied before the service is executed, and that constitutes the essential part of its definition, a precondition also includes the specification of the following properties:

- Error message
- Agent list
- Comments

The error message is a text that is shown to the user at run-time when the precondition is not satisfied.

The agent list (which, as discussed later, defines an action together with the service) restricts the checking of the precondition to those cases for which the service is launched by one of the agents in the list.

The comments (optional) allow documenting the precondition.

Example.   *Within the car rental system being described, no vehicle is to be retired until it attains a given kilometre count, such as 50,000 km. If an attempt is made to retire a vehicle with a lower kilometre count, then a message must be shown indicating that only vehicles with a kilometre count above 50,000 can be retired.*

To accomplish this, the following precondition (see Table 7.9) can be associated to the event "Retire" of class "Vehicle".

Table 7.9 Precondition of event "Retire".

Agents	
Formula	Kilometres > 50000
Error Message	Vehicles cannot be retired until they have made 50,000 km
Comments	Vehicles must serve for at least 50,000 km before they can be retired (for re-sale or junk), in order to maximise performance

Since no agent list is given, this precondition is checked every time that service execution is attempted, regardless of the agent.

Preconditions are also often used to control a service's arguments, to assess that no wrong values are provided for its execution.

Example.   *When a vehicle is rented, the "Rent" event requires, among others, the arguments "p_atrRentalDate" and "p_atrReturnDate", which represent, respectively, the date on which the vehicle is rented and the date on which the vehicle is expected back. Evidently, the return date must be later than or, at most, the same as the rental* *date. In order to control this, a precondition such as that shown in Table 7.10 can be used.*

Table 7.10 Precondition of event "Rent".

Agents	
Formula	*p_atrReturnDate >= p_atrRentalDate*
Error Message	*The expected return date must be later than or equal to the rental date*
Comments	*Controls the expected return date*

The graphical representation of preconditions is achieved in UML by associating each precondition to its service via the "precondition" stereotype in the context of the service declaration, together with the formal specification of the precondition.

7.1.3 Integrity Constraints

The specification of attributes and services in a class allows for the characterization of the properties that are relevant to the modelling being done, and the collection of actions that can modify these during the lifetimes of the class' objects respectively.

This is not all. The values of the attributes of an object (and, consequently, the state of that object) can be restricted by a series of properties that need to be satisfied in all or some of the states of the object. These properties must be appropriately specified, together with the class' attributes and services in order to fully characterize the class definition. These properties are called integrity constraints.

An *integrity constraint* is the expression of a semantic condition that must be preserved in every valid state of an object. There are two kinds of integrity constraints:

- *Static.* They are first-order, closed, well-formed formulae that are evaluated within a single object state[5] but which must hold in every valid state of the object's lifetime. This well-formed formula (wff) can use constant values, functions and attributes that are visible from the class (owned, inherited or transitively visible via association, aggregation or composition relationships). The atoms use the usual logical-relational operators such as "<", ">" and "=". Formulae are built using the logic connectives AND and OR.

Example. *In objects of class "Vehicle", the kilometre count must be always greater than zero and never above 300,000. This is represented in the following integrity constraint:*

Kilometres > 0 AND Kilometres <= 300000

where the corresponding wff is built using the attribute Kilometre and the required relational operators ('<=','>') and logic connectives (AND).

---

[5] They are evaluated within the model that represents the object's state. As is usual in object-oriented environments, this model is characterized by the set of values associated to the object's attributes at the relevant point in time.

- *Dynamic.* They are well-formed formulae that involve more than one state and for which, in addition to the structure described for static integrity constraints, temporal operators (typical of temporal logic) are required. Temporal logics are first-order classical logics that have been extended with certain temporal operators, which are intended to enrich the standard expressiveness of the previous static integrity constraints.

  Basically, well-formed formulae in dynamic integrity constraints are used to express conditions about past or future states of the object. If f and f' are well-formed formulae, as described in the previous bullet point, then well-formed formulae for dynamic integrity constraints can be obtained by extending these with the conventional temporal operators sometimes f, always f, f until f', f since f', with their usual temporal logic semantics (Harel 1984).

Example. *In class "Client", attribute "PendingBalance" represents the amount of money owed by a particular client. If this amount reaches the 1,800 € limit, then it cannot grow beyond it.*

$$ALWAYS\ (PendingBalance < 1800)\ SINCE\ (SOMETIMES\ PendingBalance > 1800)$$

An integrity constraint (either static or dynamic) can be defined using the following properties:

- Formula
- Error message
- Comments

The formula expresses the condition that must be satisfied. The error message is a text that is shown to the user at run-time when the constraint is not satisfied. The comments can be used to document the constraint.

Example. *Returning to the previous examples, the full specifications of the constraints illustrated in these are shown in Tables 7.11 and 7.12.*

Table 7.11 Static integrity constraint for class "Vehicle".

Formula	*Kilometres > 0 AND Kilometres < 300000*
Error Message	*The vehicle's kilometres count must be between zero and 300,000*
Comments	*Controls the vehicle's kilometre count*

Table 7.12 Dynamic integrity constraint for class "Client".

Formula	*ALWAYS (PendingBalance < 1800) SINCE (SOMETIMES PendingBalance > 1800)*
Error Message	*This client has already surpassed the allowed pending balance of 18,000 €*
Comments	*Controls clients' defaulting*

An alternative to using the logic connective AND is to specify multiple integrity constraints. In fact, it is possible to specify more than one integrity constraint for a given class, which is equivalent to the single constraint that would be obtained by linking them with AND connectives. Specifying multiple constraints allows giving more detailed error messages.

Example.   *Let us assume that the static integrity constraint of class "Vehicle" is to be decomposed into two different constraints:*

Kilometres > 0
and
Kilometres < 300000

Each of them would carry a different error message:

"Kilometres count must be a positive number."
and
"Kilometres count cannot be above 300,000."

In contrast with the case of derived attributes, the order of definition is not semantically relevant for integrity constraints, because all of them must be satisfied. However, it is considered a meaningful analysis practice to specify the most generic integrity constraints first, and then progress towards the most specific ones.

UML does not define a strict syntax for integrity constraints. This can be accomplished by using a string enclosed in curly braces and associated to a diagram element (such as a class or a relationship); or it can be alternatively expressed in natural language, in a formal language such as OCL, or even as a program code fragment.

The situation is different for OO-Method, since that ambiguity does not exist: integrity constraints have precisely defined syntax and semantics, and are specified in the context of a class according to such a formal definition. Graphically, the "constraint" stereotype is used to depict integrity constraints within a class' collection of properties.

7.2 Relationships Between Classes

Once the conceptual primitives for classes have been characterized, the next step is to determine what kinds of relationships can be established between the classes of a Conceptual Schema. This is particularly important, since the kind of relationships that can occur between classes is what marks the difference between different Conceptual Modelling proposals.

Typical and fundamental relationships between classes include those that determine what objects can see or do when they act as agents on objects of server classes (with regard to attribute visibility and also service execution); those that establish the way in which two classes are associated, perhaps involving a directional whole/part relationship; and those that determine which properties of an existing class can be reused in the definition of a new, semantically related class. In order to cover these three aspects, OO-Method defines three different kinds of relationships between classes, which entail different semantics.

- Agent relationships, representing which objects are authorised to activate which services.
- Association, aggregation and composition relationships, representing semantically bidirectional relationships between classes (associations) as well as stricter cases of aggregation (with whole/part semantics) and composition (a certain kind of "strong" aggregation).
- Specialisation relationships, representing the inheritance relationships usually found in object-oriented environments.

The details of each of these kinds are described in the next sections.

7.2.1 Agents and Agent Relationships

Modelling a society of interacting objects implies taking into account the client/ server relationships that occur among the classes in the Conceptual Schema. Such a client/server perspective has been pointed out by several authors, and chiefly by the RDD (Responsibility-Driven Design) proposal of Wirfs-Brock (Wirfs-Brock et al. 1990), in which are described the dual roles or responsibilities played by objects of a class.

Server and Agent Classes

When acting as a server, a class offers to the Object Society a set of services that can be activated. When acting as a client, the class' objects behave as activators of services provided by other classes (or the same class). This client perspective is represented in OO-Method by the concept of agent. Agents are objects that activate services offered by classes to the society of interacting objects being modelled.

Nowadays, there exist multiple approaches to the notion of agent, many of them having incompatible semantics, since a standard, universally accepted set of definitions does not exist. The inclusion of the notion of agent, simple but also expressively rich, is a good connection point between OO-Method and other proposals that are specifically agent-oriented. In fact, OO-Method's approach combines the concepts of object and agent in a rather balanced manner, giving a highly useful perspective for the resolution of organizational systems.

From the specification language viewpoint, every service defined in an OO-Method class must have an associated agent or agents, which are the only ones that are allowed to activate that service.

This information can be incorporated graphically, enriching the expressiveness of the Class Diagram notation by the addition of a dependency relationship stereotyped with the reserved word "agent", which links the header of the agent class (playing the role of client) to the service in the appropriate class (which plays the role of server). Figure 7.6 shows an example of agent declaration for the case study being used.

Example.   *The Rent-a-Car system contains a class "Client" that acts as agent; this class can rent and return vehicles. Figure 7.6 shows this graphically.*

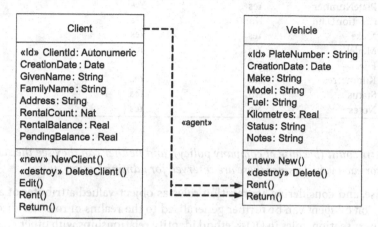

Fig. 7.6 Graphical notation for the agent relationship.

It is a very important characteristic of OO-Method that active and passive classes (clients and servers respectively) are declared in a homogeneous way. The model expressiveness thus obtained is, object-wise, higher than in conventional approaches, since these usually show in their Class Diagrams only the server perspective of classes, using different models and notation to express agent relationships. This results in decreased locality and clarity in the resulting specification.

The fact that every service has an associated agent class or classes makes it possible that the specification granularity for any particular service is the combined service plus agent. Such a combination of service plus service-activating agent is called *action*. We will show how actions allow very useful specification facilities when the Dynamic and Functional Models of OO-Method are introduced.

The notion of agent can be generalised to the realm of attributes, letting a class determine which attributes of another class are visible for it. This simple and practical mechanism for view definition makes the specification of security aspects a very convenient task, always within the expressive framework of OO-Method. For the sake of simplicity, and unless stated otherwise, it is assumed that an agent class has visibility over all the attributes of the corresponding class in the Conceptual Schema. By "corresponding class", we refer to any class related with the agent class through an agent relationship.

Example.   *Table 7.13 illustrates the extension of the notion of agent described above. The attributes of class "Vehicle" are listed, together with their visibility restrictions for two agent classes, "Client" and "Administrator".*

It can be seen in Table 7.13 that administrators have full visibility over every attribute of vehicles. Clients, on the contrary, can only "see" part of the vehicle: plate number, make, model and fuel type. They cannot check the creation date or the

Table 7.13 Attribute visibility in agent relationships.

Vehicle (server)	Client	Administrator
PlateNumber	Yes	Yes
CreationDate	No	Yes
Make	Yes	Yes
Model	Yes	Yes
Fuel	Yes	Yes
Kilometres	No	Yes
Status	No	Yes
Notes	No	Yes

kilometre count (because of company policy), and neither can they see the status or notes for each vehicle, since these are reserved for administration staff.

Likewise, and considering aggregation roles as object-valued attributes of a class, the notion of agent can be further generalised to the realms of roles. As discussed in the next section, roles in OO-Method identify relationships with other classes in the Conceptual Model. A class relates to another class via a role. By so extending the notion of agent, the analyst is able to specify what structural relationships can be navigated by an agent. Like in the case of attributes, and unless the contrary is stated, it is assumed that an agent class can "see" all the roles of the corresponding class in the Conceptual Schema.

Example.   *Table 7.14 illustrates the extension of the notion of agent described above. The roles of server class "Vehicle" are listed, together with their visibility restrictions for agent classes "Client" and "Administrator".*

Table 7.14 Role visibility in agent relationships.

Vehicle (server)	Client	Administrator
Rentals	No	Yes
Type	Yes	Yes

Each vehicle is related (via the role "Rentals") to the rental contracts in which it has participated, and to a specific vehicle type (via the role "Type"). Administrators can query the type of any vehicle, and also its rental list, whereas clients can access only the vehicle type.

The extension of the agent notion to attributes and roles allows for the definition of vertical visibility restrictions on the instances of the class. This extension limits the part of the object state that is visible to a given agent class.

In addition to such vertical visibility restrictions, the notion of agent can be further extended to include horizontal restrictions. The horizontal visibility of an agent class over a server class is given by a well-formed Boolean formula. Thus, the population of the server class that is visible to the agent class is restricted to those instances that satisfy such a formula.

Example. *Some examples of the horizontal visibility restriction mechanism are given here. As we know, clients perform rentals. Logically, and for privacy reasons, each client can access only the information pertaining to his/her own rental contracts, not being able to access rental contract information of other clients. At the same time, administrators have access to all the rental contracts, regardless of the owner client.*

Therefore, no horizontal visibility restriction must operate on class "Administrator", since administrators can observe the complete rental population.

However, the "Client" class must be subject to the horizontal visibility restriction that follows:

Client = AGENT

where "Client" is the role via which a rental is related to the client who made it, and the reserved word "AGENT" represents the instance of the agent class corresponding to the current user of the system. Since the horizontal visibility restriction is declared in the context of the relationship between the agent class "Client" and the server class "Rental", "AGENT" represents the instance of the "Client" class that corresponds to the currently connected user.

Finally, the *effective visibility* of a class over another is the result of the intersection of the vertical visibility restrictions (which attributes and roles are visible) and the horizontal visibility restrictions (which instances are visible).

As far as services are concerned, visibility restrictions affect which services can be executed on which instances. Putting together all this information, we can conclude that these Agent Relationships concretely determine the contracts that establish what objects of a class can see and do to objects of other classes. This client–server perspective applied in this context of Object-Oriented Conceptual Modelling allows for the precise definition of the notions of interface and view in OO-Method, which are introduced next.

Interfaces

An interface is comprised of a given agent relationship between two classes (one acting as agent; the other acting as server) plus the effective visibility defined by it. In this way, each agent class has an interface for each of the classes in which it can access attributes or execute services.

Since given class can be agent of multiple servers, the set of interfaces in which it participates determines the potential visibility of the class over the system. We use the word "potential" because, as we explain in the following section, it is possible to define subsets of such interfaces, called Views, by using the View mechanism.

Views

A view is a set of interfaces. Views are defined in two steps:

- Select the agent classes that will participate in the view.
- Select the interfaces for each agent class.

The selection of agent classes determines which profiles can interact with the system, whereas the selection of interfaces for each agent class determines the effective visibility that each profile will have on the system when it connects.

Example.   *Our system has two kinds of users: clients and administrators. Clients can query the catalogue of available vehicles, access their personal details and check their rentals, as well as make and confirm bookings. Administrators can access all the information in the system and perform every kind of service. To accomplish this, interfaces between all the classes in the system and the "Administrator" class are created. For the "Client" class, however, only interfaces with those classes that it may access ("Vehicle", "Rental" and "Client") are created.*

For each of these interfaces, the attributes that clients can query, the services that clients can execute and the roles that clients can navigate (as shown in Tables 7.13 and 7.14, and in Fig. 7.6) are selected.

Once the interfaces of classes "Client" and "Administrator" with the rest of the system are created, a view for these interfaces is created.

If no view is explicitly defined, it is assumed that an implicit view exists, which includes all the agent classes in the system with all their interfaces.

A view defines, first of all, the collection of agents that can connect to the system and the visibility of each of these. Since a view is a union of interfaces, the visibility of a view must be restricted at run-time to that of the connected agent, i.e. to that determined by the interfaces of the view for the agent class, but not the rest of the interfaces of other agent classes.

The concept of view is revisited in the section dealing with the Presentation Model. In fact, the Presentation Model defines the abstract interaction mechanisms that the system offers to the connected user. Since the user is connected as an instance of an agent class, these interaction mechanisms are restricted to the effective visibility of this user as an instance of the agent class.

7.2.2 Association, Aggregation, and Composition

It is evident that the classes in a Conceptual Schema are not isolated components. Relationships with precisely defined semantics occur among them, reflecting the complexity inherent to any real system. In other words, the specification of classes described so far contains only datum-valued attributes, which take values over certain domain or known data types. In addition to these, the specification must be completed by adding object-valued attributes, which are represented as semantic relationships between classes.

The need to appropriately represent the notion of semantic relationship between classes is a well-known problem in Software Engineering. From the most traditional approaches in the field of Data Semantic Modelling, to the most modern OO methods of software modelling and production, and including the most advanced proposals on OO specification languages, the definition of the semantic relationships between classes varies depending on the criteria that are used when the meaning of "putting together" objects is established. Interestingly, and after so many years and so many proposals, the specific kinds of inter-class relationships that a particular approach offers is still the major distinctive element of any methodological proposal.

In any case, a rigorous method must establish the kind of inter-class relationships that can be used, as well as their precise meaning. In our context, the conceptual primitives of association, aggregation and composition are defined. From a notational point of view, the graphical representation of these primitives is done using the recommendations derived from the UML standard.

Association

OO-Method clarifies the semantics of the different kinds of relationships (association, aggregation and composition) by using a taxonomy. First, the concept of association, the most generic one and not necessarily directed, is defined using the following bidirectional properties:

- Minimum and maximum cardinalities. The specification of minimum and maximum cardinalities is well known, especially through the prevalent Entity-Relationship Model, which has popularised its usage.
- Role names. These indicate how the instance or instances of one of the classes in the association are identified when seen from one instance of the other class of the association.
- Temporality. This indicates whether the association is static or dynamic. For each direction, an association is said to be static when the associated object cannot change over time, and dynamic otherwise. By "change over time", we mean that the associated instances can vary over time during the lifetime of the objects that participate in the relationship.

Cardinality

Looking at an association from the perspective of one of the two involved classes, specifying the cardinality means determining how many objects of the associated class (i.e. the class on the "other side") can be simultaneously related with an instance of this class. This is done by stating the lower bound (minimum cardinality) and the upper bound (maximum cardinality). Cardinalities can be seen as restrictions on the objects that participate in the relationship, and must be satisfied all the time throughout the lifetimes of these objects.

The usual minimum cardinality is 0 or 1, which is often textually expressed by phrases such as "accepts nulls" or "does not accept nulls". However, any constant natural value can be specified as a minimum cardinality.

Frequent maximum cardinalities are 1 or many (often represented by an "M" letter). Textually, this is often expressed as "uni-valued" or "multi-valued" although, like in the previous case, any natural value greater than 1 can be used, rather than "M", to specify a precise upper bound when necessary.

Obviously, the maximum cardinality is always greater than or equal to the minimum cardinality.

There is another property closely related to cardinality: the propagation behaviour of deletion operations on an object that is associated to a collection of objects. This property is specified whenever the association between two classes has a maximum cardinality of 1 in one direction, and maximum cardinality greater than 1 in the opposite direction (which is usually known as "one to many"). In such cases, the action to be performed on the objects on the "many" side whenever an object on the "one" side is deleted must be specified. The most frequent alternatives are:

- Not allow the operation
- Delete the association instance without deleting the objects themselves
- "Cascade" the appropriate deletion operation to the associated objects

Roles

Each end of an association relationship can be identified by the name of the class at that end. However, this is insufficient in two cases: when the association is reflexive (since both ends connect to the same class, and therefore their identifier would be the same), and when more than one association exists between a given pair of classes (since all the association ends of each class would have the same identifier).

In UML terms, a role is the identifier of a navigable association end, and can be seen as an object-valued property of the class at the opposite end of the association. The property's multiplicity determines, in this case, the maximum cardinality of the corresponding association end.

Temporality

Given one association end and the object at this end, this property allows for two possible values:

- *Static*, if the association is constant once established – in other words, if, once the relationship has been established, the object at the opposite end cannot be changed for another.
- *Dynamic*, if the object at the opposite end can be changed for another object over the lifetime of the object at this end.

The transition from a null value (no association exists) to existence is considered a special case of static association. As we will explain later, and from the perspective of the running software product, the association value is not established by the creation event of the involved class, but there is an instantiation event for the relationship that occurs only once – hence, the static characteristic. If the problem space (conceptual schema) defines an association as dynamic, then the solution space (software product) must contain the appropriate services to update the instances that participate in the association.

The graphical notation used to represent an association between classes in the Class Diagram associated to an Object Model in OO-Method is, again, that proposed by the UML standard: a solid line between the boxes corresponding to the associated classes. This line is labelled with the association name, and each end of the line is labelled with the role that the class at that end plays with respect to the class at the opposite end.

Example.   *Figure 7.7 shows an example of the graphical notation used to represent an association between classes in the Class Diagram. The ends of the solid line linking the two classes are labelled with the role names. In the example, "Class1" is related to "Class2" through the role "ClassRole2", and "Class2" is related to "Class1" through the role "ClassRole1".*

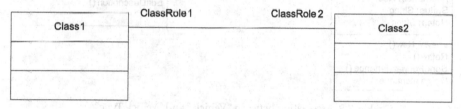

Fig. 7.7 Graphical notation for associations.

The non-available modelling elements are incorporated by using the extension mechanisms provided by UML, namely stereotypes.

Cardinality and temporality are declared for the corresponding association ends or roles. The basic cardinality primitives are included by UML. Temporality primitives are specified by introducing the appropriate stereotype: "static" and "dynamic" are added to each association end to indicate, respectively, a static or dynamic behaviour.

Example.   *Figure 7.8 shows the graphical depiction of cardinalities for an association relationship. The association end with role "ClassRole1" shows a cardinality of "0..1", meaning that any instance of "Class2" can be related, at most, to one instance of "Class1", and to none as a minimum. In other words, each instance of "Class2" is optionally related to a single instance of "Class1".*

At the other end, the cardinality is "1..1", indicating that any instance of "Class1" is related with exactly one instance of "Class2".

Example.   *Figure 7.9 shows an example of the graphical notation used to depict the association between classes "Vehicle" and "VehicleType". The figure shows that every vehicle has one type (cardinality "1..1" at the "Type" end), whereas a vehicle type can correspond to multiple vehicles (cardinality "*" at the "Vehicles" end).*

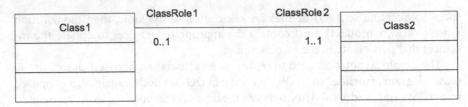

Fig. 7.8 Graphical notation for roles and cardinalities of associations.

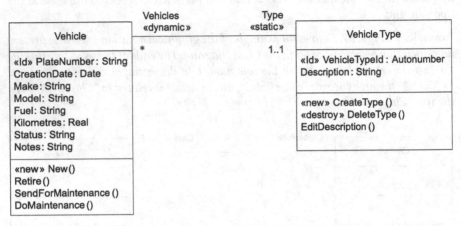

Fig. 7.9 Association between "Vehicle" and "VehicleType".

Aggregation

The semantic relationships between classes that we have called associations are intrinsically bidirectional. Consequently, their characteristic properties are bidirectional, too. However, Information Systems often include associations that exhibit an explicit directionality in order to indicate that one of the involved classes acts as a composite, and the other class as a component.

When such a "part-of" relationship is introduced, a direction (from the composite, or "whole", to the component, or "part") is established, and the association is specialised into a constructor that we call *aggregation*. The basic semantics of aggregations derive from such a directionality caused by the "part-of" characteristic.

In this sense, the utility of aggregations in OO-Method Class Diagrams is that they enable us to clearly visualise the "part-of" relationship that appears in many real systems. The graphical representation is an empty (white) diamond touching the box that represents the composite class.

Example.   *Figure 7.10 shows an example of the graphical notation that is used to depict aggregation of classes in Class Diagrams. The ends of the solid line that links the two classes are labelled with role names. The example shows that every instance of "Class1" is related to zero or more instances (cardinality "0..*") of "Class2" through the role "ClassRole2", and that every instance of "Class2" is related to zero or one instances (cardinality "0..1") of "Class1" through the role "ClassRole1".*

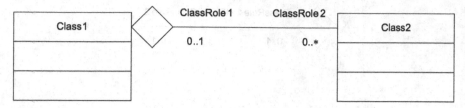

Fig. 7.10 Graphical notation for aggregations.

The specific semantics implied by the concept of aggregation are not trivial. It is clear that aggregation has all the properties of association, since it is defined as a specialisation of it. Which are the additional properties that characterize its semantics?

There are two essential properties that answer this question:

1. The impossibility of having aggregation cycles at the instance level. In this way, reflexive "part-of" relationships, in which an object is part of itself, are avoided.
2. The existence of Identification Dependency of the part with regard to the whole.

Identification Dependency

Identification Dependency allows expressing that the identifier of the component class is built using the identifier of the composite class, adding some attribute of the component class if necessary. This is considered to be a property of aggregation, since it breaks the bidirectionality typical of association that we have described in the previous section. Identification dependency is asymmetric, and the directionality that it induces assigns it to what we call aggregation.

The specification of an Identification Dependency requires the satisfaction of an important restriction: the cardinality of the component class must be "1..1" (minimum and maximum cardinalities equal one). This is a logical consequence of its definition: if the identifier of the component class requires the identifier of the composite class, then a composite object must exist and be unique for each component object.

In addition, the specification of an Identification Dependency prevents the relationship from being dynamic at the composite end; if the component identification is made from the identification of the composite, then this must be constant. Otherwise, the identification of the component would vary as the associated composite changes.

The graphical notation for an Identification Dependency consists of marking the component class role with the reserved word "ID", and introducing the corresponding UML stereotype. As with previous cases, this is a modelling element the semantics of which are precisely defined.

Example. *Figure 7.11 shows an example of the graphical notation used to depict identification dependency. The relationship end corresponding to the composite class has been marked with the "ID" letters (standing for "Identification Dependency"), and the cardinality at the opposite end is "1..1".*

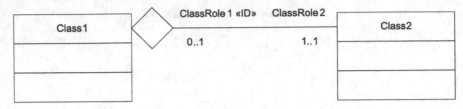

Fig. 7.11 Graphical notation for identification dependency.

Example. *Figure 7.12 shows an example of the graphical notation used for the aggregation relationship between classes "Rental" and "Vehicle". A rental has exactly one vehicle (cardinality "1..1"), and a vehicle may participate in multiple rentals (cardinality "0..*").*

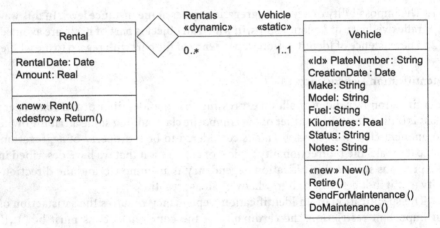

Fig. 7.12 Aggregation between "Rental" and "Vehicle".

To conclude this section, let us describe some terms often associated with the specification of aggregation relationships. When dealing with a textual specification of a conceptual schema, these terms are employed, rather than their associated cardinalities, to avoid using plain numbers. For the sake of comprehension, the cardinality of the component class can be textually expressed when defining an aggregation by using terms such as "flexible"/"strict" and "disjoint"/"not disjoint", with the following semantics:

- *Flexible / Strict.* An aggregation is *flexible* if an object of the component class can exist without being involved in the aggregation (minimum cardinality of zero at the composite end). If the existence of an object of the component class can be understood only as a part of a composite object, then the aggregation is said to be *strict*.
- *Disjoint / Not Disjoint.* An aggregation is *disjoint* if a component object cannot be shared by multiple composite objects, i.e. a component object cannot be ag-

gregated into multiple composite objects. In this case, the maximum cardinality at the composite end is one. Otherwise, the aggregation is said to be *not disjoint*.

In addition to these two pairs of terms, "null"/"not null" and "uni-valued"/"multi-valued" specifications (with their usual meanings) can be used to characterize the minimum and maximum cardinalities of a composite class with regard to its components.

Table 7.15 Equivalence between graphical and textual syntax for cardinalities.

Flexible/ Strict	Disjoint/ Not Disjoint	Null/ Not Null	Uni-valued/ Multi-valued	Cardinality of Composite	Cardinality of Component
Flexible	Not Disjoint	Null	Uni-valued	0..*	0..1
Flexible	Not Disjoint	Null	Multi-valued	0..*	0..*
Flexible	Not Disjoint	Not Null	Uni-valued	0..*	1..1
Flexible	Not Disjoint	Not Null	Multi-valued	0..*	1..*
Flexible	Disjoint	Null	Uni-valued	0..1	0..1
Flexible	Disjoint	Null	Multi-valued	0..1	0..*
Flexible	Disjoint	Not Null	Uni-valued	0..1	1..1
Flexible	Disjoint	Not Null	Multi-valued	0..1	1..*
Strict	Disjoint	Null	Uni-valued	1..1	0..1
Strict	Disjoint	Null	Multi-valued	1..1	0..*
Strict	Disjoint	Not Null	Uni-valued	1..1	1..1
Strict	Disjoint	Not Null	Multi-valued	1..1	1..*
Strict	Not Disjoint	Null	Uni-valued	1..*	0..1
Strict	Not Disjoint	Null	Multi-valued	1..*	0..*
Strict	Not Disjoint	Not Null	Uni-valued	1..*	1..1
Strict	Not Disjoint	Not Null	Multi-valued	1..*	1..*

Historically, these terms were introduced by the first versions of the OASIS OO Specification Language, which has been the conceptual origin of the method presented in this book. Table 7.15 summarizes the equivalence between this textual representation of cardinalities of aggregation relationships and the usual graphical notation.

Composition

Composition is a particular case of aggregation in which more specific restrictions are enforced. Two additional properties are introduced in order to characterize the "strong" aggregation that is called *composition*. These are:

- The fact that every component object participating in an instance of this aggregation belongs to exactly one composite object.
- The cascading deletion and modification of the part when the whole is deleted or modified.

This kind of strong aggregation, which we call *composition*, is graphically depicted using a diamond, like in the previous case, but now filled (black), following the notation proposed by UML for these modelling elements. Doing that, the UML characterization is preserved – from a syntactic point of view – for dealing with these important class relationships. Additionally, precise semantics are associated to these, making clear what association, aggregation and composition mean from a strict, conceptual modelling perspective.

Example.   *Figure 7.13 shows the graphical notation used to depict a composition relationship between two classes in a Class Diagram. The ends of the solid line linking the boxes corresponding to the involved classes are labelled with role names. The figure indicates that every instance of "Class1" is related to zero or more instances (cardinality "0..*") of "Class2" through role "ClassRole2", and each instance of "Class2" is related to exactly one instance of "Class1" (cardinality "1..1") through the role "ClassRole1".*

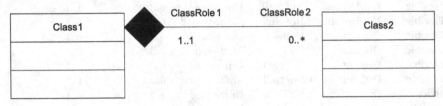

Fig. 7.13 Graphical notation for compositions.

Composition makes it impossible for component objects to exist outside their composite object, once the relationship is established. Every component object remains totally encapsulated by the aggregation, once this is defined. The state of the component object can be altered only by local services, appropriately coordinated by the services provided by the composite object. Consequently, component objects can be accessed only through their composite object.

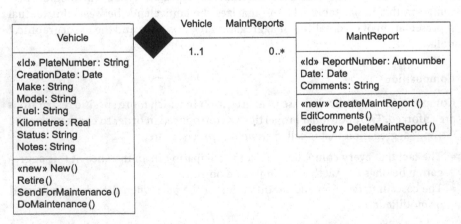

Fig. 7.14 Composition between "Vehicle" and "MaintReport".

Example. *Figure 7.14 shows an example of the graphical notation used to depict the composition relationship between a vehicle and its maintenance reports. Class "Vehicle" participates in the relationship as composite, and "MaintReport" as component. In fact, any vehicle is "made of" zero or more maintenance reports, and each report belongs to one, and only one vehicle. This is true at any point in time during the lifetime of every maintenance report: from the moment when a maintenance report is created, it is permanently linked to its vehicle. If the vehicle is eliminated, then all its maintenance reports will also be destroyed. The composition is the adequate conceptual primitive to represent this situation.*

The main characteristics of association, aggregation and composition have now been introduced. However, if we wish to precise their semantics, there are additional aspects to be considered. In particular, in the next sections we will analyse:

- how to deal with derivations in associations,
- how creation and destruction class events are affected by the specification of association relationships that affect them,
- how to manage dynamics (insertion, delete and change events) associated to associations, and
- which semantic relationship exist between shared events and associations.

Derivations in Associations

Derivation is a very important aspect of any modelling framework. We have discussed how the specification of derived attributes of a class is a relevant property. The definition of associations between classes allows for the generalisation of the notion of datum-valued derived attribute (i.e. with an associated data type) to that of object-valued derived attribute (i.e. with an associated object type).

The specification of object-valued derived attributes provides better expressiveness, making possible multi-valued associations functions such as *sum*, average (*avg*), minimum and maximum of a value set (*min*, *max*), counts (*count*), and so on, all of them with their usual semantics. Also, iteration operators can be used.

In many cases, the specification of derived information in the context of an association may need referring to properties that affect all the objects involved in an instance of such an association. In order to accomplish this, operators that can iterate over the elements of a collection (such as *for all member of ...*) are necessary. This expressiveness is useful – and it is required for modelling purposes – in different contexts of an OO-Method specification: in Functional Model evaluations, in service preconditions, in Dynamic Model triggers, or in the integrity constraints and transactions defined at the class level, as already explained.

Example. *The class "Client" has a derived attribute "PendingBalance", which adds up the amount of money owed by a particular client. The derivation formula is:*

SUM(Rentals.Invoice.Amount) WHERE (Rentals.Invoice.Payed = FALSE)

Example.   *The class "Client" has a derived attribute "RentalCount" that represents the number of rentals that a particular client has completed. The derivation formula is:*

COUNT(Rentals)

Creation Events and Associations

Association relationships (including the specific cases of aggregations and compositions) alter the semantics of the participant classes. For a class' creation events, their semantics may involve the creation of relationships with objects of other classes, and even the creation of additional objects. These semantics depend on the properties defined for each relationship in which the class of the object being created participates.

When an instance of a given class "A" is to be created, the association, aggregation and composition relationships that this class has with other classes must be examined. For each class "B" related to class "A", the following questions must be asked:

1. Does the creation of an instance of "A" imply the creation of instances of "B"?
2. Does the creation of an instance of "A" allow the creation of instances of "B"?
3. Does the creation of an instance of "A" allow selecting existing instances of "B"?

The answer to question 1 is affirmative if the new instance of "A" needs to be associated to at least one instance of "B", and either the relationship is static at the "A" end, or the existing instances of "B" already satisfy the maximum cardinality at the "A" end and, therefore, cannot be related to any additional instance of "A" (including the one being created).

The answer to question 2 is affirmative if instances of "B" need to be related to one instance of "A", at most, in order to exist, since that instance of "A" is the one being created.

The answer to question 3 is affirmative if an instance of "B" can be related to one or more instances of "A" any time after its creation, and therefore already existing instances of "B" can be selected and associated to the instance of "A" being created.

Answering these three questions will establish whether a newly created instance of "A" needs to be related to one or multiple instances of "B" (depending on the cardinality at the "B" end), and whether those instances of "B" are to be created together with the instance of "A" or, on the contrary, they are selected from the existing ones.

Moreover, and since the association, aggregation or composition relationship is binary, the three same questions must also be asked in the opposite direction. This means considering what happens when an instance of "B" is created, as far as "A" is concerned.

Depending on whether instances of "B" are to be created or selected when an instance of "A" is created, the creation event of "A" may include an object-valued argument that represents the necessary data to perform such creations or selections.

Example.   *The example in Fig. 7.9 shows the relationship between "Vehicle" and "VehicleType". The arguments of the creation event of "Vehicle" include the object-valued "p_agrVehicleType", the domain of which is "VehicleType", representing the type of vehicle to be associated to the vehicle being created. This argument appears implicitly in the creation event, since the minimum cardinality for this relationship end is one, and points to the object that is to be associated to the vehicle being created. Depending on the minimum cardinality specified for the opposite end, this vehicle type object must be selected or created within the same execution context.*

The ramifications of having affirmative answers to the aforementioned three (actually, six) questions are complex, and would constitute material for another work. Therefore, we will not explore them further in this book. The significant fact remains that, once the semantics of the potential valid situations are fixed, the right strategy to represent every such valid situation in the selected final software product can be properly defined. In the line of argumentation of this book, this is what makes it possible for us to evoke a complete conceptual model-transformation process: the existence of precise mappings between conceptual primitives and their corresponding software representation counterpart.

Destruction Events and Associations

Similarly to creation events, but now applied to destruction events, association, aggregation or composition relationships alter the semantics of the participant classes. A class' destruction events may involve the destruction of relationships with other objects, or even the destruction of other objects themselves. As we have said for creation events, this depends on the properties specified for each relationship in which the class of the object being destroyed participates.

When an instance of a given class "A" is to be destroyed, association, aggregation and composition relationships with other classes must be examined. For each class "B" related to "A", the three following questions must be asked:

1. Does the deletion of an instance of "A" imply the deletion of related instances of "B"?
2. Does the deletion of an instance of "A" allow the deletion of related instances of "B"?
3. Does the deletion of an instance of "A" allow deleting relationships to existing instances of "B"?

The answer to question 1 is affirmative if an instance of "B" needs to be related to at least one instance of "A".

The answer to question 2 is affirmative if no cardinality rules are violated when deleting instances of "B" related to the instance of "A" being destroyed.

The answer to question 3 is affirmative when an instance of "B" can be related to no instance of "A", and this relationship is dynamic at the "A" end.

Depending on the answers to these questions, it is possible to determine whether the related instances of "B" must be deleted whenever an instance of "A" is deleted, or whether relationships from "A" to "B" must be deleted but the objects preserved.

In addition, and for the same reasons as in the case of creation events, it is necessary to ask the three aforementioned questions for both ends of each relationship. That means asking what happens to instances of "A" whenever an instance of "B" is deleted.

Example.   *Figure 7.14 shows a composition relationship between class "Vehicle" (composite) and class "MaintReport" (component). The semantics of this relationship affect the destruction event of the composite class (i.e. "Vehicle"), so that every time a vehicle is deleted, every maintenance report related with it will also be deleted.*

Like in the case of creation events, the ramifications of this are many and, for the sake of brevity, we will omit further discussion here. All that together would characterize the transformation process associated with the specification of association relationships.

Insertion, Deletion and Change Events

One of the properties of association relationships allows us to specify whether the relationship is static or dynamic for each of its ends. If the relationship is dynamic for a given end, then the objects that participate in it can change over the lifetime of the object at the opposite end.

Three kinds of events need to be introduced in order to modify the relationships between objects that participate in a dynamic relationship:

- Insertion events, which associate an object of the class at the dynamic end of the relationship with an object at the opposite end.
- Deletion events, which break the association between an object of the class at the dynamic end of the relationship and an object at the opposite end.
- Change events, which break the association as in the previous point, and create a new one like in the first point.

These are implicit events, and their appearance is subject to the cardinalities of each relationship and also subject to its dynamic property. This kind of automatic appearance of information reinforces the expressiveness of OO-Method. These implicit events represent a behavioural pattern induced by structural properties (those associated to the relationship that create them). Methodologically, this is an interesting point, because structure and behaviour are mutually related in a precise way.

Deletion events appear whenever the minimum and maximum cardinalities at both ends of a relationship allow an instance at the dynamic end to stop being associated with an instance at the opposite end. If this were not so, i.e. if no deletion event existed, then the insertion event would become a change event in the case of a minimum cardinality of zero at the non-dynamic end of the relationship, or a regular insertion event otherwise.

Insertion, deletion and change events are shared by the two classes that participate in a relationship, and always have two object-valued arguments: the first one refers to the object of the class at the non-dynamic end, and the second one to the object of the class at the dynamic end.

Example.   *Let us add a new class, "Extra", to represent the extras that can be added to a vehicle, e.g. air conditioning, power windows, etc. An association between "Vehicle" and "Extra" is also added, with cardinalities "0..*" at both ends, and the "Extra" end is marked as dynamic so that extras can be added to and removed from a vehicle, as necessary. Figure 7.15 depicts this.*

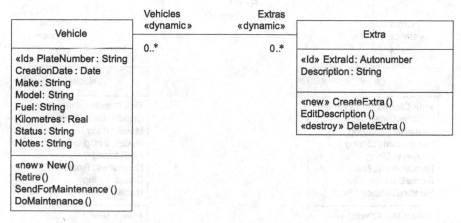

Fig. 7.15 Dynamic association between "Vehicle" and "Extra".

Two events appear, "InsertExtra" and "DeleteExtra", which allow us to add an extra to a vehicle and remove an extra from a vehicle respectively.

If the minimum and maximum cardinalities at the "Vehicle" end were both one, then no deletion event would appear, since this cardinality would force every extra to be permanently associated to a vehicle. This relationship could not be broken, or the cardinality rule violated. In that case, however, the insertion event would become a change event, since it would be possible to move an extra from one vehicle to another.

Shared Events and Associations

Some special situations related to associations and shared events are now described in order to finalize the analysis of relationships.

A frequent modelling primitive is that in which an event shared by two component classes becomes an event owned by the composite class of which the two component classes are part.

It is not necessary to show this explicitly in a diagram, since it is assumed by default. Shared events of component classes can appear as events owned by the associated composite class. In fact, it is frequent that some of these events in the composite class (initially defined as belonging to the component classes) are specified as creation or destruction events of aggregation instances.

Example.   *Figure 7.16 shows an example in which services "Rent" and "Return" are creation and destruction events of class "Rental" respectively, and are also shared by component classes "Client" and "Vehicle".*

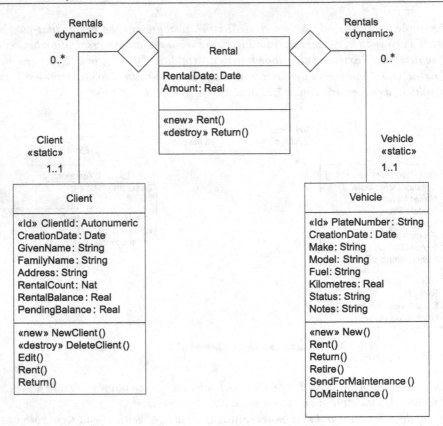

Fig. 7.16 The events "Rent" and "Return" of "Client" and "Vehicle" are also creation and destruction events of "Rental".

It is also worth mentioning that all the events that appear within a class as a consequence of the dynamic character of an association are also events shared by the associated classes. As we have already pointed out, this makes the specification of the services of a class more precise and simpler. More precise, because the shared events have the same name, and their local effects in each component class is specified without any ambiguity. Simpler, because such events appear automatically within the appropriate class whenever the static/dynamic characteristic of each association end is specified.

Example.   *An example of this situation can be found in the dynamic relationship between "Vehicle" and "Extra" that is depicted in Fig. 7.15.*

The section of this book devoted to the generation of the software product that is functionally equivalent to the Conceptual Schema shows that the precision of this model information is what makes it possible to associate specific software representations to each conceptual primitive, which constitutes the basis for the Model Compiler.

Having described the conceptual patterns or primitives of OO-Method with regard to association, aggregation and composition, we move on to describing another modelling constructor that is essential in object-oriented modelling environments: specialisation.

7.2.3 Specialisation

General Issues

The specification of inheritance relationships is a fundamental characteristic of every object-oriented approach. Inheritance between classes can be defined straightforwardly as that conceptual primitive that enables us to define a subclass (or child class) as a class that inherits behaviour and structure from a different class (called the superclass or parent class).

Since the child class can add its own properties or modify the inherited ones, the appropriate specification of inheritance implies the unambiguous determination of its semantics and the precise characterization of how properties inherited from a parent class can be altered by child classes.

One of the most practical dimensions that can be used to characterize the kind of inheritance that any given method offers is modifiability. Modifiability was introduced by Wegner and Zdonik (1988) and Messeguer (1990), and deals with how inherited attributes and services can be modified. There exist four alternatives, sorted from less to more flexibility on the basis of modification:

- *Behavioural compatibility*. This requires that instances of the subclass behave like instances of the superclass for each of their services and arguments.
- *Signature compatibility*. This only requires that the signature of the subclass be syntactically compatible with that of the superclass, and therefore be more flexible than the previous option. This alternative preserves the declarations of services and service arguments but allows for the modification of their definition (usually done through preconditions and post-conditions).
- *Name compatibility*. This only requires that the service names remain unchanged. Arguments can be added, removed and renamed, and their types changed.
- *Cancellation*. This is the least strict kind of inheritance, since it allows "forgetful" classes, i.e. those that omit properties from their parent class.

The precise specification of inheritance requires determining which of the above-mentioned options is chosen.

Inheritance in OO-Method

The inheritance relationships that OO-Method provides as conceptual constructors are specialisation and generalisation.

- *Specialisation* is oriented to dealing with "downwards" inheritance, i.e. the derivation of child classes from a given parent class.

- *Generalisation* is the opposite of the latter, and is usually employed to deal with "upwards" inheritance, i.e. the definition of parent classes from common properties of pre-existing (child) classes.

Specialisation and Generalisation represent different directions within an inheritance hierarchy. They are dual, meaning that, if a parent class has two child classes (downwards view or specialisation), then the shared properties of these could be generalised so that the parent class is obtained (upwards view or generalisation). Which of the two views is used depends on the kind of problem being analysed and the modelling context.

Typically, specialisation is used whenever general, broad classes are first perceived and modelled; these classes will become parent classes once they are refined using a top-down approach. Generalisation, on the other hand, is used when specific, detailed classes are first modelled, and converted into child classes of more general parent classes using a bottom-up approach.

Specialisation

OO-Method provides two conceptual primitives associated with the concept of specialisation: specialisation can be temporary or permanent, depending on whether an object is specialised during part of its lifetime or during its complete lifetime respectively.

- *Temporary or role specialisation.* In this case, an object of the parent class "starts acting like" the child class whenever a given role[6] creation event or carrier event (defined within the parent class) is triggered. Alternatively, the object will also take the role of the child class whenever a specialisation condition defined over the parent class' attributes is met. The object leaves the role whenever a freeing event is triggered or the specialisation condition stops being true. This type of specialisation has the following characteristics:
  1. The carrier event in the parent class consequently acts as creation event of instances of the child class.
  2. When an object stops playing a role, it continues behaving as defined by the parent class. According to the modifiability options described earlier, the child class in this situation requires signature compatibility with the parent class: in this way, the child class is forced to preserve the declaration of services and service arguments from the parent class, although it can adjust their behaviour to the characteristics required by the child class, being able to alter without restrictions any property inherited from the parent class.

---

[6] The notion of "role" in this context must not be confused with the notion of "role" in the context of associations. This notational overload is far from ideal but, unfortunately, the term "role" has been widely and systematically used in both contexts and, therefore, this word has two different meanings. Assuming that the context of the discussion is always clearly stated, we have preferred leaving the dual meaning of the word "role", rather than introducing a new term.

3. The child class can also define its own set of identifier attributes (alias); if it does not, then it inherits the identification mechanism defined for the parent class.

- *Permanent or universal specialisation.* This type of specialisation occurs when an object belongs to a specialised class from the moment the object is created. This is so because a *specialisation condition* over the attributes of the parent class is satisfied. This condition must be compulsorily specified for a permanent specialisation.

  1. It must be noted that the object is a member of the population of the child class and also of the parent class during its whole lifetime. As far as modifiability is concerned, the child class requires, in this case, behavioural compatibility with its parent class, in order to guarantee that the behaviour of the object remains unaltered regardless of whether it is seen as an instance of the parent or child class. Properties of the child class may be modified only if the modifications result in a more restrictive behaviour. For example, if an integrity constraint of the parent class is altered by the child class, then the latter must make the constraint more restrictive, in order to guarantee that the constraint is always satisfied for the parent class if it is satisfied for the child class.

  2. In addition, the child class can also define its own set of identifier attributes (alias). If it does not, then it inherits the identification mechanism defined for the parent class.

The graphical representation of the specialisation between classes is achieved by an arrow flowing from the child class (or classes) to the parent class (or classes), as shown in Figs. 7.17, 7.18 and 7.19. This coincides with the notation proposed by the UML standard. For temporary specialisations, this arrow is labelled with:

- A condition containing variable attributes (at least one), which specialises the instances of the parent class.
- Or, alternatively, the appropriate *carrier* and/or *freeing* (*liberator*) events. Carrier events are treated as *new* events of the child class, and at least one must exist if the specialisation occurs by event. Freeing events are treated as *destroy* events of the child classes, and they can be omitted. If no freeing events are defined, then objects of the parent class can take the corresponding role but cannot leave it, so that they keep playing it until they are destroyed.

These labels can be represented with the adequate UML stereotypes, to keep UML notation. Note that carrier events belong necessarily to the parent class, since no object of the child class (on which the event may be triggered) exists until the event is triggered. In fact, as we have said above, they can be seen as object creator events for the child class, which are also declared in the parent class as private events. Freeing events, on the contrary, may belong to either the parent or the child class.

Example. *Figure 7.17 shows the notation for temporary specialisation by condition.*

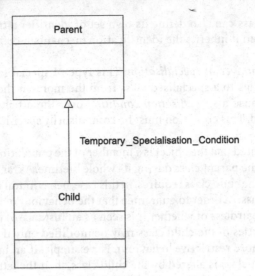

Fig. 7.17 Graphical notation for temporary specialisation by condition.

Example.   *Figure 7.18 shows the notation for temporary specialisation by event.*

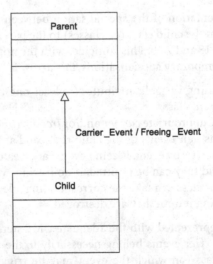

Fig. 7.18 Graphical notation for temporary specialisation by event.

In the case of permanent specialisations, the arrow must be labelled with a condition over constant attributes of the parent class. No non-constant attribute can be involved in this condition.

Example.   *Figure 7.19 shows the notation for permanent specialisation by condition.*

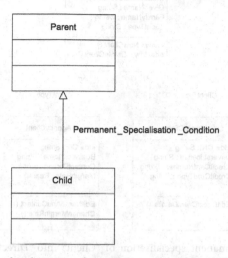

Fig. 7.19 Graphical notation for permanent specialisation by condition.

In every case, the specification of additional decorators (conditions or carrier/ freeing events) is graphically done by using the appropriate UML stereotypes that represent the corresponding modelling elements. As with the rest of the conceptual patterns described so far, OO-Method significantly facilitates and enhances the usability of the UML standard, since it characterizes a precise set of modelling elements that are sufficient to construct an object-oriented Conceptual Schema.

Example.   *Figure 7.20 shows the permanent specialisation of class "Client" into classes "DirectClient" and "AgencyClient". Clients in our rent-a-car system can be individuals (i.e. direct clients) or other car rental companies (i.e. agency clients). This difference must be taken into account whenever a new client is entered into the system, since the details specific to its client type will be required as well as the details common to all types of clients.*

Example.   *Figure 7.21 shows the temporary specialisation by event of class "Vehicle" into "RetiredVehicle". A vehicle may be retired for various reasons (such as kilometre count limit or sale), using the "Retire" service of class "Vehicle". Only when this service is triggered does an instance of "Vehicle" take the role of (i.e. is specialised into) "RetiredVehicle". The specialised instance will behave as a "RetiredVehicle" from that point on.*

Generalisation

Generalisation in OO-Method is quite simple. When a class is to be modelled as a generalisation from a set of child classes, this generalisation can be stated as being

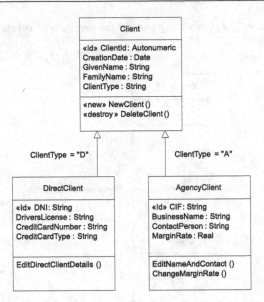

Fig. 7.20 Disjoint permanent specialisation of "Client" into "DirectClient" and "Agency-Client".

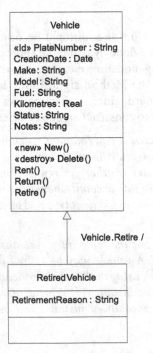

Fig. 7.21 Temporary specialisation by event of "Vehicle" into "RetiredVehicle".

disjoint if an instance of the parent class is an instance of one, and only one, of the child classes, or as *non-disjoint* otherwise.

In order for the generalisation to be possible, a collection of identical properties must be shared by the participating (child) classes; these properties become properties of the parent class. The parent class, in turn, can add its own emergent properties, taking into account that they will also become (via inheritance) properties of the child classes.

The graphical representation of generalisation requires the specification of the disjoint/non-disjoint characteristic besides the parent class.

Example.   *Figure 7.22 shows the graphical notation for generalisation.*

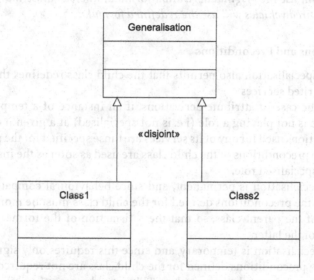

Fig. 7.22 Graphical notation for generalisation.

In order to better understand how specialisation works, the details of some modelling situations involving it (derivations, preconditions, integrity constraints and transactions or operations) are discussed below.

Specialisation and Derivations

Temporary (or role) specialisation permits the child class to redefine derivations of attributes inherited from its predecessor classes. This allows the child class to change the way in which a derived attribute determines its value.

If an instance of a temporarily specialised class is not playing a role (i.e. is not specialised) at a given moment, then the derivations used to determine the value of its attributes are those specified for the parent class. However, the derivations of the child class are used as soon as the instance starts playing the specialised role.

Example.   *Class "Vehicle" contains the derived attribute "RentalCount", which has the following derivation formula:*

   COUNT(Rentals)

At the same time, class "Vehicle" is specialised into "RetiredVehicle" via the carrier event "Retire". Let us imagine that the rental history for retired cars is not to be considered; to attain this, the "RetiredVehicle" class would redefine the previous derivation using the following formula:

   0

In this way, the rental count for a retired vehicle is always zero. Those vehicles that are not retired will use the original derivation formula, whereas those that are playing the role of retired vehicles will use the redefined formula.

Specialisations and Preconditions

Temporary specialisation also permits that the child class redefines the preconditions of inherited services.

Like in the case of attribute derivations, if an instance of a temporarily specialised class is not playing a role (i.e. is not specialised) at a given moment, then the preconditions used for any of its services are those specified for the parent class. However, the preconditions of the child class are used as soon as the instance starts playing the specialised role.

If the specialisation is permanent, and since behavioural compatibility is required, then the preconditions defined for the child class must be more restrictive than those of the parent class, so that the satisfaction of the former implies the satisfaction of the latter.

If the specialisation is temporary, and since this requires only signature compatibility, the preconditions defined for the child class are not required to be more restrictive than those of the parent class. This provides more flexibility in the use of the specification conceptual construct, what it is considered to be a required, relevant aspect for the temporary characteristic from a semantic perspective.

Specialisation and Integrity Constraints

In addition to derivations and preconditions, a temporarily specialised class can redefine the integrity constraints of its parent.

If an instance of a temporarily specialised class is not playing a role (i.e. is not specialised) at a given moment, then the integrity constraints used to determine whether the object is in a valid state are those specified for the parent class. However, the integrity constraints of the child class are used as soon as the instance starts playing the specialised role.

If the specialisation is permanent, and since behavioural compatibility is required, then the integrity constraints defined for the child class must be more restrictive than those of the parent class, so that the satisfaction of the former implies the satisfaction of the latter.

If the specialisation is temporary, and since this requires only signature compatibility, then the integrity constraints defined for the child class are not required to be more restrictive than those of the parent class.

Since integrity constraints are defined at the class level, and specialised class may introduce integrity constraints that do not redefine any inherited ones, an object must always satisfy the integrity constraints defined for all the classes of which it is an instance and that represent an active role.

Specialisation and Transactions/Operations

Services are inherited via specialisation. For both permanent specialisation, which requires behaviour (and, therefore, signature) compatibility, and temporary specialisation, the required signature compatibility prohibits that service names and name type and number of service arguments be modified.

In the case of temporary specialisation, which does not require behaviour compatibility, the effect of services may be redefined in child classes. Event redefinition is explained in the sections dealing with the Functional Model. Redefinition of transactions and operations is explained here.

A child class can redefine the formula of a transaction or operation defined in the parent class. If an instance of a temporarily specialised class is not playing a role (i.e. is not specialised) at a given moment, then the formula to be used for any redefined transaction is that specified in the parent class. However, the formula of the child class is used as soon as the instance starts playing the specialised role.

Example.   *Class "Client" is permanently specialised by condition into "DirectClient" and "AgencyClient". All three classes have events designed to edit their variable attributes; these events are named "Edit", "EditDirect" and "EditAgency". The class "Client" also defines a local transaction named "TEDIT", which is used to edit the variable attributes of a client regardless of its specific type (i.e. direct or agency).*

The "TEDIT" transaction requires the necessary arguments to set the value of the variable attributes of both "DirectClient" ("CreditCardNumber", "CreditCardType" and "Title") and "AgencyClient" ("ContactPerson" and "MarginRate"). The list of arguments of "TEDIT" is shown in Table 7.16.

Table 7.16 Arguments of the "TEDIT" transaction of class "Client".

Argument name	Data type
pt_thisClient	Client
pt_GivenName	String
pt_FamilyName	String
pt_Address	String
pt_CreditCardNumber	String
pt_CreditCardType	String
pt_Title	String
pt_ContactPerson	String
pt_MarginRate	Real

In order to achieve different effects of the local transaction depending on whether the client is a direct or agency client, the local transaction is redefined within classes "DirectClient" and "AgencyClient", so that the transaction is composed of events "Edit" (for the attributes of "Client") plus "EditDirect" (for the emergent attributes of "DirectClient") in the case of "DirectClient", and of "Edit" and "EditAgency" (for the emergent attributes of "AgencyClient") in the case of "AgencyClient". The arguments of the transaction remain unchanged.

The redefined transaction formula in "DirectClient" is:

Edit(pt_thisClient, pt_GivenName, pt_FamilyName, pt_Address) .
EditDirect(pt_thisClient, pt_CreditCardNumber, pt_CreditCardType, pt_Title)

The redefined transaction formula in "AgencyClient" is:

Edit(pt_thisClient, pt_GivenName, pt_FamilyName, pt_Address) .
EditAgency(pt_thisClient, pt_ContactPerson, pt_MarginRate)

Multiple Inheritance

There is nothing that prevents the specification of multiple inheritance in OO-Method by connecting a child class to multiple parent classes. The typical issues of name clashing and repeated inheritance are solved by labelling every conflictive property in the child class with a prefix corresponding to the parent class from which the definition is inherited.

Example.   *An alternative model of clients could be obtained by having class "Client" specialised from both "DirectClient" and "AgencyClient", rather than the other way around. In this case, and if both "DirectClient" and "AgencyClient" had a "Name" attribute, the "Client" class would access each of these by using expressions such as "DirectClient.Name" and "AgencyClient.Name". These expressions would resolve the ambiguity.*

7.2.4 Parallel Composition

Not all the properties specified during the modelling of Organizational Information Systems belong to the context of a single class; some are general properties at the Conceptual Schema level. For the object-oriented perspective inherent to OO-Method to be coherent, it is necessary that the method permits the specification of such Conceptual Schema-level properties. This can be achieved by viewing the complete Conceptual Schema as a class, with its own attributes, services and integrity constraints. Formally, this class is obtained by parallel composition of all the classes specified within the associated Organizational Information System.

Consequently, and in addition to the more conventional association and inheritance relationships, OO-Method provides a Parallel Composition relationship that provides formal support for the definition of a Conceptual Schema as a class obtained from the other classes in the system. For this purpose, the parallel composition operator often used in Process Algebras (Milner 1980; Hoare 1985) is adopted.

Since an instance of a class can be modelled as an observable process, the process resulting from the parallel composition of all these processes (objects) formally represents a conceptual schema seen as an instance of the parallel composition class.

Parallel composition is very useful, since it provides a specification context that is appropriate for those properties that are general to the whole system and can be used by any class. These properties include global attributes and functions, the global services that modify them, and the integrity constraints that check the validity of instances of the resultant global class.

From a notational point of view, it is not necessary to graphically depict the global class, since it represents the very Conceptual Schema that is already being defined. Being able to specify global properties when necessary is considered sufficient.

The global class, obtained by parallel composition, has the following characteristics:

- Access or visibility over the rest of the classes in the system.
- An implicit identification function. Note that this class will have a single instance at run-time, namely the executing system.
- A basic Statechart Diagram.
- Attributes: constant, variable and derived.
- Services: events, (global) transactions and (global) operations.
- Optionally, preconditions on services.
- Functional Model: optional evaluations that relate their variable attributes with the defined events.
- Participation in triggers as source or destination.
- Participation in projection interfaces as server class.
- Presentation patterns of the following kinds:
  - Instance Interaction Units
  - Service Interaction Units
  - Display Sets
  - Action Patterns

At the same time, restrictions on the global class include:

- It cannot participate in association relationships, including aggregation and composition.
- It cannot participate in specialisation/generalisation relationships.
- Global services cannot be accessed from local services (including transactions and operations) of any class in the system.
- Its State Transition Diagram cannot be changed.
- It cannot participate in projection interfaces as actor.
- It has no creation or destruction events.
- Presentation patterns of the following kinds are not allowed:
  - Population Interaction Units
  - Master/Detail Interaction Units
  - Filters

- Order Criteria
- Navigation Patterns

7.2.5 Visibility Between Related Classes

From within any class that participates in an association, aggregation or composition relationships, attributes of related classes can be referred to as long as there is a valid path, and using the dot notation: *<role_name>.<attribute_name>*

By having role names in association ends, they can be used instead of the name of the related class. Furthermore, they resolve ambiguity when a class is related to another class through multiple associations.

Example.   *Classes "Rental" and "Vehicle" are related by an association with ends labelled as "Rentals" and "Vehicle". From any rental (i.e. any instance of class "Rental"), the plate number of the associated vehicle can be accessed using the following expression:*

>   *Vehicle.PlateNumber*

The semantics of the resulting expression depend on the cardinality of the association end being navigated. If the cardinality is "1..1", then the value associated with the attribute name is perfectly determined.

Example.   *In the previous example, the association end on "Vehicle" has a cardinality of "1..1". Since a rental has one and only one vehicle, the expression:*

>   *Vehicle.PlateNumber*

is deterministic.

If, on the contrary, the maximum cardinality for the association end that is navigated to is greater than one, then multiple instances can be returned when the association is navigated. In this case, a non-determinism issue appears.

Example.   *The "Rentals" end of the association between "Rental" and "Vehicle" has a multiplicity of "0..*", since a given vehicle can participate in multiple rental contracts over its lifetime. Therefore, if the money amount of a rental contract is to be determined from a given vehicle, the expression:*

>   *Rentals.Amount*

is invalid, since it is nondeterministic. Which is the rental contract being referred to?

This issue can be solved by using a grouping operator (sum, min, max, for all, ...) plus an optional object selection condition (where).

Example.   *If the maximum amount of the rental contracts of a given vehicle is to be found, then the following expression can be used:*

>   *MAX(Rentals.Amount)*

Example. *If the money amount of a contract done on the 23/06/2004 is to be found, then the following expression can be used:*

GETONE[7] (Rentals.Amount) WHERE (Rentals.RentalDate = '23/06/2004')

Other semantic considerations can be made about minimum cardinalities. If non-determinism issues can arise depending on maximum cardinalities, then the value of minimum cardinalities can cause non-existence issues.

In fact, if the minimum cardinality for the association end being navigated to is lower than one (i.e. zero), then it is possible that no related object exists. Therefore, an expression such as: *<role_name>.<attribute_name>*

may not evaluate correctly at run-time if the association end represented by the role name has a minimum cardinality lower than one.

Example. *A rental can have no invoice at certain points in time. This is captured by the cardinality "0..1" at the "Invoice" end of the association between classes "Rental" and "Invoice". The following expression within the "Rental" class:*

Invoice.InvoiceDate

will fail when trying to access the invoice date if no related invoice exists.

In order to avoid these situations, it is recommended that the existence of the related object be checked before access is attempted.

Example. *If a new attribute "InvoicedOn", of type "Date", were to be added to class "Rental" in order to store the date on which each rental is invoiced, then a derivation such as:*

Invoice.InvoiceDate

could not be used, since it would fail for those rentals with no associated invoice.
One possible solution is to use a pair of derivations, as shown in Table 7.17.

Table 7.17 Derivation conditions that check object existence.

Condition	Effect
EXISTS(Invoice) = TRUE	Invoice.InvoiceDate
	NULL

The effect of the first derivation would only be computed if the condition is met, which guarantees that an associated invoice always exists. If no invoice is associated to the rental, then NULL is obtained via the second derivation.

---

[7] Syntactically, OO-Method allows for the definition of set-domain functions (functions of which the domain is a set of objects). Among these, SUM, MAX, MIN, AVERAGE, GETONE and COUNT are provided, with their classical semantics. The complete and detailed definition of valid formulas can be found in Pastor and Molina (2006).

The usage of role names to access attributes of related classes can be extended, with the same notation and considerations, to navigate through related objects in a chain:

<role_name 1>.<role_name 2>... <role_name n>.<attribute_name>

Example. *There is an aggregation relationship between "Rental" and "Vehicle", and there is an association between "Vehicle" and "VehicleType". This means that attributes of class "VehicleType" can be accessed from class "Rental" using an expression such as:*

Vehicle.Type.Description

Note that maximum cardinalities of the association ends being navigated to are always one in this example, so that the expression above is deterministic.

Example. *Class "Rental" also has an aggregation relationship to class "Client". If the name of the client who rented a vehicle is to be accessed from the "Vehicle" class, then an expression such as:*

Rentals.Client.FamilyName

would not be valid because of non-determinism issues, since a vehicle can participate in multiple rentals.

In addition to the visibility over attributes of related classes using role paths, it is also possible to refer to a specific class. This is particularly useful when grouping operators are used that work on objects, rather than attribute values.

Example. *Let us assume that the number of rental contracts for each vehicle is to be stored. Class "Vehicle" could be modified by adding an attribute "RentalCount", the derivation of which would have no condition and the following formula:*

COUNT(Rentals)

It is also common to use this kind of object-valued path expression to select instances on which a given service is to be executed repetitively, or to initialize object-valued arguments.

Example. *A client can have multiple active rentals, and he/she may wish to return all his/her rented vehicles at the same time. To implement this, the "Return" service of class "Rental" can be repeatedly invoked. Alternatively, a local transaction "RETURNALL" in class "Client" can be defined, using the following formula:*

FOR ALL[8] Rentals DO Rentals.Return(Rentals)

---

[8] Additionally to the data language, OO-Method introduces a process language, where special kinds of well-formed formulas are provided through the use of the FOR ALL quantifier acting on selected objects for the execution of particular services. These formulas have the structure *FOR ALL class-name WHERE class-condition DO class-event*. This is the type of formulas used in this example. Again, we refer the reader to Pastor and Molina (2006) for further details.

This means that the "Return" service of class "Rental" is to be executed on each rental of the calling client. Let us examine the details.

"FOR ALL Rentals" specifies which rentals are being selected, namely those reuchable through the role name "Rentals" of the "Client" class.

"Rentals.Return" specifies the service to be executed, i.e. the "Return" service of the class retrieved through the "Rentals" role of "Client", namely "Rental".

Finally, the "Return" service of class "Rental" has a single, object-valued input argument, of type "Rental", representing the rental that is subject to returning.

Although a role with cardinality greater than one is being used for the initialization of this argument, this case does not pose non-determinism problems, since the FOR ALL operator solves this. Our example involves the iteration over all the rentals related to the calling client, assigning the particular rental retrieved within each pass of the loop to the symbol "Rentals". This conceptual pattern will be taken into account by the Model Compiler for the correct generation of the appropriate software. This is possible as long as the semantics of the conceptual pattern are precisely defined.

The visibility between classes related by association, aggregation or composition is considered to be bidirectional in OO-Method. This choice may incite debate, but the fact that an association (or aggregation or composition) exists between two classes alters their behaviour as a consequence. Two unrelated classes cannot "see" each other's properties. If an association is created between them, however, then their behaviours can be modified depending on the state of the associated class. Like two persons who decide to live together share reciprocal visibility, two classes that "decide" to associate are subject to the same conditions.

The role names that allow classes to access related classes or their attributes are always subject to the existence of the object from which the path expression is used.

This is particularly relevant for the preconditions of creation services (usually events, but also transactions). It is a common error to think that attributes of related classes can be accessed from the creation event of a class; since any precondition associated to an event must be satisfied before the event begins to execute, and the object does not exist before the creation event is executed, the object does not exist when the precondition is being evaluated, and therefore is not associated to any other objects.

Example.   *Let us assume that no vehicle with a kilometre count greater than 100,000 km is to be rented out. To capture this, the following precondition is added to the "Rent" event:*

Vehicle.Kilometres < 100000

Since "Rent" is the creation event of class "Rental", the rental object to be created does not exist when its precondition is evaluated and, therefore, no relation to an instance of "Vehicle" will be available.

Such problems are solved by using a different kind of path expression. We have explained that attributes of a class can be accessed through a role name or a sequence of role names that navigate associations between classes. There is another kind of path expression, which begins with an object-valued service argument, rather than a role name. An object-valued argument represents an object and so, using a similar notation, attributes of that object can be accessed:

   <argument_name>.<attribute_name>

Roles can also be accessed:

   <argument_name>.<role_name>.<attribute_name>

and role sequences can be used:

   <argument_name>.<role_name 1>.<role_name 2>...
   <role_name n>.<attribute_name>

Both attribute values of an object and the objects themselves can be accessed using navigation paths like these.

Example.   *The previous example shows an incorrect precondition. In order to solve the problem, we should take into account that the "Rent" event of class "Rental" requires (among others) the object-valued argument "p_agrVehicle", which refers to the vehicle being rented out. Using this information, the precondition can be rewritten as:*

   p_agrVehicle.Kilometres < 100000

Although the association to the vehicle has not been made when the precondition is evaluated, the corresponding vehicle can be accessed through the argument that refers to it.

Specialisation relationships entail simpler scenarios, since a single object (although two classes) is involved. Depending on the active class in the specialisation hierarchy and the specialisation kind, properties that can be referenced within any given target class include those of the class together with those of its parent class. If a property is redefined by the target class, then the redefined semantics are considered.

Example.   *Class "Vehicle" is specialised into "RetiredVehicle", which can access the properties of "Vehicle" directly. For example, the following expressions are valid within "RetiredVehicle":*

   PlateNumber (access to the "PlateNumer" attribute)
   Type.Description (access to the description of the associated vehicle type object)

This is so because the child class "RetiredVehicle" inherits all the properties from its parent class, including the attribute "PlateNumber" and the association with class "VehicleType" (labelled with the role name "Type").

The dot notation is used to access the properties of related classes, even when they are not in the same specialisation hierarchy (inheritance network).

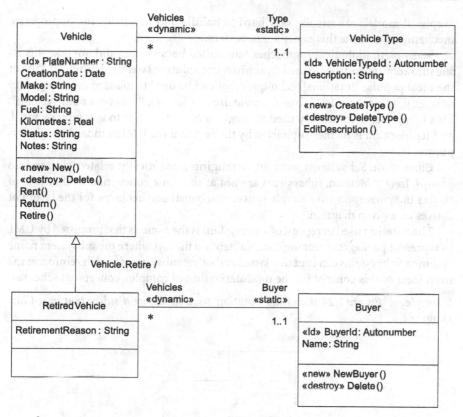

Fig. 7.23 Inter-class visibility combining specialisation and association.

Example. *Let us imagine that a vehicle can be acquired by the buyer once the vehicle is retired.*

In order to capture this, the class "Buyer" is added to the model, and an association between "RetiredVehicle" and "Buyer" is incorporated as shown in Fig. 7.23.

The attribute "Description" of class "VehicleType" could be accessed from class "Buyer" through the following expression:

Vehicles.Type.Description

to which the appropriate condition should be added, in order to avoid non-determinism issues related to multi-valuedness, as described earlier.

7.3 Complexity Management

Reality is complex, and real-life systems are easily composed of hundreds of classes. When a system is being modelled in which the number of classes is very high, the need to adequately manage the resulting "diagrammatic explosion" arises. Large graphical models are usually very hard to handle and maintain, and appropriate mechanisms to make this easier are necessary.

Many methodological approaches have failed because they did not take this issue into account and, consequently, appropriate solutions were not provided. One of the most popular notational techniques that can be used to manage the complexity of large graphical models is based on the use of Clusters, Packages or Subsystems[9]. This comprises a commonly used strategy to give structure to a complex model, and its adoption is further supported by the fact that the UML standard also incorporates it.

Clusters or Subsystems work by arranging semantically related classes into groups. In OO-Method, subsystems are not at the same conceptual level as that of classes but correspond to a simple syntactical construct that helps for the layout of classes on a given diagram.

The notation used to represent a subsystem is the same as that proposed by UML to represent packages: a rectangle with a "tab" on the top, where the subsystem name is shown. Subsystems can contain classes and other subsystems, which reinforces the usefulness of this concept for the modularization of complex conceptual schemas.

Example.   *Figure 7.24 shows the notation used to depict a subsystem in a Class Diagram.*

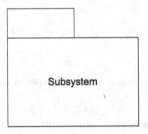

Fig. 7.24 Graphical notation for subsystems.

Since clusters (or subsystems) are not part of the system, but simply a mechanism to organize the Conceptual Schema, only a usage relationship between subsystems is defined. A usage relationship is depicted by a solid line that connects two rectangles representing subsystems, denoting that there exists a relationship between two classes defined in different subsystems. If required, the line representing the usage relationship can be labelled with some information about this kind of relationship.

Example.   *Figure 7.25 shows the graphical representation of the relationship between class "Rental" and the "Clients" subsystem.*

In addition, and within any given subsystem, dashed and "greyed out" strokes can be used to represent model elements that belong to a different subsystem. This can provide the required locality of information when it is convenient to

---

[9] These terms are used as synonyms.

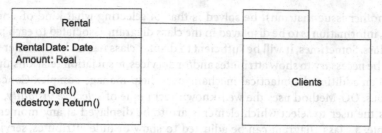

Fig. 7.25 Relationship between class "Rental" and the "Clients" subsystem.

visualise graphically particular relationships that exist between a given class and other classes belonging to other subsystems.

Example.   *Figure 7.26 shows the graphical representation of the relationship between class "Client" of subsystem "Clients" and class "Rental" of a different subsystem.*

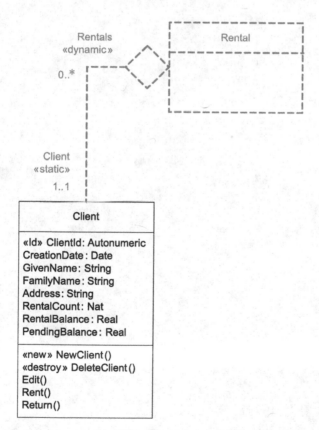

Fig. 7.26 Relationship between class "Client" of subsystem "Clients" and class "Rental" of a different subsystem.

Another issue that must be solved is that of selecting what kind of, and how much, information is to be displayed in the class diagram associated to each particular class. Sometimes, it will be sufficient to display class names but, at other times, it will be necessary to show attributes and/or services, association relationships, etc.

As an additional syntactical mechanism to help manage complex Conceptual Schemas, OO-Method uses the well-known technique of *selective visibility*, which allows the user to select which elements are to be displayed at any moment. For example, a Class Diagram can be adjusted to show or hide attributes, services or associations so that visual complexity is kept at a minimum and always under the control of the user. These characteristics must be taken into account by any CASE environment supporting OO-Method.

8

Dynamic Model

Using the Object Model, we can specify the static architecture of the system classes, determining:

- The component classes and their properties, namely attributes, services and integrity constraints.
- The relationships between classes, namely association / aggregation / composition and specialisation / generalisation.
- The agent relationships, which determine who is authorised to do what, and to see what.

Obviously, this information is very important for the successful construction of a Conceptual Schema. Nevertheless, some parts are still missing from the puzzle of representing a System via a correct and complete Conceptual Schema. Once the static class structure is fixed, the specification must be completed by adding dynamic (related to intra-object control and inter-object communication), functional (characterization of service functionality) and presentation (characterization of the interaction mechanisms between user and system) aspects. It is necessary to view this under the global perspective of the Conceptual Schema, which unites all the abovementioned views (static, dynamic, functional and presentation).

In this section, we start by the specification of the conceptual primitives that are required to characterize the dynamic aspects. Specifically, the following aspects must be determined:

- Once the services available for each class are specified in the Object Model, it is necessary to decide in which order they may occur. In other words, it is necessary to determine which service sequences are allowed as valid lifetimes for the objects of each class.
- It is also necessary to determine which communication mechanisms are possible amongst objects of different classes. In particular, two mechanisms are particularly relevant:
  - How global transactions, which glue together services from different classes but comprise a single unit of execution, can be specified.

– Which services must be automatically activated in certain objects whenever
  some trigger conditions are met within other objects.

This captures the information that will be specified by the Dynamic Model of OO-
Method, which is described now. In summary, the Dynamic Model will represent
those aspects of the organizational system that refer to intra-object control, i.e. the
determination of the potential service sequences that may occur during an object's
lifetime, and to the interaction between objects that may occur in order to compose
inter-object execution units. The set of primitives or conceptual constructors that
OO-Method offers to specify all this information is presented now.

Following our strategy of adopting the notational standard defined by UML,
we use the most adequate diagram types for graphical depictions. As we see in
this section, a State Transition Diagram is used to describe the possible event
sequences for each class, and an Interaction Diagram (a Collaboration Diagram,
more specifically) is used to describe the communication and interaction between
objects.

8.1 State Transition Diagram

As we have said, one of the main objectives of the Dynamic Model is to define the
behaviour of objects over time, explicitly indicating the valid sequences of events
that may occur during an object's lifetime. These are known as *possible lifetimes* of
the objects of the class. In order to describe the valid sequences of events, a State
Transition Diagram is used for each class. In these diagrams, states are used to
represent each of the different *situations* in which an object of the associated class
can be found, and to support the potential state transitions.

State Transition Diagrams are very important in the model, since they establish
when an object can accept or must reject a service request that an agent object tries
to activate, depending on their state (their particular *situation*). In other words,
given a specific state, only a subset of all services can be activated. The states of
diagrams of this type therefore constrain the potential valid transitions.

From a philosophical viewpoint, the existence of each object of a class passes
through a sequence of states that characterize its life. The current state of an object
is the result of its lifetime history up to the moment. From this perspective, an
object's lifetime can be seen as the sequence of services that have occurred for
the object. In addition, an object's current state determines what can happen to
the object in that precise instance; in other words, the set of services that can be
potentially activated for an object depends on the state of that object at that precise
moment.

The graphical representation of the State Transition Diagram of each class
includes:

- *States*, shown as circles that contain a name for the state.
- *Transitions*, shown as labelled arrows between two states, named "source state"
  and "destination state" or, more simply, "source" and "destination".

Example.   *Although the notation for each of the elements that compose state transition diagrams is introduced first, the reader can refer now to the example in Fig. 8.5 to obtain an overall view of the diagram type being discussed.*

8.1.1 States

As we have said, the graphical representation of the dynamic model of OO-Method consists of a state transition diagram for each class, in which states appear as circles containing the state name. States in this diagram represent each of the different situations in which an object of the associated class may find itself at any point during its lifetime. States have the following types:

- *Pre-creation state.* Represents the situation in which objects are immediately before they are created. Only creation events (new) leave states of this type. No incoming transitions can exist. It is graphically depicted by two concentric circles, as Fig. 8.1 shows.

Fig. 8.1 Graphical notation for a pre-creation state.

- *Destruction state.* Represents the situation in which objects are immediately after they are destroyed. Only destroy events (destroy) come into states of this type. No outgoing transitions can exist. States of this kind are depicted by a black filled circle surrounded by a larger circle (bull's eye), as Fig. 8.2 shows. State changes associated with pre-creation and destruction states are considered to be strong state changes, because they take the object from non-existence to existence, and vice versa.

Fig. 8.2 Graphical notation for a destruction state.

- *Simple state.* These have a name, and both incoming and outgoing transitions are possible, originating from the activation of services (events or local transactions). They are depicted by a circle labelled with a representative name, as Fig. 8.3 shows.

Graphically, a state transition diagram cannot show more than one pre-creation state. With regard to destruction states, this may be zero or one, since it is not

Fig. 8.3 Graphical notation for a simple state.

required that an object has a destruction state. If no destruction event is specified, objects that cannot be deleted become possible; they are "immortal" objects. There is no limitation to the number of intermediate states.

8.1.2 Transitions

State transitions represent a change of state of an object. This is the way to represent the move from one situation to another caused by the activation of a service by an agent, i.e. as the consequence of the activation of an action.

Graphically, transitions are depicted by a solid line with an arrowhead from the source state into the destination state. The arrow is labelled with an action and, optionally, with a control condition, as explained by Fig. 8.4 and below.

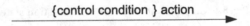

Fig. 8.4 Graphical notation for a state transition.

It must be recalled that an *action* is a service plus a list of agents that may activate it. The syntax to represent an action is as follows:

[Agents]: Service

where *Agents* may be:

- A list of names of agent class, which constrains the service agent list (all the classes authorised to act as agents of the service) to the subset of classes given by the list.
- An empty list, so that no agent (regardless of whether any agent has been defined for the service) is allowed to execute it. This situation represents that the action is part of a transaction and has no external visibility (internal action). Otherwise, an action without an associated actor cannot be activated.
- A list with the * symbol (asterisk) as the only element, which refers to all the classes that are agents of the service.

Example.   *In our system, there is a "rent" service for class "Vehicle", of which classes "Client" and "Administrator" are agents. An action for which the "rent" service can be executed for all the agents of the service is represented as follows:*

   [*]: rent

Example.   *An action for which the "rent" service can be executed in the context of a transaction with no explicit agent attached to it (regardless of whether an agent for the "rent" service has been specified) is represented as follows:*

   rent

Note that, since the agent list is empty, the square brackets and the colon are omitted.

Example.   *An action for which the "rent" service can be activated only by instances of one of its class agents (for example, instances of the class "Client") is represented as follows:*

   [Client]: rent

Understandably, state transitions that start from a pre-creation state must be labelled with actions that correspond to creation services (creation events or local creation transactions for which the first service is a creation service).

State transitions that end at a destruction state must be labelled with actions that correspond to destruction services (destruction events or local destruction transactions for which the last service is a destruction service, since the object ceases existence immediately after a destruction event, and no additional services can be executed on it).

No transitions labelled with creation service actions can originate from a simple state. Similarly, no destruction service actions can end at simple states.

A transition may begin and end at the same state. This is the case when, for any given action, the characterization of different situations (corresponding to the initial and final states) is not considered to be relevant from a dynamic modelling perspective. A change of state associated to the execution of the action may exist but, in these cases, the situation represented by the final state is the same as that of the initial one.

Example.   *Consider a class "Person" with the services "BeBorn", "GetMarried", "HaveChild" and "GetSeparated". In the state transition diagram for this class we will have, in addition to pre-creation and destruction states, the simple states "Single", "Married" and "Separated", since we assume to be interested in characterizing the person's marital status as relevant. The "BeBorn" service labels a transition originating at the pre-creation state and finishing at the "Single" state. The "GetMarried" service labels one transition from the "Single" state and into the "Married" state, and another transition from "Separated" to "Married". Finally, the "GetSeparated" service labels a transition from "Married" to "Separated". This is sufficient to capture the valid lifetimes of any person instance as far as his/her marital status is concerned.*

Whether or not the person has children is not considered relevant from this perspective, since a person can have children irrespective of his/her marital status, and having children does not imply a marital status change. Therefore, the "HaveChild" service labels transitions from "Single" to "Single", from "Married" to "Married", and from "Separated" to "Separated". Alternatively, this characterization (having or not having children) could be represented decomposing the state transition diagram into two different subdiagrams, composed using an AND composition for determining the object's state.

A **control condition** is a well-formed formula (wff) that is used to determine the destination state that is achieved after executing an action that labels multiple transitions with the same source state but different destination states. The wff is constructed using constant values, object attributes (including those visible in related objects) and arguments to the service of the action. The syntax for a control condition involves using the *when* keyword to separate the action from the control condition:

>   *[Agents]: Service when Condition*

Example.   *The state transition diagram for the "Vehicle" class includes:*

- *the simple state "VRegular"*
- *the simple state "VAirCon"*
- *the action [Administrator]: InsExtras*
- *a transition labelled with the action just mentioned from "VRegular" to "VRegular"*
- *a transition labelled with the same action from "VRegular" to "VAirCon"*

Whenever an "Administrator" agent executes the "InsExtras" service to add an extra to the vehicle, and if the vehicle is in the "VRegular" state, how can we determine the final state of the vehicle?

   Control conditions can be added to both transitions in order to resolve this ambiguity. The transition from "VRegular" to "VAirCon" has this condition added:

>   *pvc_Extra.Description = "air conditioning"*

where "pvc_Extra" is the object-valued argument to the insertion event "InsExtra" that represents the extra being added to the vehicle, and "Description" is an attribute of the "Extra" class.

   The transition from "VRegular" to "VRegular", in turn, has this condition added:

>   *pvc_Extra.Description <> "air conditioning"*

In this way, it is easy to distinguish precisely the two situations in which a vehicle can be found: "VRegular" (regular vehicle), in which a vehicle remains as long as air conditioning is not added as an extra; and "VAirCon" (air-conditioned vehicle), to which a vehicle transitions as soon as an air-conditioning extra is added.[1]

8.1.3 Basic Statechart Diagram

Every class has, by default, a basic state transition diagram that is built from the services of the class. This basic state transition diagram represents the essential

---

[1] It is worth mentioning that control conditions could have been avoided in this example by introducing "InsAirCon" as an independent event. This would have constituted a different modelling alternative. For the sake of the example, we have opted for using the "InsExtras" event with a description argument that refers to the kind of extra being selected (such as "air conditioning"). It is not our intention to discuss here the subjectivity factor already treated above and that is inherent to conceptual modelling, which often results in different conceptual schemas for the very same problem, depending on the point of view of the person doing the modelling.

valid lifetimes for the objects of that class, which begin with a creation event, continue with an intermediate state, on which most services operate, and finalize with a destruction event. The basic state transition diagram (shown in Fig. 8.5) is composed of three states (pre-creation, destruction and an intermediate simple state), and the following transitions:

- those starting at the pre-creation state and arriving at the intermediate state, for every creation service.
- those starting at the intermediate state and arriving at the destruction state, for every destruction service.
- those implementing a "loop" on the intermediate state, for all other services.

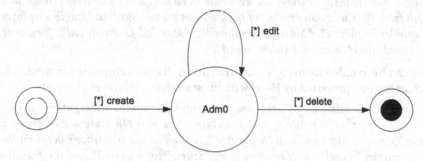

Fig. 8.5 State transition diagram (STD) for the "Administrator" class as an example of a basic STD.

If such a basic state transition diagram obtained by default is considered to be sufficient as far as modelling is concerned, then it is not necessary to modify it. If, on the contrary, states and transitions need to be refined in order to obtain a more detailed description of the possible valid lifetimes of the objects of the class, then the basic state transition diagram constitutes an excellent starting point, since it contains all the necessary information to approach the fleshing-out process.

8.1.4 Managing Complexity in State Transition Diagrams

We have explained how State Transition Diagrams are useful to characterize the valid lifetimes of objects with regard to the state changes caused by the occurrence of services. These states in the diagram are not associated to any particular sets of values for the object's attributes, but represent relevant situations in which an object can be found due to the sequence of services executed up to that moment (and not because of changes of the values of the object's attributes).

Sometimes, it is useful to distinguish between different subsets of states of an object in the problem domain. This happens with the description of global object state as seen in the AND composition of a set a substates, where the different valid paths for different ordered occurrences of class services are specified.

Example.   *Consider a class "Person". We wish to distinguish between two types of states: those that refer to the person's marital status ("Single", "Married", "Separated") and those that refer to the person's employment situation ("Employed", "Unemployed").*

If we had to represent different spaces or subsets of states in a single state transition diagram, then a number of states equal to the Cartesian product of the states of each subset would be necessary; in turn, these would cause a large number of necessary state transitions. This would mean a considerable increment in the complexity of the state transition diagram, which would affect its creation, maintenance, readability and comprehensibility.

Example.   *In order to represent the situation outlined in the previous example in a single State Transition Diagram, we would need to create six different states, which result from the Cartesian product of the states in the two subsets: "Single-Employed", "Single-Unemployed", "Married-Employed", "Married-Unemployed", "Separated-Employed" and "Separated-Unemployed".*

This can be avoided by using a state transition diagram composition mechanism such as the one proposed by Harel with his statecharts (Harel et al. 1987).

Example.   *Continuing with the case from previous examples, it is possible to model an AND state that is made of two OR states. The first OR state would group the states "Single", "Married" and "Separated", as well as the transitions between these ("get_married" labels the transition from "Single" to "Married" and the transition from "Separated" to "Married"; "get_separated" labels the transition from "Married" to "Separated"). The second OR state would group the states "Employed" and "Unemployed" as well as the transitions between these ("find_job" labels the transition from "Unemployed" to "Employed", and "quit_job" labels the transition from "Employed" to "Unemployed"). The creation service of class "Person" labels the transition from the pre-creation state to the AND state, and the destruction service labels the transition from the AND state to the destruction state. This can be seen in Fig. 8.6.*

8.1.5 Operations and State Transition Diagrams

When we explained how actions label a state transition, we stated that an action consists of a service plus a list of agents that may activate that service. Also, we have said that classes can have three different kinds of services: events, transactions and operations.

Operations do not participate in State Transition Diagrams. The reason is simple: both events and transactions follow an "all or nothing" policy for their execution. If something fails during the execution of an event or transaction, all the changes done are undone and the system is left in the same state as that immediately before the execution. This includes state transitions. An event or transaction that causes a state change in an object from state A to state B leaves the object in state A if the execution fails, or in state B if the execution succeeds.

Operations, however, do not follow this policy, and therefore a failure during the execution of any of its component services does not cause the system to revert to

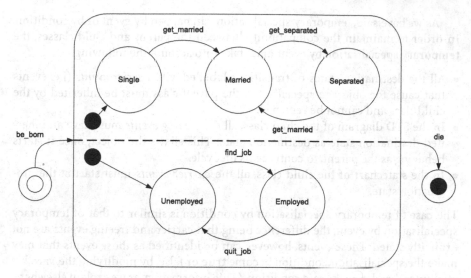

Fig. 8.6 Usage of Harel statecharts adapted to OO-Method State Transition Diagrams.

the previous state. For this reason, operations are not used to label actions in a State Transition diagram, delegating the triggering of transitions to their component services as long as they are not, in turn, operations.

8.1.6 Specialisation and State Transition Diagrams

This section describes how an object's valid lifetime is the sequence of services (events or transactions) that take place for it. This is represented via a State Transition Diagram in OO-Method, which is related to the State Diagram in UML.

We have also stated that, when a class is specialised, the child class inherits the static structure as well as the behaviour of the parent class. Given two classes, PC (parent class) and CC (child class), the following must be taken into account:

- All the attributes and services defined for PC are also attributes and services of CC. In addition, CC can incorporate new attributes and services.
- If the lifecycle specified for CC is restricted to the services defined for PC only, a subset of the lifecycle specified for PC must be obtained. Consequently, we can say that the lifetime of an instance of CC is a valid lifetime when this instance is seen as an instance of PC. Specifically, and in the case that CC is a permanent specialisation of PC, its lifecycle (restricted to the services defined for PC) must coincide with that of PC. If, on the contrary, CC is a temporary specialisation of PC, then its lifecycle (restricted to the services defined for PC) may be a subset of the lifecycle of PC.

In other words, if the states not inherited from the parent class and the transitions labelled with actions of services not inherited from the parent class were removed from the State Transition diagram (STD) of the child class, then the resulting STD would be equivalent to the STD of the parent class.

As we have said, temporary specialisation can happen by event or by condition. In order to maintain the compatibility between the parent and child classes, the temporary specialisation by event must take into account the following:

- All the destination states of transitions labelled with *carrier events* (i.e. events that cause the object to specialise) in the parent class must be inherited by the child class and cannot be renamed.
- In the STD diagram of the child class, all the *freeing events* must have an inherited destination state as destination state. This allows the object, once it starts behaving as the parent, to continue its lifecycle.
- In the statechart of the child class, all the *carrier events* must start at the pre-creation state.

The case of temporary specialisation by condition is similar to that of temporary specialisation by event, the difference being that carrier and freeing events are not explicitly stated. These events, however, can be identified as those events that may make the specialisation condition become true or false, by modifying the variable attributes that define the said condition. (This information, as we explain elsewhere, is specified in the Functional Model).

8.2 Object Interaction Diagram

We have explained how the intra-object control mechanisms associated with the valid lifetimes of a class can be specified. Inter-object interaction mechanisms must now be determined. The need to model object interactions in the system leads us to introduce an object communication/interaction diagram.

The Model of Objects supported by OO-Method involves two mechanisms for inter-object communication: *triggers* and *global transactions* (*global operations*).

- *Triggers.* A condition on an object's state becoming true may cause this object to trigger events or transactions on itself or on other objects in the system. This communication mechanism is called *Trigger* in OASIS (Pastor 1992; Pastor and Ramos 1995).
  The syntax of a trigger in OASIS is:

  <destination>::<condition>:<service>

  where *<destination> := self | object | class | for all*
  Each of these options is discussed below. Also, service arguments can be initialized to constant values or values of attributes of the class causing the trigger.
- *Global Transactions and Global Operations.* Within a transaction, the sequence of services that become activated constitutes a unit of execution. If the events, transactions or operations that compose it belong to the same class, then the transaction is a local transaction (operation). If the sequence is composed of events, transactions or operations of multiple classes, then the transaction is a global transaction (operation; Pastor and Ramos 1995). The former case corresponds

to an intra-object transaction, while the latter corresponds to an inter-object transaction.

Formally, a global transaction (operation) may be seen as a local service of a class that would be obtained by aggregating all the classes that contribute services to the global transaction. This aggregate class would have at least one relevant emergent property, namely the abovementioned global service seen as a local service within the aggregate class. For the sake of simplicity, global services can be seen as services of the parallel composition class that is the Conceptual Schema, already introduced, this making an appropriate context for the specification of any property of a general kind.

Every global transaction (operation) has a name assigned, and arguments may be defined as well. The arguments of the component services can be initialized to constant values or arguments of the global transaction (operation). The details of this are explained in another section.

Now, we describe the notation of the interaction diagrams that are used in OO-Method to represent the communication/interaction between classes in the system. The adopted notation is a subset of the standard proposed by UML (UML 2004) for Collaboration Diagrams. As on previous occasions, the primitives used by these Collaboration Diagrams adapted to OO-Method are precisely defined, and their semantics are not ambiguous. This makes their use much simpler than that of generic Collaboration Diagrams, as described by UML.

For this notation, a class is depicted as a box labelled with the underlined text Instance:ClassName across the top. The Instance label denotes a specific object of the class (optionally), whereas the ClassName label refers to a class in the system. The latter must always be specified, and the former is necessary only if multiple objects of the same class are interacting. In this way, the diagram conveys that inter-action happens between objects (instances of the class "ClassName") and allows for the individual identification of each object via the "Instance" label. Arrows flowing from a class box to other boxes (or to itself) depict communication/interaction. Now, we augment the information about the graphical notation, explaining how the different kinds of communication/interaction that have been introduced can be depicted correctly and clearly.

8.2.1 Triggers

The triggering of a service occurs as a consequence of the satisfaction of a condition on the state of an object. The label associated with the communication/interaction arrows has the following format: *[<destination>::]<condition>:<service>*. The definition of a trigger involves the following properties:

- Definition Class, which is the class in terms of which the trigger condition is specified.
- Trigger Condition, which is a well-formed Boolean formula involving constants, functions and attributes of the definition class (or related classes). The trigger is activated in every instance of the definition class for which the condition is satisfied.

- Destination, which refers to the entity that receives the triggered service, and that determines the trigger kind. Possible options for this destination type are:
  - Self, if the service being triggered is to be executed on the same object as that satisfying the trigger condition.
  - Object, when the service being triggered is executed on a specific object of a class, which does not need to be the same class as that for which the trigger condition is satisfied. In this case, the identifier (or identifiers) of the object on which the service is to be executed must be provided.
  - Class, when the service being triggered is executed on the complete population of a class (i.e. all the instances of that class). As in the previous case, this class does not need to be the same class as that for which the trigger condition is satisfied.
  - For All, when the service being triggered is executed on a subset of the population of a class reached through a sequence of role names from the definition class. This fourth option is, in fact, a special case of the third, in which the destination population is a subset of the class' population, rather than the whole set.
- Path to Destination, which is a deterministic sequence of role names that are visible from the definition class.
- Object Selection Clause, which is a well-formed Boolean formula that may involve constants, functions and attributes of the class reached by navigating the role name sequence from the definition class (or related classes). This clause restricts the set of objects on which the triggered service is executed to those reached from the definition class through the role name sequence that also satisfies the condition.
- Destination Class, which is the name of the class of the object or objects on which the triggered service is executed. This class depends on the destination kind:
  - Self: The destination class is the same as the definition class.
  - Object: The destination class may not coincide with the definition class.
  - Class: The destination class may not coincide with the definition class.
  - For All: The destination class is the one reached from the definition class through the role name sequence indicated by the "Path to Destination", or a predecessor of such a class.
- Service, which is the name of the service that is triggered, plus initialization values for its arguments.
- Comments, which is an optional property that allows documenting the trigger definition.

The graphical specification of triggers is undertaken, as we have said, using a Collaboration Diagram, in which each kind of trigger is depicted as shown below. Depending on the destination, triggers are graphically depicted in one of the following four ways:

- *SELF*: If the trigger is directed to the same object as that where the condition is satisfied, then an arrow is used going out of the box representing the class, and coming into the same box and labelled with the word "self". The trigger condition and the service to be executed, together with its initialized arguments, are shown afterwards.

Example.   *In order to implement the fact that vehicles must be retired once they travel 100,000 km, the following SELF trigger can be modelled. The properties of this trigger can be seen in Table 8.1 below, and graphically in Fig. 8.7.*
    The trigger condition

Kilometres > 100000 AND Status <> "B"

specifies when the triggered service

Retire(pt_thisVehicle, "Retired after travelling 100,000 km")

will be activated and where (SELF indicating that the same object satisfying the trigger condition will be the recipient of the triggered service).

Table 8.1 Trigger to SELF in class "Vehicle".

Definition Class	Vehicle
Trigger Condition	Kilometres > 100000 AND Status <> "B"
Destination	SELF
Path	
Object Selection	
Destination Class	Vehicle
Service	Retire(pt_thisVehicle, "Retired after travelling 100,000 km")

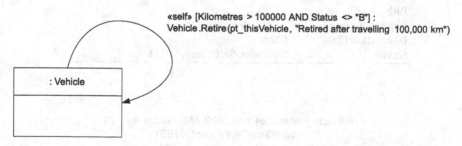

«self» [Kilometres > 100000 AND Status <> "B"] :
Vehicle .Retire (pt_thisVehicle, "Retired after travelling 100,000 km")

: Vehicle

Fig. 8.7 Trigger to SELF in class "Vehicle".

As shown, the trigger condition not only checks that the number of travelled kilometres is over 100,000, it also checks that the vehicle's status is not "B" (meaning retired vehicles), so the "Retire" service is not invoked repeatedly. The "Retire" services sets the attribute "State" to the value "B", so it is invoked only once for the vehicle.
    The "Retire" service has two arguments: "pt_thisVehicle", of type "Vehicle", refers to the vehicle to be retired; "pt_Reason", of type "String", describes the reason why the vehicle is retired and, in this example, is initialized to the literal "Retired after travelling 100,000 km".

- OBJECT: If the trigger is directed to *a specific object* of a different class (or other object of the same class), then an arrow is used going out of the box representing the class where the condition is satisfied, and coming into the box representing the destination class, and labelled with the syntax described earlier. The identity of the specific object is provided by initializing the object-valued argument of the triggered service to the destination object.

Example.   *Let us imagine that the system must send a sale offer to any customer who has just returned a vehicle that has travelled over 100,000 km. This can be achieved through the introduction of a trigger to OBJECT having the aforementioned client as destination.*

In order to implement this, the event "SendSaleOffer(p_thisClient, p_Vehicle)" of class "Client" is used. The argument corresponding to the destination object ("p_thisClient") is initialized to the instance of "Client" associated to the instance of "Vehicle" on which the trigger condition is satisfied (namely that the travelled distance is above 100,000 km and that the vehicle is not retired).

The second argument, representing the vehicle that is offered on sale, is initialized precisely to the instance of "Vehicle" that satisfies the trigger condition (using the reserved word "THIS"). The properties of this trigger can be seen in Table 8.2 below and, graphically, in Fig. 8.9.

Table 8.2 Trigger to OBJECT in class "Vehicle".

Definition Class	Vehicle
Trigger Condition	Kilometres > 100000 AND Status <> "B"
Destination	OBJECT
Path	
Object Selection	
Destination Class	Client
Service	SendSaleOffer(Client, THIS)

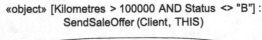

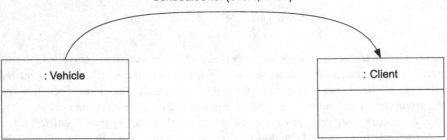

Fig. 8.8 Trigger to OBJECT in class "Vehicle".

- CLASS: If the trigger is directed to *all objects* of the same class, then the same approach is used as in the case of *self,* but using the reserved word *class,* rather than *self* as trigger destination (the message may be intended for any class in the system).

Example.   *If a vehicle is retired and has never been offered on sale, then the system must offer it on sale to every existing client. As this involves the whole population of class client, to accomplish this a trigger to CLASS executing the service*

   "SendSaleOffer(p_thisClient, p_Vehicle)"

for each client in the system can be used. The properties of this trigger can be seen in Table 8.3 below and, graphically, in Fig. 8.9.

Table 8.3 Trigger to CLASS in class "Vehicle".

Definition Class	Vehicle
Trigger Condition	Status = "B"
Destination	CLASS
Path	
Object Selection	
Destination Class	Client
Service	SendSaleOffer(p_thisClient, THIS)

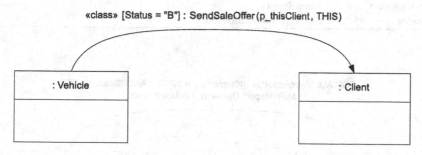

Fig. 8.9 Trigger to CLASS in class "Vehicle".

In this case, the "p_thisClient" argument (representing the client that receives the sale offer) is not initialized, since the semantics of the trigger to CLASS will initialize it to each instance of the class "Client" in turn. However, the "p_Vehicle" argument is initialized to the reserved word "THIS", thus indicating that the vehicle that satisfied the trigger condition will be offered to each of the clients.

- FOR ALL: If the trigger is directed to *a subset of the objects of a class,* the same approach is used as in the previous case but, rather than the *class* reserved word, an expression like that shown below is used:

<path>[where <path_condition>]

where

  path is a deterministic role name sequence from the class defining the trigger, which determines the subset of objects that will receive the trigger, and

  path_condition is an optional Boolean expression on attributes of the class reached by *path* that restricts the subset to only those objects that satisfy the condition. Therefore, and as we have already said, this fourth case is, in fact, a special case of the third case (trigger to CLASS).

Example.   *Assume that the system must delete the maintenance report history whenever a vehicle is retired because it has travelled over 100,000 km. Assume also that the "Retire" service, which changes the vehicle status to "B", is triggered when this kilometre value is surpassed, as we described in a previous example.*

  It is now possible to introduce a trigger for the "delete" service in class "MaintReport" that affects only those instances related to the vehicle that satisfies the trigger condition, as shown in Table 8.4 below and, graphically, in Fig. 8.10.

Table 8.4 Trigger FOR ALL in class "Vehicle".

Definition Class	Vehicle
Trigger Condition	Kilometres > 100000 AND Status <> "B"
Destination	FOR ALL
Path	MaintReports
Object Selection	
Destination Class	MaintReport
Service	Delete(p_thisMaintReport)

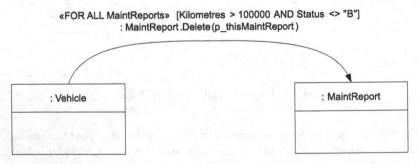

«FOR ALL MaintReports» [Kilometres > 100000 AND Status <> "B"]
: MaintReport .Delete(p_thisMaintReport)

: Vehicle   : MaintReport

Fig. 8.10 Trigger FOR ALL in class "Vehicle".

In this case, the path "MaintReports" determines that the population of objects of the destination class (namely "MaintReport") for which the "Delete" service (of the same class) is invoked corresponds to those objects related to the vehicle that satisfies the trigger condition via the "MaintReports" role.

Constants, functions and attributes of the object satisfying the trigger condition (or other objects related to it) can be used for the arguments of the service to be triggered.

If the service to be triggered has an object-valued argument that represents the object for which the service is invoked (as is the case for all non-creation services), then such an argument does not need to be initialized explicitly, since the specification of the trigger destination (self, object, class, for all) carries out this initialization implicitly. Any other arguments of the service to be triggered, however, must be initialized.

Triggers represent internal activity in the system. Services are triggered when the appropriate trigger conditions are satisfied, without the user being aware of this. For this reason, it is convenient that every argument of the service to be triggered be appropriately initialized by the trigger definitions, so that the system does not need to require additional information from the user in order to trigger the services.

8.2.2 Global Transactions and Global Operations

We have mentioned the need to specify services with a granularity larger than a single class, in order to capture those cases in which a system service is composed of events or transactions that belong to multiple classes, all of them constituting a single unit of execution. OO-Method introduces the notion of global transaction or global operation in order to capture this mechanism, and its specification context is the Dynamic Model being discussed. Specifically, a global transaction (operation) is a "molecular" unit of execution (composed of multiple services), in which the component services may belong to different classes that do not need to be related.

From a methodological point of view, a global service is the conceptual representation of a given organizational task, modelled at a higher level of abstraction than the Conceptual Model. Business Processes, together with their associated tasks and activities, agents, resources, etc. are primitives in the Business Process Model or Workflow Model in the context of Organizational Modelling, which comprises the ultimate source of the services that appear in the Conceptual Schema. In fact, work is being carried out on OO-Method in order to extend its basic model-transformation metaphor to the transformation of Business Process Models into Conceptual Schemas. This work is beyond the scope of this book, but additional information can be found in Estrada et al. (2003), and Martinez et al. (2004).

In MDA terms, the core idea involves using a high-level Organizational Model as a PIM, which appropriately represents system requirements, and developing the appropriate mappings between conceptual primitives so that this model can be transformed into another, lower-level PIM (PIM–PIM transformation). The resulting PIM is the Object-Oriented Conceptual Schema that is described in this book and that serves as the starting point for the final transformation from PIM (Conceptual Schema) into the corresponding Product Software (PIM–PSM transformation).

Returning to our current discussion, a global transaction (operation) has a system-wide unique name. This name may coincide with the name of a service or class. If this happens, then no clash occurs, since local services (defined within classes) are prefixed with their class name when referred to from global transactions (operations).

In addition, a global transaction (operation) has the following optional properties, with their usual semantics:

- Alias
- Comments
- help message

Being services, global transactions (operations) may carry arguments. As with local services, the properties of an argument of a global transaction (operation) are:

- a name
- a data type
- a data size, for arguments of type "string"
- a default value (optional)
- a flag indicating whether null values are accepted
- an alias (optional)
- a help message (optional)
- comments (optional)

The name of the argument must be unique in the context of the global service.

The default value is a well-formed formula, similar to those of local transactions/operations, of a type that is compatible with the argument. If a default value is provided for an argument, then the system will use it as a suggested value, the agent in charge of activating the service being able to change it.

In addition, arguments of a global service are one of two kinds:

- Input arguments. Their value must be determined for the global service to execute. The agent in charge of activating the service is responsible for assigning a value to them.
- Output arguments. They take a value as a consequence of execution, once the global service finishes successfully. Their value is expressed through a value expression, which is a well-formed formula built from input arguments and/or properties of any object in the system. In addition, conditions can be incorporated into its specification, so that the value of an output argument can depend on their satisfaction.

Example.   *It is possible to combine the deletion of a vehicle and a client into a single service, using the global transaction*

   "*DELETEVEHICLEANDCLIENT(ptg_Vehicle, ptg_Client)*",

which receives two object-valued arguments that represent, respectively, the vehicle and client that are to be deleted. This global transaction composes transactions "DELETEVEHICLE(pt_Vehicle)" and "DELETECLIENT(pt_Client)" of classes "Vehicle" and "Client" respectively, as the following formula shows:

   DELETEVEHICLE(ptg_Vehicle) . DELETECLIENT(ptg_Client)

This formula shows that the arguments "pt_Vehicle" (from the local transaction "DELETEVEHICLE") and "pt_Client" (from the local transaction "DELETE-CLIENT") are initialized, respectively, to the arguments "ptg_Vehicle" and "ptg_Client" of the global transaction "DELETEVEHICLEANDCLIENT".

The considerations to be made for the value expressions of output arguments of global services are the same as those made for output arguments of local services, so we will not repeat these here.

The specification of a global transaction or operation needs to define the corresponding service composition through a formula, as do local transactions and operations.

The syntax used to specify such formulae is, basically, the same as that used for local transactions and operations. There is a single difference, due to the special nature of these services. Since these are global services, they can be seen as being defined for the class that represents the complete Conceptual Schema. As we have said before, this class is obtained by parallel composition of all the system classes, and is implicitly related to them.

This global class relates to a system class A via a role name A, so that every role name sequence that appears within the specification of a global transaction or operation must always start with a role name that matches the name of a class in the system.

Example.   *Let us assume that a service to delete all vehicles, clients and rentals is needed. The classes "Vehicle", "Client" and "Rental" already have local transactions "DELETEVEHICLE", "DELETECLIENT" and "DELETERENTAL", which implement the deletion of a vehicle, client and rental respectively. Using global transactions, it is possible to compose these three services into a single unit of execution, and make them run not on a single instance of each class but on the complete population of objects of each class.*

Thus, a global transaction "DELETEAVC" is introduced with no arguments and the following formula:

> *FOR ALL Rental DO Rental.DELETERENTAL(Rental) .*
> *FOR ALL Client DO Client.DELETECLIENT(Client) .*
> *FOR ALL Vehicle DO Vehicle.DELETEVEHICLE(Vehicle)*

Note that role sequences used with the collection iteration operator "FOR ALL", in the case of global transactions, must start with the name of a class, rather than the name of a role. This is so because global transactions are not defined (and, therefore, executed) within any particular class. Instead, we can see the whole conceptual model as a single class that relates to every other class via "roles" of which the names coincide with the name of each class.

Let us examine the first action of this global transaction in detail (the other two are similar).

The "FOR ALL Rental" part iterates over the complete object population of the "Rental" class.

The "DO Rental.DELETERENTAL" part selects the service to be executed (in this case, "DELETERENTAL" of class "Rental", since "Rental" is the class name preceding the service name "DELETERENTAL").

Finally, the argument "pt_thisRental" of local transaction "DELETE RENTAL" is initialized to the same role sequence as that used in the "FOR ALL ..." part, thus indicating that the rental on which the local transaction "DELETERENTAL" is to be executed corresponds to each iteration of "FOR ALL Rental".

Since the implicit relationship with each of the classes in the system gives visibility and access to the complete population of each class, global transactions and operations often use the *FOR ALL* operator with a *WHERE* clause in order to restrict the population on which services must be executed.

Example.   *It is possible to delete from the system all those vehicles that have been retired, by using a global transaction on the "Vehicle" class restricted to those instances with a retired status. This global transaction, called "DELETERETIRED-VEHICLES", does not need arguments, and is defined by the following formula:*

FOR ALL Vehicle WHERE Vehicle.Status = "B"
DO Vehicle.DELETEVEHICLE(Vehicle)

This formula restricts the population of vehicles on which the FOR ALL clause iterates to those of which the status equals "B" (meaning retired).

A different alternative would be to define object-valued arguments in the global transaction (operation) that represent the objects on which we wish to act.

Example.   *It is possible to issue invoices for all rentals of a given vehicle by using a global transaction "ISSUERENTALINVOICES(ptg_Vehicle)", to which the vehicle of which the rentals must be invoiced is passed as an argument. The formula of this global transaction is as follows:*

FOR ALL Rental WHERE Rental.Vehicle = ptg_Vehicle
DO Rental.IssueInvoice(Rental)

Note how, in this case, the population of "Rental" on which the FOR ALL clause iterates (and, therefore, on which the service will be executed) is restricted to those rentals associated to the target vehicle by the comparison to the object-valued argument "ptg_Vehicle".

The graphical representation of global services in a Conceptual Schema is now described. Using a Collaboration Diagram as a starting point (like in the case of triggers), arrows are drawn between the boxes corresponding to the classes that participate in the global interaction, representing the service activation sequence, and are labelled with each service to be executed.

Each global service is assigned a unique number. Arrows belonging to the same service are labelled with the same number. This number allows the modeller to visually track the component transitions of a global service.

Arrows are labelled using the following format:

   [GlobaServiceNumber] :: [Condition :] Service

where

- *GlobalServiceNumber* is the number identifying the global service.
- *Condition* represents a guard of necessary condition for the service to execute.
- *Service* can be a service local to a class or a global service, declared preserving the valid syntax for services in this context.

Example.   *Figure 8.11 shows the graphical notation for a global transaction, of which the textual representation would be class1.service1.class2.service2 (the concatenation of service1 provided by class1 and service2 provided by class2).*

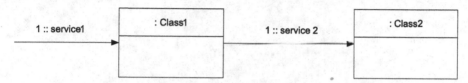

Fig. 8.11 Graphical notation for a global transaction.

Functional Model

Up to this point, the Conceptual Schema contains the architectural declaration of the classes in the system, including the definitions of all the classes and inter-class relationships with all their properties, which have been described in previous chapters in the context of the Object Model of OO-Method. In addition, the Dynamic Model adds detail to these properties by specifying the valid lifecycles for the objects of any given class and by specifying the aspects related to inter-object communication via the appropriate triggers and global services.

It can be argued that all these specifications cover most aspects of the relevant information to be modelled within a Conceptual Schema. However, something is still missing: the specification of the functionality of each service in terms of how it affects the local state of the object or objects involved in its execution.

This is precisely the objective of the Functional Model of OO-Method, which is presented in this section. The Functional Model is used to specify the effects that events have on object state.

It is worth noting that the specification of these properties is a problem poorly solved by most object-oriented approaches. Some approaches simply ignore the issue, performing the definition of event semantics in any free-form language. Others address the problem from the opposite side, advocating that functional specifications be done in some programming language such as C++ or Java. This approach is particularly improper, since it introduces a notation belonging to the solution space into the problem space, thereby violating the basic tenet of modelling: the independence of the model with regard to the specific technologies that may be used to implement it.

This issue can be followed even further back, being present in the evolution and current state of UML. Some very successful proposals such as OMT (Rumbaugh et al. 1991) suggested that the functional model should be based on Data Flow Diagrams (DFDs), which were extensively used in the context of Structured Analysis. The usage of this technique, in any of its variants, within object-oriented approaches has been strongly criticized for being too operational and imprecise, and for giving a perspective of the system too different from that of the two other models (object and dynamic). Both object and dynamic models partition a system into objects with a local state and behaviour. Functional models, on the other hand, split state and behaviour and partition the system into data stores and processes. Any data store can contain fragments of the state of any object, and a process may carry out (part of) the work of an operation. As a conclusion, it is very hard to establish a precise mapping between the functional view provided by DFDs and the static and dynamic views provided by object and dynamic models respectively. It is symptomatic that later versions of OMT did not involve using DFDs as a functional modelling mechanism, and did not incorporate any other technique that would replace them.

The UML standard and the collection of methods that currently revolve around it are victims of this evolution. No precise technique exists that can specify the detailed functionality of the services of a class. Sometimes, it is suggested that the notation provided by some diagrams (such as Interaction Diagrams or State Transitions Diagrams) can be used. Other times, the formal support of OCL is recommended. Some works have been done on the definition of a formalism that can characterize the functional view; for example, action semantics in the UML 2.0 superstructure (UML 2004) propose a collection of semantically defined actions for this purpose. All aspects considered, however, the truth is that what to specify and how to do this are always decided freely by the engineer. The primitives necessary to specify the body of the services are not determined, and the precise semantics for their usage and integration within the Conceptual Schema are not given.

These issues are solved by the Functional Model in OO-Method, which is presented here. The proposed approach is based on the declarative specification of event effects, as already suggested by the first versions of OO-Method's formal background, namely the OASIS formal specification language (Pastor and Ramos 1995). In this approach, the declaration of the functionality of a service is based on the definition of a set of axioms in a Dynamic Logic that has been specially adapted to the particularities of object-oriented modelling.

The formalism that underpins these dynamic-logic axioms is hidden as far as the specification is concerned, in order to make the modelling job easier for the engineer. The Functional Model of OO-Method expresses the system functionality without having to use the OASIS formal notation explicitly. To achieve this, a collection of information templates are introduced that, depending on the kind of attribute, enable us to adopt a simple and powerful declarative schema that captures all the information necessary to describe the effects of an event on the objects of the system. The necessary conceptual primitives of the Functional Model are described in the next sections. Such basic concepts allow us to specify precisely the value changes that an object's attributes undergo as a response to certain events, and these are the following:

- Evaluations (seen as the specification atom of the effect of an event on an attribute)
- Evaluation conditions
- Evaluation categories

9.1 Event Effect Specification Using Evaluations

The engineer must be able to define with ease and clarity how the occurrence of an event affects the value of each of the variable attributes of an object. An attribute is declared as variable when its value can be altered as a consequence of one or more events, which are said to be "relevant" for this particular attribute.

Therefore, each variable attribute of an object has a collection of associated relevant events, which may make its value change. Seen from the opposite side, each event is associated to a set of variable attributes that it can modify.

Each <variable attribute, event> pair can have an associated evaluation. An evaluation is a well-formed formula that determines the value that the variable attribute of a class takes whenever the event (in the same class) occurs. This formula can involve constants, functions, attributes of the class (or related classes) and event arguments.

Example.   One of the most basic uses of evaluations is to link event arguments to the variable attributes of the class, so that the semantics of the event are simply to set the attributes to the values given by its arguments.

Class "Client" has an event "Edit(p_thisClient, p_GivenName, p_FamilyName, p_Address)" that is used to modify the values of the variable attributes "GivenName", "FamilyName" and "Address" of a particular "Client" instance. This instance is represented within the event by the object-valued argument "p_thisClient". The other three arguments are used to set the values of the corresponding attributes of "Client". The evaluations that define this behaviour are shown in Table 9.1.

Table 9.1 Evaluations of event "Edit" of class "Client".

Event	Attribute	Evaluation effect
Edit	GivenName	p_GivenName
Edit	FamilyName	p_FamilyName
Edit	Address	p_Address

This table shows that the value of the "p_GivenName" argument would be assigned to the "GivenName" attribute, the value of the "p_FamilyName" argument to "FamilyName", and the value of "p_Address" to the "Address" attribute.

9.2 Evaluation Conditions

Assigning a single evaluation to a given variable attribute for a given event is often not expressive enough. Usually, the same event can modify the associated attribute differently, depending on whether certain conditions are met or not.

It can be argued that different events can be introduced to cater for this need, so that each event has a single effect on each attribute. Compared to the possibility of assigning multiple evaluations to each <variable attribute, event> pair, however, this approach is quite weak. Also, creating multiple artificial events with the same conceptual meaning is not a recommended prospect, as this goes against the main goal of modelling: the natural representation of real-world concepts.

Therefore, it is necessary to determine which of the multiple evaluations associated to a single <variable attribute, event> pair is to be chosen when the event occurs. This is done using evaluation conditions, which are well-formed formulae that represent the conditions under which the associated evaluation is used. These formulae are defined in terms of the state of the object at the exact moment in which the event is triggered.

Only the evaluation for which the evaluation condition holds is chosen. In order to guarantee that only one evaluation condition can be satisfied, evaluation conditions must be mutually exclusive. If a <variable attribute, event> pair has a single evaluation, then no evaluation condition can exist for it, since it is always applicable.

If a <variable attribute, event> pair has more than one evaluation, then all of these but one must have an evaluation condition. The evaluation with no condition is the *default evaluation*.

Example.   *The rental rates for any given tariff are updated periodically, being incremented by a percentage that depends on the kind of vehicle associated to the tariff. An increment of 2% is used for regular cars, 5% is used for vans, and 9% for industrial vehicles. An event "UpdateRentalRates(p_thisTariff)" is created in class "Tariff", and some evaluations are defined for this event and the attribute "RentalRate", as shown in Table 9.2.*

Table 9.2 Evaluations of event "UpdateRentalRates" of class "Tariff".

Event	Attribute	Evaluation condition	Evaluation effect
UpdateRentalRates	RentalRate	VehicleClass = "R"	RentalRate * (1 + 0.02)
UpdateRentalRates	RentalRate	VehicleClass = "V"	RentalRate * (1 + 0.05)
UpdateRentalRates	RentalRate	VehicleClass = "I"	RentalRate * (1 + 0.09)
UpdateRentalRates	RentalRate		RentalRate

*This table shows that the modification done on the value of "RentalRate" depends on the vehicle class to which the tariff applies. For example, if a particular tariff instance applies to regular vehicles ("VehicleClass = "R""), then the "RentalRate" attribute is incremented by 2%, as shown by the corresponding evaluation effect "RentalRate * (1 + 0.02)".*

Note that the value of "RentalRate" inside the evaluation effect formulae is that of the attribute immediately before the event is triggered. This is the case even when the evaluations for an attribute are not mutually exclusive (such as in this example), and more than one of them are applicable. Note also that, in our example, all the evaluations except for one have a condition. The evaluation with no condition is chosen only if none of the evaluation conditions are satisfied, thereby guaranteeing that the event always has some effect on the value of the attribute.

9.3 Categorization of Evaluations

A variable attribute can be modified by multiple events (at least one), and an event can modify multiple attributes. It is important that the specification of evaluations is made in a simple and effective way. In order to describe the manner in which an event may modify the value of an attribute, OO-Method introduces three evaluation kinds or categories: *state*, *cardinal* and *situation*.

This classification can be used to facilitate the description of evaluations by taking into account how an event modifies the value of an attribute. For each category, a data entry template helps the engineer to specify the necessary information to guarantee that the evaluation specification is correct.

The three evaluation categories are described now.

- *State evaluations* are those in which the event makes an attribute change its value into a new value that is independent of the values previously held. Such a new value is computed from event arguments. Formally, a State Evaluation represents a dynamic logic axiom where the value of an attribute in the final state (after the event occurrence) does not depend in any way on the value in the initial state. This is not the case for the other types of evaluations.

Example. *Evaluations for event "UpdateRentalRates" of class "Tariff" of this category would be those specifying a precise value for the modified attribute (Rental-Rate). This value will be fixed by an argument of the relevant event (in this case, the p_NewRentalRates argument assumed declared for the UpdateRentalRates event).*
This would be declared as has been shown in Table 9.1.

- *Cardinal evaluations* are those in which the event has an increment or decrement effect, quantifiable through a function over the value of the associated attribute, the event arguments, and the object's attributes. In addition, an attribute initialization effect can also appear. The effect of the event depends on the value of the attribute immediately before the event occurs. The increment or decrement of a unit is a special case assumed by default.

Example. *Table 9.2 shows state evaluations for event "UpdateRentalRates" of class "Tariff". These evaluations can be expressed in an equivalent form using a cardinal approach, as shown in Table 9.3.*
In this case, the conditional evaluations are described by an increment action (shown by a "+" sign) on the "RentalRate" attribute, and the increment amount is expressed as the evaluation effect. At the same time, the default evaluation is described by an initialization action (shown by an "=" sign) on the same attribute that sets its value to the same value as it used to have. Note that the cardinal evaluations shown in Table 9.3 are equivalent to the state evaluation shown in Table 9.2.

- *Situation evaluations* are those in which the associated attribute takes a value within a well-defined domain. Each of the values that the attribute may take represents a situation that can be described by the attribute. The new value that is assigned to the attribute may depend on its previous value, like in the case of

Table 9.3 Cardinal evaluations of event "UpdateRentalRates" of class "Tariff".

Event	Attribute	Evaluation condition	Action	Evaluation effect
UpdateRentalRates	RentalRate	VehicleClass = "R"	+	RentalRate * 0.02
UpdateRentalRates	RentalRate	VehicleClass = "V"	+	RentalRate * 0.05
UpdateRentalRates	RentalRate	VehicleClass = "I"	+	RentalRate * 0.09
UpdateRentalRates	RentalRate		=	RentalRate

cardinal evaluations. In this case, however, there exists a discrete domain from which the attribute can take values.

Example.   *Class "VehicleType" has a "VehicleLevel" attribute of type string, the possible values of which are "T", "M" and "E", depending on the vehicle being a top-, mid- or entry-level one. The event "UpdateLevel" operates on this attribute in a cyclical manner, setting its value to mid-level if it is entry-level, to top-level if mid-level, and back to entry-level if top-level. Table 9.4 shows the situation evaluations that relate the "VehicleLevel" attribute to the "UpdateLevel" event.*

Table 9.4 Situation evaluations of event "UpdateLevel" of class "Vehicle".

Event	Attribute	Previous value	Evaluation effect
UpdateLevel	Level	"E"	"M"
UpdateLevel	Level	"M"	"T"
UpdateLevel	Level	"T"	"E"

The evaluation classification feature is a convenient strategy to specify the dynamic-logic axioms on which evaluations are based. These axioms are of the form $f[e()]f'$, where f characterizes the current state, e the triggered event, and f' the resulting state. The potential complexity of the underlying formalism is thus hidden from the engineer's view, who has to use only the provided templates to specify evaluations of any kind.

9.4 Creation Events and the Functional Model

It is not necessary to use a class' creation events within the Functional Model, since their evaluations are implicit and cannot be altered. The reason for this is that the semantics associated to creation events are precise and well known.

We have stated that creation events involve a datum-valued argument for each of the class' variable or constant attributes marked as requiring data on creation[1].

The implicit evaluation of a creation event guarantees that the following activities are performed correctly:

---

[1] Note that a constant attribute may take a default value; in this case, it is not necessary to mark the attribute as requiring data on creation.

- Argument values are assigned to variable attributes marked to require values on creation[2].
- Argument values are assigned to constant attributes marked to require values on creation.
- Default values (or null values, if no defaults are specified and nulls are allowed) are assigned to variable attributes not marked to require values on creation.
- Default values are assigned to constant attributes not marked to require values on creation.

It must be emphasized that default value formulae for attributes cannot refer to attributes of related classes, since related objects can be accessed only once the object has been created and its associations established. At that moment when default attribute formulae are evaluated, this has not happened yet.

Example.   *The attributes of class "Vehicle" includes "PlateNumber", "Creation-Date", "Make", "Status" and "SalePrice", as summarized in Table 9.5.*

Table 9.5 Some of the attributes of class "Vehicle".

Name	Type	Require on creation	Nulls allowed	Default value
PlateNumber	Constant	Yes	No	
CreationDate	Constant	No	No	getSystemDate()
Make	Variable	Yes	No	
Status	Variable	No	No	"D"
SalePrice	Variable	No	Yes	

Focusing on these attributes as an example, the creation event of class "Vehicle" involves arguments "p_PlateNumber" and "p_Make". The effect of the creation event on the attributes shown in Table 9.5 is as follows:

- *Assign the value of argument "p_PlateNumber" to the constant attribute "Plate-Number".*
- *Assign the value returned by the "getSystemDate()" function (i.e. the current date) to the constant attribute "CreationDate".*
- *Assign the value of argument "p_Make" to the variable attribute "Make".*
- *Assign the default value "D" to the variable attribute "Status".*
- *Assign a null value to the variable attribute "SalePrice".*

---

[2] The specific characteristics of the value associated to each argument are determined in the context of the Presentation Model, as explained elsewhere.

9.5 Destruction Events and the Functional Model

Destruction events of a class do not need to be used within its Functional Model either, because they cause the destruction of an object. Modifying the values of an object that is about to be destroyed makes no sense. In addition, the semantics associated to destruction events are precise and their effects are well known.

9.6 Specialisation and the Functional Model

Some rules must be followed within the Functional Model to guarantee that the specified compatibility is maintained between parent and child classes:

- All the attributes inherited by a permanently specialised class can be modified by events of the child class but not by events of the parent class. Evaluations on attributes of the parent class and for events of the same class must be defined within that class. These evaluations cannot be redefined by the child class in order to preserve the behavioural compatibility that is associated to permanent specialisation.
- In temporary specialisation scenarios, it is possible for the child class to redefine the evaluations of the parent class. In these cases, the child-redefined evaluations are used when the event is triggered. The required signature compatibility is thus supported.

Example.   When a rental is entered into the system, an invoice is created. An invoice can only be cashed once it is issued. This situation is captured through the temporary specialisation of class "Invoice" into "IssuedInvoice". This specialisation is attained through the "Issue" event of class "Invoice". Since this is a temporary specialisation, it is possible for "IssuedInvoice" to redefine evaluations on attributes inherited from "Invoice". Specifically, "IssuedInvoice" redefines the evaluations on the "Paid" attribute of "Invoice" for the "Pay" event of "IssuedInvoice", as shown in Table 9.6.

Table 9.6 Evaluations on attribute "Paid" of class "Invoice" as redefined by "IssuedInvoice".

Event	Attribute	Evaluation condition	Evaluation effect
Pay	Paid	Issued = true	True
Pay	Paid		False

- In temporary specialisation by event scenarios, the carrier events of the child class are subject to implicit evaluations under the same considerations as for creation events, which have been already described. In fact, these events act as creation events of the new state of the object seen as an instance of the child class.

Example.   *The carrier event of "IssuedInvoice" is "Issue", that is, the execution of the "Issue" event has the effect of specialising the invoice object into an issued invoice object. The "IssuedInvoice" class has the two own attributes shown in Table 9.7.*

Table 9.7 Owned attributes of class "IssuedInvoice".

Name	Type	Require on creation	Nulls allowed	Default value
IssueDate	Variable	Yes	No	getSystemDate()
TaxRate	Constant	Yes	No	0.17

Consequently, the carrier event "Issue" has the following arguments:

- *"p_thisInvoice", of data type "Invoice", which refers to the invoice to issue.*
- *"p_IssueDate", which provides a value for the variable attribute "IssueDate" of class "IssuedInvoice".*
- *"p_TaxRate", which provides a value for the constant attribute "TaxRate" of class "IssuedInvoice".*

Note that the carrier event "Issue" has arguments "p_IssueDate" and "p_TaxRate", since, like in the case of a regular creation event, these arguments are used to initialize the values of attributes marked to require data on creation. The implicit evaluations of this carrier event are those that assign the value of "p_IssueDate" to the attribute "IssueDate", and the value of "p_TaxRate" to the attribute "TaxRate".

9.7 Transactions, Operations, and the Functional Model

OO-Method's Functional Model allows us to fully specify how events affect the state of objects, i.e. the collection of values of their attributes. Also, we have explained that the atomic execution units (i.e. events) can be composed into molecular execution units (i.e. transactions and operations) that, in turn, can be composed into molecular units again.

We have additionally explained that (atomic or molecular) services of classes can be composed into molecular execution units at the global level; in turn, these can be composed into larger global molecular units.

Therefore, the *Functional Model* (which allows us to specify the functionality of events), together with the specification of *Local Transactions and Operations* of classes and the Interaction Diagram, which is part of the Dynamic Model that encompasses the specification of *Global Transaction and Operations*, constitute the three mechanisms used to specify the complete functionality of an information system.

OO-Method thus enables us to specify the semantics of events with precision, providing simple and effective mechanisms for the composition of simple, atomic execution units into larger, molecular ones. In this way, we can state that OO-Method allows for the precise specification of service semantics, either events or transactions/operations. Starting from events that provide the basic building functional blocks, more complex business processes can be represented through the adequate specification of transactions and/or operations.

Example.   *In a previous example related to the specification of local transactions, it was stated that the local transaction "RETURNVEHICLE(pt_Vehicle)" of class "Vehicle" has the following formula:*

$$RETURNVEHICLE(pt\_Vehicle) = Return(pt\_Vehicle) .$$
$$SendForMaintenance(pt\_Vehicle)$$

This means that the semantics of transaction "RETURNVEHICLE" involve chaining the execution of "Return" (initializing its "pt_Vehicle" argument to the transaction's argument of the same name) and "SendForMaintenance" (with a similar argument initialization). However, what are the semantics of services "Return" and "SendForMaintenance"? Since both of these are events, their semantics are specified in the Functional Model through one or more evaluations. We can see that the specification of the semantics of any service is fully and precisely achieved in OO-Method, using evaluations in the Functional Model in the case of events, and service composition by formulae in the case of transactions and operations.

Presentation Model

The specification of the static and dynamic aspects achieved by the models described so far is, without any doubt, essential for the appropriate characterization of a system. In fact, this is the focus of the best known modelling approaches in Software Engineering, often based on data and process specification models. However, this is not sufficient.

Some basic aspects are still needed, namely those related to the manner in which users will interact with the running system, studied in recent years by the Human–Computer Interaction (HCI) community. From this community, some proposals have been made to model user interfaces, usually based on some kind of task modelling. However, the lack of generic approaches that integrate user-interface modelling aspects with other views of the Conceptual Schema is remarkable. Taking into account the relevance of the user interface in the final product, it is surprising that conventional modelling approaches neglect this area and leave it to be tackled at design or implementation phases, often obtaining operational environments that do not comply with basic usability rules and, for this reason, unsuccessful software products.

The issue has an interesting philosophical facet: the inclusion of HCI aspects in the specification of a system implies the recognition that the way in which users see and interact with the world must be a part of the description of that world. This is why the specification constructed through the three models already described (object, dynamic and functional) must be complemented by that for a fourth one that can integrate the properties of the user interface into the existing Conceptual Schema.

For this purpose, OO-Method incorporates the Presentation Model, which extends the conventional views discussed above. This is a User Interface Abstract Specification Model, since it captures the necessary aspects of the user interface without delving into implementation issues.

Adopting an MDA perspective, the Conceptual Schema Compiler transforms the Abstract Interface Model (a Platform-Independent Model or PIM) into a Concrete Interface Model (a Platform-Specific Model or PSM). This PSM contains the software elements that implement, on the target platform, the abstract specifications included in the PIM.

In addition, this proposal constitutes a bridge between the modelling and software production methods used in Software Engineering and those used in the HCI field, allowing us to effectively combine techniques and approaches that have been used by two different communities that, despite having tried to solve the same problems, have frequently ignored each other's advances. In fact, the proposals from HCI that try to model tasks are indeed reinventing, at a very basic level, some functional modelling mechanisms that are well known in Software Engineering.

Likewise, many Software Engineering methods that try to model the interaction between people and computers are proposing solutions of arguable usability that have been already studied and surpassed by the HCI community. OO-Method combines the knowledge and experiences of both communities in a balanced way.

OO-Method's Presentation Model is made of a collection of interface patterns, which are described in this section. Interface patterns enable us to specify the properties considered relevant to determine how the user–system interaction must occur. It is worth noting that this specification is done at the modelling stage, and the conceptual primitives utilised are integrated with the other primitives used for other modelling views in OO-Method.

The Presentation Model is defined in terms of already known concepts, mostly from the Object Model. It provides a methodological guide to represent the user interface in an abstract and design-independent way, ensuring the semantic integration of user-interface aspects with those from static and dynamic models.

Always respectful with the "OO-Method metaphor", the construction of a presentation model allows the engineer to define user interfaces in a homogeneous and platform-independent fashion. This is achieved by taking each interface pattern that is specified in the problem space (conceptual schema) and associating to it a software representation that is adequate in the solution space (final software product).

10.1 General Structure

The Presentation Model is structured in three levels. From more general to more specific, these levels are:

- *LEVEL 1: System Access Structure*
  - Action Hierarchy Tree
- *LEVEL 2: Interaction Units*
  - Simple
    - o Service
    - o Instance
    - o Population
  - Composite
    - o Master / Detail

- *LEVEL 3: Basic Elements*
  - Entry
  - Defined selection
  - Argument grouping
  - Argument dependency
  - Filter
  - Order criterion
  - Display Set
  - Available actions
  - Navigation

The first level establishes the way in which the user interacts with the system, organizing the access to system functionality through a tree-shaped abstraction in which non-leaf nodes are aliased groups of leaf nodes, which represent interaction units at the second level.

The second level defines system interaction units and the navigation between these. An interaction unit determines the scope of the interaction between the user and the system, which entails one of the following:

- Executing a service.
- Querying the population of a class.
- Visualising the details of a specific object.
- The grouping of a collection of pre-existent interaction units into a composite interaction unit, following a master/detail structure.

There exist four types of interaction units, which correspond to the four scenarios listed above. Some of these are simple (or "atomic") whereas some others are composite (or "molecular"). Each of the simple types can be modified by third-level patterns, called basic elements, which provide the precise semantics necessary in order to specify the details of each interaction unit, as discussed below.

The navigation diagram is expressed at level two, and enables us to represent the valid sequences of interaction units for any given user type. This diagram is particularly relevant in the context of web application development.

With regard to the third level, it is composed of patterns called basic elements, which are the building blocks from which interaction units are constructed. Usage of basic elements is not orthogonal, and they cannot be combined in an arbitrary way; on the contrary, each of them has a restricted application scope that depends on the kind of interaction unit.

Figure 10.1 shows the 3-level structure that we have just introduced. It is important to remark that the level-2 presentation patterns characterize the basic types of interaction to be modelled:

- the context of a service execution (Service Interaction Unit),
- the visualisation of a particular instance (Instance Interaction Unit),
- the visualisation of a set of objects (Population Interaction Unit).

These three fundamental Interaction Units are complemented with a Master-Detail Interaction Unit, as a concrete example of how composed scenarios of interaction

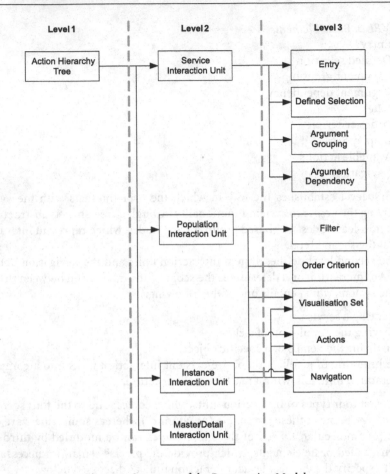

Fig. 10.1 Structure of the Presentation Model.

can be constructed by combining pre-existing interaction units. Under this approach, other composed conceptual primitives could be incorporated if required for enriching the expressiveness of the OO-Method Presentation Model.

The other two levels complement this one, by structuring how to access to the basic Interaction Units (level 1) or fixing which lower-level, elementary patterns can be applied to define them precisely.

Each of the patterns in the Presentation Model is described in detail in the following sections, going from the most specific to the most general ones. Once the global picture has been given, such a bottom-up approach hopefully provides improved clarity, since it starts by describing the basic building blocks of human–computer interaction to then combine these into second-level interaction units and eventually into top-level entities.

10.2 Basic Elements

Presentation basic elements are the building blocks from which abstract user interfaces can be constructed. They represent specific aspects of the interaction between a human and a system, and can be composed into interaction units.

Some of these basic elements are closely linked to the execution context of a service and, consequently, are generally used within a Service Interaction Unit. This is the case, for example, for Entry and Defined Selection elements, which determine (respectively) how service argument data can be entered and which value (from within a predefined set) a given service argument can take. These basic elements can also be used in different contexts, as we explain when we introduce the Filter element. The usage of some other basic elements, such as Argument Grouping and Argument Dependency, is meaningful only in the context of a service execution.

In any case, and for the sake of completeness, the appropriate usage context is given for each basic element.

10.2.1 Entry

The Entry basic element captures the relevant aspects of data to be entered by the user, for example, when providing values for service arguments. Interaction aspects that can be specified include edit masks, valid value ranges, and help and validation messages.

The properties that define the Entry basic element are:

- Name.
- Data type.
- Edit mask.
- Valid value range.
- Default value.
- Help message.
- Validation message.
- Comments.

The name must be unique in the system, and is used to identify the element.

The data type is used to control type compatibility when using the basic element.

Example. *An entry element of type "Integer" can be assigned to a service argument of type "Integer" or "Real" (since "Integer" can be cast into "Real"), but not to one of type "String".*

The edit mask determines the format that the data show when the user enters them.

Example. *An entry element of type "String" is assigned to a "String" argument corresponding to a telephone number, and the edit mask*

> *##.###.###*

is provided. This mask would allow the following values to be entered:

96.123.456
12.345.678

but not the following ones:

12345678
12345

The valid value range enables us to define and control which values can be entered.

Example.   *The "Rent" event of class "Rental" includes, among others, the argument "p_atrDayCount" of type "Nat". If the number of days for any given rental is so constrained to the range 1 to 29, then a valid value range can be specified with these limits. This would avoid users entering a value for this argument that is outside the permitted bounds.*

The default value lets the system suggest a predefined value to the user.

Example.   *Let us imagine that statistics show that most vehicles are hired for a period of 7 days. In order to speed up the data entry process, the entry element assigned to the "p_atrDayCount" argument can have a default value of 7, so that this value is suggested to the user, who can still change it if necessary.*

The help message works as usual, specifying a text that can be shown to the user to provide some information about the meaning of the data to be entered.

Example.   *The argument "p_atrVehicleClass" of event "CreateTariff" of class "Tariff" is a string of size 1, which can take the values "R" (for regular cars), "V" (for vans) or "I" (for industrial vehicles such as trucks). An entry element associated to this argument would be helpful to the user by explaining the range of possible values and the meaning of each one.*

The validation message is a piece of text that is shown to the user when a validation error occurs on the entered data.

Example.   *Let us return to the example of the argument "p_atrDayCount" of event "Rent", which had a valid value range between 1 and 29. A validation message can be added with the text "Rentals cannot span more than 29 days."*

Comments allow the engineer to specify additional information that is considered useful for documentation purposes.

The modelling elements to which an entry presentation element can be assigned are:

- Class attributes.
- Datum-valued service input arguments.
- Datum-valued filter variables.

Example.   *The event "CreateVehicle" of class "Vehicle" includes the argument "p_atrKilometres", which is used to initialize the "Kilometres" attribute of that class. An entry element is assigned to that event with the following properties:*

- *Name: E_Kilometres*
- *Data type: Real*
- *Edit mask: ##,###.##*
- *Valid data range:*
- *Lower bound: 0.00*
- *Upper bound: 99,999.99*
- *Default value: 0.00*
- *Help message: Please enter a real number between 0.00 and 99,999.99*
- *Validation message: Only real values between 0.00 and 99,999.99 can be entered*
- *Comments: This element helps the user in the entry of kilometre values*

The most frequent usage scenarios of entry elements are the assignment of values to arguments and filter variables (described in the section dealing with the Filter element[1]). It is also possible to use these to assign a value to an attribute; in this case, every service argument related to that attribute (such as those of creation services) implicitly uses that entry element, unless a different entry element is explicitly assigned.

In any of the three cases, the entry element is a good example of the convenience of the User Interface Abstract Specification features provided by OO-Method's Presentation Model. Attributes or service arguments are augmented with presentation basic elements during modelling and in the Problem Space. Using this information, the Conceptual Schema Compiler can generate those appropriate software components in the Solution Space that best implement the model.

Object-valued service arguments cannot have entry elements associated, since they do not correspond to discrete values but to object references. The mechanisms used to enter object references are different to those used to enter discrete values.

10.2.2 Defined Selection

The interaction between a user and the system does not only involve entering data; very often, the user needs to select a value from within an existing collection. The Defined Selection basic element enables us to define, beforehand, the set of valid values for the associated model element. The set thus defined behaves as an enumerated type.

The properties that define a Defined Selection basic element are:

- Name.
- Data type.
- Value set.
- Help message.
- Comments.

The name must be unique within the system, and is used to identify the element.

The data type is used to control type compatibility when using the basic element.

---

[1] An intuitive explanation is that a filter variable is entered in order to select a subset of the population of a class.

Example.   *A defined selection element of type "Integer" can be assigned to a service argument of type "Integer" or "Real" (since "Integer" can be cast into "Real"), but not to one of type "String".*

The value set is a list of pairs <*Code, Label*>, where *Code* is a valid value for the model element to which the defined selection element can be assigned, and *Label* is an alias for that value. This label or alias is the text that is shown to the user, keeping the actual value hidden from his/her sight. Since the values handled by information systems (such as codes, abbreviations or mnemonics) are sometimes meaningless to the average user, this presentation element is useful to assign meaningful labels to such values for the sake of comprehension.

Example.   *The "Status" attribute of class "Vehicle" is a string of size 1 that represents the status of the vehicle. Possible values include "D" for available, "A" for rented out, "R" for being serviced, and "B" for retired. A defined selection element can be assigned to this attribute with the value set shown in Table 10.1.*

Table 10.1 Value set of the defined selection element assigned to attribute "Status" of class "Vehicle".

Code	Label
D	Available
A	Rented out
R	Being serviced
B	Retired

In this way, every time the system prompts the user to select a value for this attribute, meaningful labels such as "Available" or "Rented Out" are shown, rather than apparently meaningless letters such as "D" or "A".

The help message is a piece of text that is shown to the user with information about the data type and meaning of the model element to which the defined selection element is assigned.

Example.   *The defined selection element introduced in the previous example can be completed with an appropriate help message, such as the following:*
"A vehicle is 'available' from the moment of its creation. It moves to being 'rented out' when a rental on it is entered. It moves to 'being serviced' whenever it is sent to the maintenance garage, and to 'retired' when it is withdrawn from the vehicle pool."

Finally, comments enable the engineer to document the defined selection element.
The model elements to which a defined selection element can be assigned are:

• Class attributes.
• Datum-valued service input arguments.
• Datum-valued filter variables.

Like in the previous case, the most frequent usage scenarios are assignment to service arguments and filter variables, as well as assignment to attributes (and the resulting implicit assignment to related services). In this case, a new Data Type is actually being defined for the attribute, since the possible range of values is being delimited.

10.2.3 Argument Grouping

The Argument Grouping basic element helps define the way in which input arguments for a given service are presented to the user.

The input arguments to a service are organized as an ordered list that establishes the order in which they are shown to the user, so that he/she can give values to them prior to the execution of the service. In addition to the ordering, this basic element enables us to arrange arguments in groups and subgroups. This aspect is needed from an interaction modelling perspective, changing the way in which this interaction will be perceived by users. Again, this is an example of how to adapt user interaction properties at modelling time.

The properties that define an Argument Grouping basic element are:

- Argument order.
- Argument groups.
- Containment relationships of groups and arguments.

As its name indicates, the argument order fixes the sequence in which the service arguments will be navigated, under the selected argument group granularity.

An argument group is defined by the following:

- Alias.
- Help message.
- Comments.

The alias is used on the user interface to identify the argument group.

The help message is a piece of text that is shown to the user to give information about the argument group and the arguments contained in it.

The comments are useful, like in previous cases, for the engineer to document the argument group; in turn, this can be useful in automatically generating the corresponding documentation.

Every Service Interaction Unit has an implicit Argument Grouping basic element that contains all the service arguments in the same order as that in which they are defined.

Example.   *The implicit Argument Grouping basic element of service "BuyVehicle" of class "Vehicle" contains all the service arguments in the same order as that in which they are defined, as shown in Table 10.2.*

The arguments in Table 10.2 appear in a single, implicit group (without a name). The order used in their definition could have been changed simply by declaring them in this context with a different order.

More complex argument grouping basic elements can be defined by introducing groups, putting arguments inside groups, and nesting groups within groups in a tree-like fashion.

Table 10.2 Default argument grouping basic element for service "BuyVehicle" of class "Vehicle".

Group	Argument
	p_agrVehicleType
	p_atrPlateNumber
	P_atrMake
	P_atrModel
	P_atrFuel
	P_atrKilometres
	P_atrCreationDate
	P_atrNotes
	P_agrExtras
	P_agrInsurance
	P_atrLocation
	P_agrOperations

Example.   *The implicit argument grouping basic element for service "BuyVehicle" of class "Vehicle" shown in the previous example can be modified by adding groups in which related arguments can be placed, and by conveniently sorting arguments inside each group. Table 10.3 shows a possible arrangement.*

Table 10.3 shows that four groups have been added with aliases "Identification" (containing only the vehicle's plate number); "Classification" (containing arguments that allow us to classify vehicles according to their type, make, model and fuel type); "Status" (grouping the arguments pertaining to the status of the vehicle); and "Miscellaneous" (which contains other arguments, such as those describing extras and insurance details as well as the operations that have been done on the vehicle).

Table 10.3 Sample argument grouping basic element for service "BuyVehicle" of class "Vehicle".

Group	Argument
Identification	
	p_atrPlateNumber
Classification	
	p_agrVehicleType
	p_atrMake
	p_atrModel
	p_atrFuel
Status	
	p_atrCreationDate
	p_atrKilometres
	p_atrLocation
	p_atrNotes
Miscellaneous	
	p_agrExtras
	p_agrInsurance
	p_agrOperations

Each argument can be directly contained in a single group at most, regardless of whether this group is nested within another group or not.

10.2.4 Argument Dependency

The Argument Dependency basic element enables us to define dependency relationships between the values or state of an input argument of a service and the values or state of other input arguments of the same service.

The Argument Dependency basic element uses ECA-type rules (event, condition, action) for each of the input arguments of the service, with the following semantics: when a given interface event occurs for a specific argument (such as entering its value or activating/deactivating it), certain action is performed if a condition is met.

This basic element enables us to specify certain dynamic behaviour for the user interface, and is always applied within a Service Interaction Unit. For this reason, and as we detail below, the terms "event" and "action" must be interpreted, in this context, as an interface event and an action that is carried out in the context of the human–machine interaction associated with the execution of the service.

An Argument Dependency basic element is defined through the following data:

- Interface Event.
- Condition.
- Actions.

The *interface event* indicates what happens to the argument to which the Argument Dependency basic element is applied. Two types of events exist:

- *SetValue(v)*, which indicates that the argument has received a value.
- *SetActive(v)*, which indicates that the argument has been activated or deactivated.

Events of both types carry an implicit argument "v" that represents:

- The value that has been given to the argument, in the case of *SetValue*.
- The activated state (v = true indicates that the argument is activated; v = false indicates that it is deactivated), in the case of *SetActive*.

Each event has an associated *agent*, which enables us to restrict the application of the Argument Dependency basic element to the activation of the event by a specific agent.

The *agent* can be:

- *User*, when the event is caused by the user.
- *Internal*, when the event is caused by the action of another Argument Dependency basic element.
- *, which encompasses both *User* and *Internal*.

The *condition* is a Boolean well-formed formula that must be satisfied in order to carry out the actions. This formula may be composed of constants, functions and service arguments.

The *actions* comprise a nonempty list of elements, each of which consists of three parts:

- Argument.
- Event.
- Formula.

Argument refers to the name of an argument of the service (possibly the same as that for which the Argument Dependency basic element is defined).

Event is the action to be performed on *Argument*. As indicated above, it can be *SetValue* (to assign a value to *Argument*) or *SetActive* (to activate or deactivate *Argument*).

Formula is a well-formed formula that indicates the value that *Argument* will receive (if *Event* is *SetValue*), or whether Argument is to be activated or deactivated (if *Event* is *SetActive*).

Example.   *Let us imagine that the acquisitions policy establishes that all the vehicles of a certain make "MakeX" must have the diesel fuel type. This means that the value "Diesel" must be automatically assigned to the argument "p_atrFuel" of service "BuyVehicle" of class "Vehicle" whenever the user enters the value "MakeX" for the "p_atrMake" argument of the same service. An argument dependency basic element can be defined to implement this behaviour, as shown below:*

Event

Agent	*Argument*	*Event*
User	*p_atrMake*	*SetValue(v)*

Condition

v = *"MakeX"*

Action

Argument	*Event*	*Formula*
p_atrFuel	*SetValue(v)*	*"Diesel"*

The "Event" section of the argument dependency basic element indicates that the rule is activated when agent "User" (i.e. the user of the system) triggers the "SetValue" event for the "p_atrMake" argument (i.e. when the user sets this argument to some value, overwriting the current one).

When this rule is activated, the "Condition" section is evaluated in order to determine whether the associated actions must be carried out or not. In our example, the condition indicates that "v" (the value assigned by the user to the "p_atrMake" argument) must equal "MakeX" for the actions to be carried out. In the example there is a single action, which assigns the value "Diesel" to the "p_atrFuel" argument.

Example.   *Continuing with the same example, it would be appropriate to deactivate the "p_atrFuel" argument after setting its value to "Diesel" to prevent the user from manually changing its value into something different (and thus violating the* *company's policies). This can be attained by adding an extra action to the argument dependency basic element shown in the previous example, which would appear as follows:*

Event

Agent	*Argument*	*Event*
User	*p_atrMake*	*SetValue(v)*

Condition

v = "MakeX"

Action

Argument	*Event*	*Formula*
p_atrFuel	*SetValue(v)*	*"Diesel"*
p_atrFuel	*SetActive(v)*	*false*

The newly added action indicates that the "SetActive" event is to be executed for the "p_atrFuel" argument with the value "false", effectively deactivating the argument. This happens once the "Diesel" value has been assigned to it, since the order of the actions is meaningful.

Note that the execution of actions as a consequence of the activation of an argument dependency basic element can result in the activation of further argument dependency basic elements and, therefore, further actions. Special care must be taken to avoid situations in which a collection of argument dependency basic elements trigger each other in an infinite loop.

10.2.5 Filter

A frequent situation is that in which a subset of the objects of a class must be selected according to some criteria expressed for the attributes of that class. The Filter basic element is introduced to capture this need, defining a selection condition over the population of a class that can be used to restrict its object population, and facilitate further object search and selection operations. Filter basic elements appear in the context of Population Interaction Units.

Example. *The rent-a-car system often provides features in which searches are performed depending on different criteria: available vehicles, pending invoices, etc. To access in every case the right population, a filter must be defined.*

Filter basic elements can also be used in the context of a Service Interaction Unit. A filter (or collection of filters) is used, contained in a Population Interaction Unit, whenever an argument of a service is object-valued (i.e. refers to a class) and a specific object is to be selected as a value to the argument. In scenarios like this, filters are not used directly but as part of a Population Interaction Unit, which is the object selection atom in OO-Method's Presentation Model.

In the most general case, searches must be parameterized with certain values that vary for each particular search operation. These parameters are called *filter variables*.

Example.   *Necessary searches in the rent-a-car system include clients by family name, invoices issued between two dates, etc. Family name and those two dates are filter variables.*

A filter is always defined for a given class. The properties associated to a Filter basic element are the following:

- Name.
- Alias.
- Help message.
- Comments.
- Formula.
- Variables.

The name identifies the basic element within the class, so it must be unique within this context, including the specialisation hierarchy of the class.

The alias is the text that serves the human user of the system to identify the search mechanism. The alias does not need to be unique, although avoiding duplicate aliases reduces confusion for the users.

The help message is a piece of text that is shown to the user to inform him/her about the purpose and working details of the search mechanism.

The comments are useful for engineers to document the Filter basic element.

The formula is the expression of the search criterion. This is a well-formed formula made of constants, functions, attributes of the class on which the filter is being defined (or related classes), and filter variables.

Example.   *Renting a vehicle is one of the most frequent use cases of the rent-a-car system. Service "Rent" of class "Rental" encapsulates this functionality, carrying the object-valued argument "p_agrVehicle", which refers to the vehicle to be rented. A population interaction unit can be associated to this argument with a filter that allows the user to select only those vehicles that are available. The formula for this filter is:*

   Status = "D"

Only available vehicles (i.e. vehicles with Status = "D") are shown to the user when a value is to be selected for the "p_agrVehicle" argument.

Filter variables represent parameters in the search criterion. They can be datum-valued or object-valued.

Datum-Valued Filter Variables

A datum-valued filter variable is defined through the following properties:

- Name.
- Alias.
- Data type.
- Default value.

- Entry basic element.
- Defined selection basic element.

The name identifies the variable in the context of its filter basic element, so it must be unique within this context.

The alias is used by the user to identify the parameter of the search criterion. It does not have to be unique, but it is recommended that it be within the context of the filter basic element.

The data type is used to control the values that the user may enter.

The (optional) default value is an expression built from constants or functions of the appropriate data type that provides a suggested initial value to the user for the search parameter.

The (optional) entry basic element (a level-3 presentation pattern) is used to validate, control the value range, and apply edit masks on the search parameter, as given by their semantics.

The (optional) defined selection basic element (also a level-3 presentation pattern) is used to restrict the values that the user may enter for the search parameter to those given by it.

Both entry and defined selection basic elements may be used, as explained, associated to a filter variable.

Example.   *Continuing with the previous example, let us stipulate that the search criteria for vehicles that can be rented include, in addition to the vehicle state, the type of fuel of the vehicle. The filter definition previously described can be extended by adding a datum-valued filter variable with the following properties:*

- *Name: v_Fuel*
- *Alias: Fuel Type*
- *Data type: String*

In addition, the filter formula of the previous example should be modified as follows:

   Status = "D" AND Fuel = v_Fuel

In this way, the instances of class "Vehicle" shown by the population interaction unit assigned to the "p_agrVehicle" argument are those that satisfy both conditions in the filter, namely that the status is available ("D") and that the fuel type of the vehicle is as indicated by the user through the variable "v_Fuel".

Example.   *A very common query in the system is locating invoices that have been issued between two given dates. In order to implement this, a filter can be defined for class "IssuedInvoice" with two variables of type "Date" named "v_FromDate" and "v_ToDate", and with aliases "From" and "To" respectively. The filter formula is:*

   IssueDate >= v_FromDate AND IssueDate <= v_ToDate

This filter limits the instances of "IssuedInvoice" to those having an issue date between (and including) "v_FromDate" and "v_ToDate".

Object-Valued Filter Variables

An object-valued filter variable is defined through the following properties:

- Name.
- Alias.
- Data type.
- Default value.
- Additional information.
- Selection.

The basic components are similar to those of datum-valued filter variables. The major difference resides in the two types of basic elements (level-3 presentation patterns) that can be used in this case, namely Display Set (additional information) and population interaction unit (selection).

The name identifies the variable in the context of its filter basic element, and so it must be unique within this context.

The alias is used by the user to identify the parameter of the search criterion. It does not have to be unique, but it is recommended that it be within the context of the filter basic element.

The data type points to a type of object, i.e. a class in the system. For practical purposes, it can take values that correspond to the attribute or attributes that act as identifiers for such a class.

The (optional) default value is an expression that provides a suggested initial value (according to the data types of the identifier attributes of the associated class) to the user for the search parameter. Consequently, the expression must be evaluate to an object-valued type, which, for practical purposes, is represented via the values associated to the identifier attributes of the class, as we have said.

The additional information is the name of a Display Set basic element (described in a section below) that has been defined for the class selected as data type of the filter variable. The final purpose here is to give the user some feedback about the object that is selected as a value for the search parameter, displaying the values of the elements in the Display Set for that object.

The selection is the name of a population interaction unit (also described in a section below) that has been defined for the class selected as data type of the filter variable. The purpose here is to provide the user with an object selection mechanism that can be used to assign a value to the search parameter.

Example.   *Another common search in the system involves finding the rentals made by a particular client. This can be implemented by a filter on class "Rental" with an object-valued variable named "v_Client", of type "Client" and with alias "Client". The filter formula is:*

   Client = v_Client

This filter limits the instances of class "Rental" to those that are related to the client referred to by "v_Client" via the role "Client".

Using Filter Variables

As we have stated, filter variables are useful to parameterize the search criterion defined by a filter formula. This does not mean that the user must give a value to each of the filter variables in order to apply the filter.

Filter variables that do not receive a value have no effect on the parts of the formula where they appear. This means that the fewer variables are specified, the less restrictive the filter is for the target object population. It is even possible that no restriction whatsoever is applied.

Example.   *Consider a filter that finds vehicles that use a particular type of fuel, with the following formula:*

   Fuel = v_Fuel

where "v_Fuel" is a datum-valued filter variable of type "String". If the user does not specify any value for this filter variable and applies the filter, then no restriction is applied over the vehicle object population, and the filter returns all the vehicles in the system.

Example.   *Let us retrieve the filter that finds available vehicles with a given fuel type. The formula is:*

   Status = "D" AND Fuel = v_Fuel

If the user applies this filter without specifying any value for "v_Fuel", then the filter acts as if the only restriction given is that of "Status = "D"", so that all available vehicle objects are returned regardless of their fuel type.

10.2.6 Order Criterion

In addition to defining search criteria that restrict the population of a class, it is also common to define how the search result is to be ordered. Ordering is often done on the values of one or more properties of the objects returned from the search, and considering ascending/descending options.

Example.   *The issued invoices returned by a search are to be displayed to the user ordered by issue date, ascending.*

Example.   *The clients returned by a search are to be displayed to the user ordered by pending balance, descending, and then by family name, ascending.*

The Order Criterion basic element is defined for any particular class through the following properties:

- Name.
- Alias.
- Help message.
- Comments.
- Elements.

The name identifies the basic element within the associated class, and so it must be unique within this context, including the specialisation hierarchy to which the class belongs.

The alias is used by the user to identify the order criterion. It does not need to be unique in the context of the class or its specialisation hierarchy, although this is recommended.

The help message is a piece of text that can be shown to the user to give him/her information on the purpose and working of the order criterion.

The comments enable engineers to document the basic element.

The elements of the order criterion are expressed as a list of pairs <*attribute, direction*>: *attribute* is the name of an attribute of the class for which the basic element is defined, or a role name sequence that ends in an attribute name of a class related to that, deterministically reachable through the role name sequence; *direction* is the way in which sorting must be performed for the element, i.e. ascending or descending.

Example.   *Sorting issued invoices by ascending issue date can be accomplished by specifying an order criterion for class "IssuedInvoice" with the following properties:*

- *Name: OC_IssueDate*
- *Alias: By issue date*
- *Help message: Invoices sorted by ascending issue date*
- *Comments: Sorts invoices by issue date, ascending*
- *Elements:*
  - *Element1:*
    - o *Attribute: IssueDate*
    - o *Direction: Ascending*

The order in which elements are specified is meaningful.

Example.   *Sorting clients first by descending pending balance and then by ascending family name can be accomplished by specifying an order criterion for class "Client" with the following properties:*

- *Name: OC_PendingAndFamilyName*
- *Alias: By pending balance and family name*
- *Help message: Clients sorted by descending pending balance and ascending family name*
- *Comments: Sort clients by pending balance, descending, and family name, ascending*
- *Elements:*
  - *Element1:*
    - o *Attribute: PendingBalance*
    - o *Direction: Descending*
  - *Element2:*
    - o *Attribute: FamilyName*
    - o *Direction: Ascending*

Agents and Order Criterion Basic Elements

Order criterion basic elements specify a collection of attributes the values of which are used to sort the result set of a search. For the ordering to be possible, the agent that represents the interactive user must have visibility over all the attributes referenced by the order criterion. This check makes the verification of the Conceptual Schema easier. If the necessary visibility does not exist, then the order criterion is not available to the user at run-time.

Example.   *Applying this consideration to the previous example, let us imagine that the agent representing the interactive user does not have visibility over the "PendingBalance" attribute of class "Client". In this case, the order criterion "OC_PendingAndFamilyName" could not be applied, since it references the non-visible "PendingBalance" attribute. This order criterion, consequently, would not be available to the user.*

10.2.7 Display Set

Once a collection of objects has been selected using search criteria and sorted using order criteria, the next step is deciding which properties of these objects are to be shown to the user, and in what order. In conventional scenarios of interaction, not every property of the selected objects is to be shown. Consequently, it is important to precisely specify the set of properties that are considered relevant in this interaction context.

The Display Set basic element is intended to solve this problem. It determines which properties of a class are to be presented to the user, and in what order. Fixing this visualisation set of properties that must be provided for any selected object, the required type of interaction is specified more precisely, according to the user intention.

Example.   *The following information about vehicles is to be shown to clients: make, model and fuel type. Information related to the vehicle's creation date or its kilometre count is not to be shown.*

This basic element is defined for a class through the following properties:

- Name.
- Comments.
- Elements.

The name identifies the Display Set basic element in the context of the class, and must be unique in this context and in the specialisation hierarchy to which the class belongs.

The comments enable engineers to document the basic element.

The elements are expressed as an ordered list of pairs <*attribute, alias*>: *attribute* is the name of an attribute of the class for which the basic element is defined, or a role name sequence that ends in an attribute name of a class related to that, deterministically reachable through the role name sequence; *alias* is an alternative name with which the attribute is presented to the user.

Example.   *The Display Set for the scenario described in the previous example is as follows:*

- *Name: VS_Vehicle*
- *Comments: Information about the vehicle for clients*
- *Elements:*
  - *Element1:*
    - o *Attribute: Make*
    - o *Alias: Vehicle's make*
  - *Element2:*
    - o *Attribute: Model*
    - o *Alias: Vehicle's model*
  - *Element3:*
    - o *Attribute: Fuel*
    - o *Alias: Fuel type*

Agents and Display Set Basic Elements

Display Sets organize the properties of objects that are shown to users. Since these properties may be subject to visibility restrictions for the agent representing the interactive user, this check must be done in advance.

In fact, if the interactive user is associated to an agent that has visibility over a subset of the elements specified by the Display Set, only those properties that are visible are actually shown. An agent class is said to have visibility over a Display Set when it has visibility over at least one of the elements referenced by it. In any case, the information stored in the Conceptual Schema permits that these scenarios be detected automatically, giving users access to only those properties over which they have visibility.

Example.   *Applying this consideration to the previous example, let us imagine that the current interactive user of the system is represented by an agent that has no visibility over the "Fuel" attribute of class "Vehicle", but has visibility over the "Make" and "Model" attributes. In this case, the "VS_Vehicle" Display Set would display only the "Make" and "Model" attributes.*

The basic elements described so far allow us to specify how objects are to be selected, sorted, and presented to the user. User interaction does not end here; there are two kinds of tasks that must be available and have not been covered yet:

- Navigating to information of objects related to the one being displayed (for example, navigating to the lines of an invoice).
- Executing a service on an object (for example, issuing an invoice).

The next sections describe basic elements that cover these needs.

10.2.8 Navigation

Defining a Display Set allows us to specify which properties of an object or collection of objects are to be presented to the user, being even able to include properties of related objects that can be reached by deterministic role name sequences.

Since classes in the system are interconnected, information is often presented to the user in a "connected" manner, so that the user can select an object and then "navigate" to a related object or objects to show their properties.

These navigations correspond to relationships between classes (associations, aggregations and composition). This is an interesting characteristic of OO-Method: any navigation action is enabled by the existence of a relationship of some kind between the involved classes. This reinforces the semantic integration between the different views or models that compose the global Conceptual Schema.

Example.   *When information is displayed about a vehicle object, related information such as extras, maintenance reports and the vehicle's type can be navigated to.*

OO-Method provides the Navigation basic element as a mechanism to define navigational properties. Once an initial class is fixed, an instance of this basic element determines an information set that can be accessed via navigation of the relationships found from the said initial class.

A Navigation basic element is defined for a class through the following properties:

- Name.
- Help message.
- Comments.
- Elements.

As usual, the name identifies the basic element within the context of the class, so it must be unique in this context and in the specialisation hierarchy to which the class belongs.

The help message is a text that can be shown to the user to give him/her information about the elements that compose the basic element.

Comments enable the engineer to document the basic element. As we have stated elsewhere, a disciplined approach to entering comments for modelling elements makes possible that comprehensive documentation be automatically generated by OO-Method tools.

Elements comprise a list of ordered triplets *<interaction_unit, path, alias>*, where *interaction_unit* is the name of an instance or master/detail interaction unit (explained in sections below) that represents the scenario associated to the object that is presented to the user. These interaction units are the nodes of the navigational graph that represents potentially valid paths. Navigation links are given by relationships between classes, which make inter-node navigation possible.

Any interaction unit referenced in this context (i.e. within an element triplet) must have been previously defined for the class reached by *path* from the class for which the basic element is defined. If *path* is empty, then the referenced interaction unit must exist for the same class as that of the navigation basic element.

The *path* component, therefore, is a deterministic sequence of role names starting with the class for which the basic element is defined. An empty *path* indicates that navigation occurs within the specialisation hierarchy to which the class belongs.

The *alias* component is an alternative name for the user to identify the navigation option. It does not need to be unique within the basic element, although this is recommended.

The navigational model obtained through the specification of navigation basic elements can be represented graphically as a graph for each user type. The resulting diagram is comparable to that used by well-known approaches to web application modelling, such as OOHDM (Rossi and Schwabe 2001), WebML (Ceri et al. 2001) or OOWS (Pastor et al. 2006), in which the specification of a Navigational Model is an essential part of the modelling task.

Example.   *The situation described in the previous example can be implemented through a Navigation basic element defined for the "Vehicle" class and with the following properties:*

- *Name: N_Vehicle*
- *Help message: Access to extras, maintenance reports and vehicle's type*
- *Comments: Allows navigation to vehicle-related information, namely extras, maintenance reports and vehicle type*
- *Elements:*
  - *Element1:*
    - o *Interaction unit: PIU_Extras*
    - o *Path: Extras*
    - o *Alias: Vehicle extras*
  - *Element2:*
    - o *Interaction unit: PIU_MaintReports*
    - o *Path: MaintReports*
    - o *Alias: Vehicle maintenance reports*
  - *Element3:*
    - o *Interaction unit: IIU_Type*
    - o *Path: Type*
    - o *Alias: Vehicle type description*

Given this specification, it is possible for the user to navigate from any vehicle object to other objects of the corresponding classes that are related with it. Specifically, the scenarios to which the user can navigate are:

- *PIU_Extras: Population interaction unit for class "Extra", related to "Vehicle" by an association via path "Extras".*
- *PIU_MaintReports: Population interaction unit for class "MaintReport", related to "Vehicle" by an association via path "MaintReports".*
- *IIU_Type: Instance interaction unit for class "VehicleType", related to "Vehicle" by an association via path "Type".*

Agents and Navigation Basic Elements

A Navigation basic element groups together the scenarios that can be traversed from a given object by the user. This collection of scenarios can be restricted depending on the visibility of the agent that represents the interactive user at any moment.

In fact, if the interactive user is mapped to an agent class that has no visibility over the role name sequences that compose the navigation basic element, then he/she is able to see only those scenarios for which visibility has been granted.

Example.   *Let us imagine that a certain agent has visibility over all the attributes of class "Vehicle" as well as its relationships with "VehicleType" and "Extra", but no visibility over the relationship with "MaintReport" via role "MaintReports". When a user represented by this agent exercises an interaction unit that shows one or more vehicle objects and that uses the navigation basic element described in the previous example, he/she will be able to navigate to the extras and vehicle type information for each vehicle, but not to the maintenance reports.*

10.2.9 Actions

The second kind of task that can be performed on an object (in addition to navigation) is executing a service on it. The simplest approach would be to allow the user to invoke, for a particular object, any service defined by the object's class (according to the specification in the Dynamic Model). However, and in order to enhance interactivity and adjust interaction to different situations, it is convenient that the set of available services is restricted and ordered by frequency of use. The Actions basic element captures this.

Example.   *When a vehicle object is displayed to the user in the rent-a-car system, actions to rent it, send it to maintenance, and retire it must be given.*

The Actions basic element is defined for a particular class and enables us to define the collection of services that are available to be executed on an object of that class. Multiple Actions basic elements can be defined for the same class, of course. The Actions basic element is characterized by the following properties:

- Name.
- Help message.
- Comments.
- Elements.

The name identifies the basic element within the context of the class, and so it must be unique in this context and in the specialisation hierarchy to which the class belongs.

The help message is a text that can be shown to the user with information about the elements that compose the basic element.

The comments enable engineers to document the basic element.

Elements comprise an ordered list of pairs <*interaction_unit, alias*>, where *interaction_unit* is usually the name of a service interaction unit (which is described below) that describes the scenario related with the execution of a service of the associated class. Although less common, *interaction_unit* can also point to an instance or master/detail interaction unit, rather than a service interaction unit.

The *alias* component is an alternative name for the user to identify the action option. It does not need to be unique within the context of the basic element, although this is recommended for the sake of clarity.

Example.   *The situation described in the previous example can be modelled by using an Actions basic element defined for class "Vehicle" and with the following properties:*

- *Name: A_Vehicle*
- *Help message: Operations for renting, sending for maintenance and retiring a vehicle*
- *Comments: Allows renting, sending for maintenance and retiring a vehicle*
- *Elements:*
  - *Element1:*
    - o   *Interaction unit: SIU_Rent*
    - o   *Alias: Rent this vehicle*
  - *Element2:*
    - o   *Interaction unit: SIU_SendForMaint*
    - o   *Alias: Send this vehicle for maintenance*
  - *Element3:*
    - o   *Interaction unit: SIU_Retire*
    - o   *Alias: Retire this vehicle*

Given this specification, it is possible for the user to navigate from any vehicle object to the scenarios that will enable him/her to invoke the associated services. Specifically, the scenarios to which the user can navigate are:

- *SIU_Rent: Service interaction unit for class "Vehicle" for the execution of service "Rent".*
- *SIU_SendForMaint: Service interaction unit for class "Vehicle" for the execution of service "SendForMaintenance".*
- *SIU_Retire: Service interaction unit for class "Vehicle" for the execution of service "Retire".*

Note that the Actions basic element constrains the set of services that can be invoked for objects of a class to a certain subset. However, it is possible that, at run-time, a particular object cannot accept a particular service being executed on it, depending on what has been specified in the state transition diagram of the corresponding class in the context of the dynamic model specification.

Example.   *Section 8.1.2 shows a sample State TransitionDiagram for class "Person" with services "BeBorn", "GetMarried", "HaveChild" and "GetSeparated". If these four services are included in an Actions basic element that is then associated to the "Person" class, it will be possible for users to invoke any of these services for any person object. However, if a particular person object is already married (i.e. it is in*

*the "Married" state as defined by its State Transition Diagram), then the execution
of this service will not be completed.*

Agents and Actions Basic Elements

An Actions basic element groups together the scenarios that allow the user to
execute services of a particular class. This collection of scenarios can be restricted
depending on the visibility of the agent that represents the interactive user at any
moment.

In fact, if the interactive user is mapped to an agent class that has no visibility
over the services that are referenced by the actions basic element, then he/she is
able to see (and invoke) only those services for which execution permission has
been granted.

Example.   *System operators have permissions over services "Rent" and "SendFor-
Maintenance" of class "Vehicle", but not over "Retire", which can be executed only by
system administrators.*

*Regular clients have permissions over "Rent" (so that direct rentals can be made),
but not over "SendForMaintenance" (which is reserved to company employees) or
"Retire".*

*When a "regular" system operator (i.e. one with no administrator privileges)
accesses an interaction unit that shows one or more vehicle objects and that uses the
Actions basic element described in the previous example, he/she will be able to rent
the vehicle or send it to the garage for maintenance, but he/she will not be able to
retire the vehicle. If the user is a client, then only rental is possible.*

*Finally, a company employee with administrator privileges is able to execute all
three services, being able to rent, send for maintenance, and retire vehicles.*

10.3 Interaction Units

The concept of Interaction Unit is crucial in the Presentation Model of OO-Method,
since it comprises the basic specification element for the interaction between the
user and the software system. An Interaction Unit describes a particular scenario
of the user interface through which users are able to carry out specific tasks (such
as executing services or searching for objects).

The user interface of the system is defined by the collection of relevant interaction units and the way in which these are structured. OO-Method provides four
different types of interaction units, which represent four different basic kinds of
interaction scenarios:

- Execution of a service.
- Manipulation of an object.
- Manipulation of a collection of objects.
- Manipulation of multiple related collections of objects.

According to these, four Interaction Units are described in the following sections:

- Service Interaction Unit.
- Instance Interaction Unit.
- Population Interaction Unit.
- Master/Detail Interaction Unit.

Each of these interaction units uses some of the basic elements defined in previous sections, according to the three-level architecture of OO-Method's Presentation Model.

10.3.1 Service Interaction Units

A Service Interaction Unit enables us to define a scenario in which the user interacts with the system in order to execute a service.

The properties of this scenario include:

- Presentation of ordered and/or grouped service arguments.
- Presentation of suggested default values for service arguments.
- Validation of argument values.
- Help information about each argument.
- Help information about the service.
- Feedback in case of error during the execution of the service.

All these characteristics are expressed using the appropriate basic elements.

Service Interaction Units are defined for a service through the following properties:

- Name.
- Alias.
- Help message.
- Comments.
- Argument grouping.

The name identifies the interaction unit and must be unique in the context of the class to which the associated service belongs and in the specialisation hierarchy of that class.

The alias is an alternative name for the user to identify the interaction unit. It does not need to be unique, although this is recommended.

Comments allow engineers to document the interaction unit.

The argument grouping is defined through the corresponding Argument Grouping basic element, as explained earlier.

We stated that basic elements of different kinds (as elementary, level-3 presentation patterns) are used by a service interaction unit in order to define the concrete properties of the associated scenario. This is accomplished through the following:

- Help information about service arguments is provided by the comments property of each argument.

- Default values for each argument are given by the default value property of each argument.
- Validation and selection functionality on datum-valued arguments are provided by related Entry and Defined Selection basic elements.
- Additional control over the value and the enabled/disabled state of each argument can be provided by Argument Dependency basic elements, as needed.
- Selection functionality on object-valued arguments is given by the appropriate Population Interaction Units. Filters are associated to these.
- Additional information on candidate objects to be selected for object-valued arguments is given by Display Set basic elements associated to each argument.
- In the case of services with datum-valued arguments that are exclusively used to assign values to the attributes of the class that owns the service (which can be determined by checking the Functional Model), an implicit State Retrieval basic element appears, which suggests as default value for each argument the current value of the associated attribute.

Example.   *Class "Vehicle" owns the "BuyVehicle" service, for which a service inter-action unit is defined with the following properties:*

- *Name: SIU_BuyVehicle*
- *Alias: Buy vehicle*
- *Help message: Acquire a vehicle for the pool*
- *Comments: Vehicle creation service*
- *Argument grouping: (see Table 10.3)*

In addition, the specification of each of the arguments of the "BuyVehicle" service includes a help message, so this information becomes available in the context of the service interaction unit "SIU_BuyVehicle".

Another property of arguments is the default value formula. In the case of the "p_atrKilometres" argument of the "BuyVehicle" service, this has been specified as the constant 0 (zero).

Each datum-valued argument, in addition, can have entry or defined selection basic elements associated to it. This is the case of "p_atrKilometres", which has been linked to the entry basic element "E_Kilometres" as shown in the example of Sect. 10.2.1.

Section 10.2.4 explains how dependency rules for the "p_atrMake" argument can be defined. These dependency rules are effective within the context of the "SIU_BuyVehicle" service interaction unit.

One of the object-valued arguments of the "BuyVehicle" service, "p_agrVehicleType", had the population interaction unit "PIU_Type" associated to it, which enables us to select a particular instance of "VehicleType" for the vehicle being created in the context of the service interaction unit "SIU_BuyVehicle".

The same argument, "p_agrVehicleType", had the Display Set basic element "VS_VehicleType" associated to it, which is composed of two elements related to the attributes "VehicleLevel" and "VehicleClass" of class "VehicleType".

Given this collection of definitions related to the service interaction unit "SIU_BuyVehicle", a user trying to execute the service "BuyVehicle" will find a scenario in which:

- *The identifying alias is "Buy vehicle".*
- *Each argument is identified by its alias, rather than its name. For example, the argument "p_atrKilometres" is shown as "Kilometres".*
- *Service arguments are arranged according to the argument grouping depicted in Table 10.3.*
- *The argument "p_atrKilometres" has an initial default value of 0 (zero) when it is first displayed.*
- *The user can modify the value of argument "p_atrKilometres" within the specified bounds of 0.00 to 99,999.00, and using an input mask with five digits to the left of the decimal point and two decimal digits.*
- *The argument "p_atrFuel" automatically receives the value "Diesel" when the user sets the value of argument "p_atrMake" to "MakeX", according to the argument dependency basic element defined in Sect. 10.2.4.*
- *The value for argument "p_agrVehicleType" can be entered by the user or be selected by him/her from the collection of objects returned by the population interaction unit "PIU_Type" associated to the argument.*
- *The level and class of the selected vehicle type are shown to the user when he/she selects a particular vehicle type instance as a value for argument "p_agrVehicleType", since these are the elements that compose the Display Set defined for this argument.*

It must be noted that a service interaction unit, plus its associated basic elements, specify the structure of a scenario for the execution of a given service, but does not define the specific manner in which the scenario is carried out or implemented.

Example.   *The scenario described in the previous example can be implemented in a number of ways. In a windowed graphical user interface, the scenario can be mapped to a window titled "Buy vehicle" (the alias of the service interaction unit) that presents a text label for each service argument showing the argument's alias (such as "Vehicle type"). Next to each label, a text box appears in which the value of the corresponding argument is shown and can be edited. Arguments are grouped in group boxes (or frames) according to the grouping structure defined by Table 10.3; these group boxes are titled using the aliases of the different grouping elements ("Identification", "Classification", "Status" and "Miscellaneous"). The selection of a vehicle type for the value of "p_agrVehicleType" is implemented by a button next to the corresponding text box so that, when clicked, a pop-up window appears that implements the population interaction unit "PIU_Type".*

An alternative implementation, also in a windowed graphical user interface, would use tabs, rather than group boxes to arrange arguments, and a drop-down box, rather than a button and a pop-up window to make the vehicle type selection.

It can be seen that the information captured in the conceptual model is independent of the final implementation, accommodating different specific solutions. In this case, there is a precise distinction between an *abstract presentation model* level, where all these abstract, implementation-independent presentation patterns are specified, and a *concrete presentation model* level, directly associated with the corresponding design and implementation decisions that will transform the abstract patterns into their associated software components – in this context, user-interface software components.

Agents and Service Interaction Units

Service Interaction Units allow the user to execute a service. Logically, the availability of the corresponding scenario is subject to the visibility that the agent mapped to the interactive user has on the service to be executed. If there is no visibility, then the service interaction unit is not available at run-time.

Example.   *The service interaction unit described in the previous section, defined on the "BuyVehicle" service of class "Vehicle", can be implemented on a windowed graphical user interface as a complete window, as we have explained. Access to this window can be provided to the user, for example, via a menu item in the application's main window. If the interactive user is mapped to a class that is an agent of "BuyVehicle", then this menu item is enabled. On the contrary, if the user is not an agent of the service, the menu item is visible but disabled. In an alternative implementation of the service interaction unit, the interactive element that gives access to the corresponding scenario could be even not visible.*

10.3.2 Instance Interaction Unit

Another type of functionality that the user interface must provide, in addition to service execution, is the appropriate management of individual objects. Instance Interaction Units is precisely OO-Method's answer to this need. This interaction unit represents a scenario in which information about a single object is displayed, including the list of services that can be executed on it, as well as the scenarios of related information to which the user can navigate. The appropriate basic elements are used to accomplish this.

Example.   *A typical situation found in the rent-a-car system involves managing a specific vehicle. This includes displaying its details (make, model, fuel type, ...), being able to navigate to related information (extras, maintenance reports, ...) and executing services on it (renting, sending for maintenance, ...). This is the working context of an Instance Interaction Unit.*

   The Instance Interaction Unit is defined for a class through the following properties:

- Name.
- Alias.
- Help message.
- Comments.
- Display Set.

- Actions.
- Navigation.

As usual, the name identifies the interaction unit and must be unique within the class and the specialisation hierarchy to which the class belongs.

The alias is an alternate name for the user to identify the interaction unit. It does not need to be unique, although this is recommended.

The help message is a piece of text that can be shown to the user with information about the corresponding scenario.

Comments allow the engineer to document the interaction unit so that automatic documentation can be generated.

The Display Set, the Actions and Navigation information are defined through associated basic elements, as explained in previous sections. They refer to the corresponding 3-level, elementary presentation patterns used as basic building blocks of the Presentation Model.

Example.   The scenario described in the previous example can be implemented by defining an Instance Interaction Unit with the following properties:

- *Name: IIU_Vehicle*
- *Alias: Vehicle Record*
- *Help message: Details and operations on a vehicle*
- *Comments: Scenario that allows the user to query details of a vehicle and perform usual operations on it*
- *Display Set: VS_Vehicle (see example in Sect. 10.2.7)*
- *Actions: A_Vehicle (see example in Sect. 10.2.9)*
- *Navigation: N_Vehicle (see example in Sect. 10.2.8)*

Given this specification, a user can access the details of a vehicle and its related information, as well as execute operations on it. The resulting scenario:

- *Is identified by the alias "Vehicle Record".*
- *Displays the make, model and fuel type of the vehicle, each of these details labelled with the associated alias ("Vehicle's make", "Vehicle's model" and "Fuel type") as defined by the Display Set "VS_Vehicle".*
- *Provides some mechanism to navigate to other scenarios where information about the vehicle's extras, maintenance reports and vehicle type can be obtained. The navigation to each of these scenarios is identified by the appropriate alias ("Vehicle extras", "Vehicle maintenance reports" and "Vehicle type description") as defined by "N_Vehicle".*
- *Provides some mechanism to execute operations to rent the vehicle, send it for maintenance or retire it from the pool. Each of these operations is labelled by the appropriate alias ("Rent this vehicle", "Send this vehicle for maintenance" and "Retire this vehicle") as defined by "A_Vehicle".*

As previously commented in the context of the Service Interaction Unit, it must be noted that an instance interaction unit (including its associated basic elements) specifies the structure of a scenario for the display and editing of the information on a given object, but does not define the specific manner in which the scenario is implemented.

Example.   *The scenario in the previous example can be implemented in a number of ways.*

In a web environment, for example, the overall scenario could correspond to an HTML page titled "Vehicle Record" (the alias of the instance interaction unit) and showing a table with two columns and three rows. The left column would display the labels "Vehicle's make", "Vehicle's model" and "Fuel type", and the right column would show the values of the attributes "Make", "Model" and "Fuel" (as dictated by the Display Set "VS_Vehicle"). Three hyperlinks would also appear, labelled as "Vehicle extras", "Vehicle maintenance reports" and "Vehicle type description", which would allow the user to jump to other HTML pages implementing the interaction units "PIU_Extras", "PIU_MaintReports" and "IIU_Type" (as described by the navigation basic element "N_Vehicle"). Finally, three buttons would appear with labels "Rent this vehicle", "Send this vehicle for maintenance" and "Retire this vehicle", which would send the user to the HTML pages in which the corresponding service interaction units would be available (as described by the actions basic element "A_Vehicle").

An alternative representation, also in a web environment, could use a drop-down list and a "Go" button to implement navigation.

Again, it can be seen that the information captured in the conceptual model is independent of the final implementation, accommodating different specific solutions.

Agents and Instance Interaction Units

Instance Interaction Units allow the user to display information about an object and access operations on it. As usual, the availability of the corresponding scenario is subject to the visibility settings for the agent mapped to the interactive user.

If the user is represented by an agent that has no visibility on the attributes included in the Display Set of the instance interaction unit, then this is not available at run-time. We have stated that an agent is said to have visibility over a Display Set if it has visibility over at least one of its elements. In this case, only the visible attributes are shown.

With regard to navigation and the performance of actions, the restrictions already explained for each of the relevant basic elements are applicable.

Example.   *The instance interaction unit described in the previous section allows a user to access the direct and related information about a vehicle as well as execute actions on it. If the interactive user is represented by an agent class that has no visibility over the "Fuel" attribute of class "vehicle", for example, then this value is not displayed but other values (such as the vehicle's make and model) are. In the case that the application is implemented using web technologies, this means that the row corresponding to the "Fuel" attribute in the web page would not be displayed. Alternatively, the row could be displayed including only the label, and not the attribute value. Similar situations appear if we consider the visibility of the agent over associations (in the case of navigation) and services (in the case of actions); the appropriate hyperlinks or buttons would be hidden or disabled, depending on the chosen implementation.*

10.3.3 Population Interaction Unit

Once the interaction units related to service execution and single object display have been defined, it is necessary to describe those that will enable the user to manipulate a collection of objects of any given class. This is called the Population Interaction Unit.

A Population Interaction Unit represents an interaction scenario where multiple objects are presented, including the appropriate mechanisms to select and sort objects, choose the information and available services to be shown, and list other scenarios that can be reached from this.

Example.   *Staff members of the rent-a-car company usually need to obtain details about their clients, including their names, address, pending balance and so on. Since the number of clients in the system is usually very high, searches are performed using different criteria (on properties such as name, pending balance, etc.) depending on the task at hand. Even using filters, the result of a search is sometimes a large number of objects, which must be organized in an understandable fashion so that the required object can be found by the user and navigated to, so that whatever specific operation that is necessary on it can be performed.*

A Population Interaction Unit is defined for a particular class through the following properties:

- Name.
- Alias.
- Instance count.
- Help message.
- Comments.
- Filters.
- Order criteria.
- Display Sets.
- Actions.
- Navigation.

As usual, the name identifies the interaction unit and must be unique within the context of the class and the specialisation hierarchy of the class.

The alias is an alternative name for the user to identify the interaction unit. It does not need to be unique, although this is recommended.

The instance count is the maximum number of objects that can be simultaneously displayed.

The help message is a text that can be shown to the user with information about the interaction scenario.

Comments allow engineers to document the interaction unit.

Filters are defined as indicated earlier. These are optional and, if none are associated to a Population Interaction Unit, then all the objects of the class will be selected. Generally, filters are an essential component of this kind of interaction units, since they enable the engineer to decide which is the relevant subset of the class population. Although the number of filters is not limited, it is not common to have a large value (such as five), for usability and efficiency reasons.

Order criteria are also defined as explained earlier. These are optional, and the same comments about their number as in the case of filters are applicable.

The Display Sets associated to this interaction unit specify which attributes of the selected set of objects must be displayed. By having more than one Display Set, the collection of attributes that is displayed can be changed dynamically. It is possible to indicate default order criteria and Display Set for each of the associated filters.

Finally, the actions and navigation are defined as explained earlier in this chapter. Actions and navigation act on the objects from the set that is selected at any given moment.

Example.   *The scenario described in the previous example can be implemented by defining a Population Interaction Unit with the following properties:*

- *Name: PIU_Client*
- *Alias: Client search*
- *Instance count: 20*
- *Help message: Client query and search*
- *Comments: This scenario enables the user to search clients by given and family names or by pending balance*
- *Filters:*
  - *F_ByGivenAndFamilyName*
  - *F_ByPendingBalance*
- *Order criteria:*
  - *OC_FamilyName*
  - *OC_PendingBalance*
- *Display Sets:*
  - *VS_Client*
- *Actions: A_Client*
- *Navigation: N_Client*

For the sake of brevity, the following comments will suffice:

- *F_ByGivenAndFamilyName is a filter (see Section 10.2.5) that selects instances of "Client" for which the given and family names match those given as filter variables.*
- *F_ByPendingBalance is a filter (see Section 10.2.5) that selects instances of "Client" for which the pending balance equals or is greater than a threshold value given as a filter variable.*
- *OC_FamilyName is an order criterion (see Section 10.2.6) for class "Client" that orders instances for attribute "FamilyName", ascending.*
- *OC_PendingBalance is an order criterion (see Section 10.2.6) for class "Client" that orders instances for attribute "PendingBalance", ascending.*
- *VS_Client is a Display Set (see Section 10.2.7) containing the attributes "Family-Name", "GivenName", "Address" and "PendingBalance".*
- *A_Client is an action basic element (see Section 10.2.9) that references the service interaction units for services "Edit" and "Delete".*

- *N_Client is a navigation basic element (see Section 10.2.9) that references a population interaction unit for class "Rental" (related to "Client" through the "Rentals" role).*

Using this collection of basic elements and interaction units, the user can access the direct and related information about a client, as well as perform operations on it. The scenario that allows this:

- *Is defined by the alias "Client search".*
- *Provides two mechanisms to find clients, since two filters exist, each one identified by its alias (see Section 10.2.5).*
- *Provides two mechanisms to sort the query results, since two order criteria are specified, each identified by its alias (see Section 10.2.6).*
- *Shows the family name, first name, address and pending balance (as defined by the "VS_Client" Display Set) for each retrieved object, which are displayed in pages of 20 (as specified by the instance count property).*
- *Provides a mechanism to navigate to another scenario where vehicle rentals for a particular client can be queried, this scenario being identified by its alias (as defined by the navigation basic element "N_Client").*
- *Provides a mechanism to execute actions to edit a client or delete it, identifying each of these actions by its alias (as defined by the action basic element "A_Client").*

Once more, it must be noted that population interaction units (including the associated basic elements and related interaction units) specify the structure of scenarios for searching and querying (the abstract specification of the user interaction), but do not define the specific manner in which these scenarios are to be implemented (the concrete user-interface implementation).

Example.   *The scenario in the previous example can be implemented in a number of different ways. In a windowed graphical user interface, for instance, a window with the title "Client search" would appear containing two tabs, one for each selection mechanisms and labelled as "Search by family name" and "Search by pending balance", for example. Each tab would present a labelled textbox for each defined filter variable (such as "Family name" in the case of family name search, and "Pending balance" in the case of pending balance search), as well as a button labelled "Search".*

Under the tab control, a drop-down list would enable the user to select the preferred order criterion. In the results area, a grid with four columns (labelled "Family name", "Given name", "Address" and "Pending balance") and a maximum of 20 rows would be displayed. A scroll bar next to the grid would enable the user to paginate up and down the result set. Selecting a row in the results grid (which would correspond to a particular "Client" object) would enable two buttons labelled "Edit" and "Delete", as well as an additional button to navigate to the client's rental window.

An alternative representation could be implemented in a web environment using hyperlinks, rather than buttons, for example.

It can be seen that the information captured in the conceptual model is independent of the final implementation, accommodating different specific solutions.

There are different concrete implementations satisfying the abstract user interaction specification obtained by using the OO-Method Presentation Patterns. Any model-transformation engine for software generation will either instantiate one of such possible implementations or it will give the user the chance to adapt the final, concrete user interface to his/her particular wishes.

Agents and Population Interaction Units

Population Interaction Units present the user with a scenario in which objects of a class can be displayed and manipulated. Therefore, it is constrained by visibility limitations of the agent class representing the interactive user.

If the interactive user is mapped to an agent class that has no visibility over the Display Set associated to the interaction unit, then this interaction unit is not available to the user at run-time.

Regarding filters, order criteria, navigation and actions, the same restrictions as those described for other interaction units also apply.

Example.   *The population interaction unit described in the examples above allows a user to search for clients, obtain information about specific clients, execute some operations on them, and check their rentals.*

If the interactive user is represented by an agent class with no visibility over the "PendingBalance" attribute, for example, then the value for this attribute is not displayed on screen, but the values for the remaining attributes are. If the scenario is implemented in a windowed environment as described in the examples, this would mean that the column corresponding to the "PendingBalance" attribute would be hidden or, alternatively, shown empty. Similar situations would arise depending on the visibility of the agent over associations (for navigations) or services (for actions), enabling or disabling the appropriate buttons.

10.3.4 Master/Detail Interaction Unit

This section introduces an interaction unit that can combine the three interaction units already described following composition mechanisms that are well established in the context of human–machine interaction. Specifically, a master/detail structure is introduced, the specification of which reuses and combines instance or population interaction units as have been described in previous sections.

According to this, the Master/Detail Interaction Unit presents the user with a scenario for the interaction with multiple collections of objects that belong to different interrelated classes. This forms a composite scenario in which two kinds of role can be defined:

- Master role, which represents the main interaction scenario.
- Detail roles, which represent secondary, subordinated interaction scenarios that are kept synchronised with the master role.

Example.   *Users of the rent-a-car system often need to see the details of a particular vehicle together with a list of its extras. Conceptually, this can be modelled as a master/detail scenario in which the master role is played by the vehicle and the extras play a detail role.*

The master role is usually implemented as an instance or population interaction unit, whereas detail roles are implemented as either instance, population, or master/detail interaction units, which enables us to nest master/detail structures to accomplish complex scenarios.

A Master/Detail Interaction Unit is defined for a class through the following properties:

- Name.
- Alias.
- Help message.
- Comments.
- Master.
- Details.

As usual, the name identifies the interaction unit, and must be unique in the context of the class and the specialisation hierarchy of the class.

The alias is an alternative name for the user to identify the interaction unit and, even though it does not have to be unique, this is recommended.

The help message is a piece of text that can be shown to the user at run-time with information about the scenario.

Comments enable the engineer to document the interaction unit so that complete documentation of the system can be automatically obtained.

The master is the interaction unit that plays the main role in the master/detail interaction unit, and it must be defined for the same class as that of the unit.

Details are given by an ordered list of triplets <*interaction_unit, path, alias*>, where *interaction unit* is the name of an instance, population or master/detail interaction unit that determines the detail scenario related with the master scenario that will be presented to the user. The referenced interaction unit must be associated to a class that is related to the class for which the master interaction unit is defined.

The path to traverse in order to reach the associated class is specified by *path*. If path is *empty*, then it is assumed that the detail interaction unit is defined for one of the classes specialised from the master class. In this way, both associations and specialisations (defined in the Object Model) are used in the Presentation Model to define master/detail structures. The *path* component, therefore, is a deterministic role name sequence rooted on the master class.

The *alias* component of the triplet is a name for the user to identify the detail scenario. It does not need to be unique within the context of the master/detail interaction unit, although this is recommended for the sake of clarity.

Example.   *The scenario described in the previous example can be implemented through a Master/Detail Interaction Unit for class "Vehicle" and with the following properties:*

- *Name: MDIU_Vehicle*
- *Alias: Vehicle and extras*
- *Help message: Details and operations on a vehicle and its extras*
- *Comments: Scenario that allows the user to query details of a vehicle plus its related extras, and perform usual operations on them*
- *Master: IIU_Vehicle (see example in Section 10.3.2)*
- *Details: PIU_Extra (a population interaction unit defined for class "Extra")*

In this case, the master role is played by an instance interaction unit for class "Vehicle", and the single detail role is played by a population interaction unit for class "Extra", reachable from class "Vehicle" through the path "Extras".

It must be noted that an instance interaction unit cannot be used as a detail scenario if an instance of the master class can be associated to multiple instances of the detail class.

Example.   *In the previous example, an instance interaction unit for class "Extra" could not have been selected as detail, since a vehicle can have multiple extras associated to it. A population interaction unit is necessary to cater for this situation.*

The opposite case is possible. If only one detail instance can be related to a master instance, then a population interaction unit can be used. However, using an instance interaction unit in this case is more reasonable, as this is the more appropriate pattern to be used when information of an individual instance is to be seen.

Example.   *A similar scenario to that in the previous example would show a vehicle (an instance of class "Vehicle") together with the details of its associated vehicle type (an instance of class "VehicleType"). In this case, the detail would be implemented by an instance interaction unit on class "VehicleType", since the maximum cardinality of "VehicleType" from "Vehicle" is 1. In other words, each vehicle can have, at most, one vehicle type associated to it.*

It must also be noted that a master/detail interaction unit can be used as detail, enabling the composition of more complex interaction scenarios.

Example.   *A plausible case would be a master/detail interaction unit with class "Rental" as master and the "MDUI_Vehicle" master/detail interaction unit as detail.*

Agents and Master/Detail Interaction Units

Master/Detail Interaction Units are subject to the same visibility limitations as for other types of interaction units described earlier. If the interactive user is mapped to a class that is not an agent of at least the master interaction unit, then the complete master/detail interaction unit is not available at run-time. Recall from Sects. 10.3.1, 10.3.2, and 10.3.3 that a class is said to be an agent of an interaction unit when the class has the appropriate visibility over the attributes and services involved in it.

Similarly, if the interactive user is represented by a class that is not an agent of some of the detail interaction units, then the affected interaction units are not available at run-time. In order to determine whether a class is an agent of a detail interaction unit, an additional verification is necessary, namely checking its visibility over each of the role names that define the path linking the master and detail classes.

10.4 Action Hierarchy Tree

Once those interaction scenarios have been described through the corresponding Interaction Units, it is necessary to determine how these interaction units are to be structured, organized, and presented to the user. This structure will characterize the top level of the user interface, establishing what could be described as the Main Menu of the typical application. The Action Hierarchy Tree serves this purpose.

The Action Hierarchy Tree defines an access tree that follows the principle of gradual approximation to specify the manner in which the interactive user can access system functionality.

This is achieved by arranging actions into groups and subgroups in a tree fashion, from the most general to the most detailed. Intermediate (i.e. non-leaf) nodes in the tree are simply grouping labels, whereas tree leaves reference pre-existing interaction units.

The interaction units referenced by tree leaves are the ones that the user will be able to access directly. The remaining interaction units will be reachable through the navigation and action mechanisms defined in these.

A different Action Hierarchy Tree may exist for each type of user. Therefore, a tree can be defined for each agent class in the system. The notion of view introduced by OO-Method lets us approach this in an adequate fashion: each Action Hierarchy Tree is defined on a particular view (which represents a way to access the elements of the Conceptual Schema), and each view can support at most one Action Hierarchy Tree. Recall that an OO-Method view is a collection of interfaces, and each interface defines the visibility relationship between an agent class and the attributes, services and association roles of a particular server class, fixing what the agent class can see (in terms of data and object-valued attributes) and execute (in terms of class services).

In summary, the root of the Action Hierarchy Tree is a node that represents the access point to all the functionality that the system can provide. Other nodes, as well as interaction units, can be hung from the root node, as well as from any other node. This can be repeated until the leaf nodes are reached, which always represent interaction units.

Example.   *The functionality of the rent-a-car system is organized mainly around the following areas:*

- *Vehicles: vehicle administration, extras, vehicle types, maintenance reports, insurance.*
- *Clients: client maintenance (direct and agency).*
- *Rentals: rental management, supplements, invoices, invoice issuing.*
- *Users: user and administrator management.*

The Action Hierarchy Tree is organized in three levels: a global level, a non-leaf node level, and a leaf-node level. Each of these levels has its own data entry template that caters for the relevant information in each case.

At the global level, the only property considered is Comments, which allow the engineers to document the global perspective.

At the non-leaf node level, each node is defined by the following properties:

- Alias.
- Help message.
- Comments.

The alias is a name through which the user can identify a cluster of functionality in the system.

The help message is a piece of text that can be shown to the user with information about the node.

The comments enable engineers to document the node.

Finally, each leaf node in the tree is defined through the following properties:

- Interaction unit.
- Alias.
- Help message.
- Comments.

The interaction unit refers to the specific interaction scenario associated to this node, which will be displayed to the user. This constitutes a basic piece of information, as it is the main link between the tree and the interaction units specified in the Presentation Model.

The alias is the name by which the user identifies the interaction scenario. By default, it is the same as for the alias of the associated interaction unit, although it can be changed.

The help message is a piece of text that can be shown to the user with information about the node.

At the leaf-node level, comments allow engineers to document the specific way in which access to the corresponding interaction scenario is achieved.

Example.   *The organization of the functionality of the rent-a-car system sketched in the previous example can be modelled as the following Action Hierarchy Tree, where there are four main nodes, representing the four areas introduced in the example: vehicles (node 1), clients (node 2), rentals (node 3) and users (profile management, node 4)*

- *Root node:*
  - *Alias: Rent-a-Car System*
  - *Help message: Car rental application*
  - *Comments: This is the root node in the hierarchy*
  - *Sub-nodes:*
    - *Node 1:*
      - *Interaction unit: PIU_Vehicles*

- ■ *Alias: Vehicles*
- ■ *Help message: Vehicle search and maintenance*
- ■ *Comments: Access to the population interaction unit for "Vehicle" for queries and maintenance operations*
- ○ *Node 2:*
  - ■ *Alias: Clients*
  - ■ *Help message: Client management*
  - ■ *Comments: This node groups interaction units for client creation and client maintenance*
  - ■ *Sub-nodes:*
    - ● *Node 2.1:*
      - ○ *Interaction unit: SIU_Create Client*
      - ○ *Alias: Create client*
      - ○ *Help message: Creates a new client*
      - ○ *Comments: Access to the service interaction unit to create a new client*
    - ● *Node 2.2:*
      - ○ *Interaction unit: PIU_Clients*
      - ○ *Alias: Client search*
      - ○ *Help message: Searches for clients and performs operations on them*
      - ○ *Comments: Access to the population interaction unit for "Client"*
- ○ *Node 3:*
  - ■ *Alias: Rentals*
  - ■ *Help message: Rental management*
  - ■ *Comments: This node groups interaction units for rental creation and rental maintenance*
  - ■ *Sub-nodes:*
    - ● *Node 3.1:*
      - ○ *Interaction unit: SIU_Rent*
      - ○ *Alias: Rent a vehicle*
      - ○ *Help message: Rent a vehicle*
      - ○ *Comments: Access to the service interaction unit to create a new rental*
    - ● *Node 3.2:*
      - ○ *Interaction unit: PIU_Rentals*
      - ○ *Alias: Rental search*
      - ○ *Help message: Searches for rentals and performs operations on them*
      - ○ *Comments: Access to the population interaction unit for "Rental"*
- ○ *Node 4:*
  - ■ *Alias: Profile management*
  - ■ *Help message: User and administrator management*
  - ■ *Comments: This node groups interaction units for the management of users and system administrators*

- *Sub-nodes:*
  - *Node 4.1:*
    - ○ *Interaction unit: PIU_Users*
    - ○ *Alias: User management*
    - ○ *Help message: User search and maintenance*
    - ○ *Comments: Access to the population interaction unit for "User"*
  - *Node 4.2:*
    - ○ *Interaction unit: PIU_Admins*
    - ○ *Alias: Administrator management*
    - ○ *Help message: Administrator search and maintenance*
    - ○ *Comments: Access to the population interaction unit for "Administrator"*

Action hierarchy trees specify how access to interaction scenarios is arranged, but do not dictate any particular implementation mechanism.

Example. *The action hierarchy tree presented in the previous example can be implemented in a windowed graphical user interface as the main menu in the application's main window. The title of the main window would be taken from the alias of the root node in the tree. The menu would contain four menu items, corresponding to the four first-level nodes in the tree, each of the items labelled with the alias of the corresponding node.*

Nodes at further levels would be implemented similarly. For example, the "Profile management" menu item would have two sub-items labelled "User management" and "Administrator management". When the menu item corresponding to a leaf node is clicked, the appropriate interaction unit is displayed to the user.

An alternative implementation, in a web environment, would use a collection of hyperlinks, rather than a menu, contained in frameset within the main web page.

It can be seen that the information captured by the conceptual model accommodates different implementations, being abstract enough to separate interaction specification from interaction implementation.

10.4.1 Agents and Action Hierarchy Trees

The Action Hierarchy Tree allows us to define the structure of the access to system functionality. Being an Action Hierarchy Tree defined for a particular view, access to the functionality described by it is restricted to the users who are mapped at run-time to the associated agent class. Therefore, the visibility over the action hierarchy tree of two different users mapped to two different agent classes defined for the same view would be determined by the interfaces of each agent class.

If the interactive user is represented by an agent class that has no visibility over at least one interaction unit grouped under a node of the tree, that node is not presented to the user at run-time. Since the same view can involve multiple agent classes, each with interfaces that imply different visibilities, an action hierarchy tree may include elements that are not necessarily available to every agent of such a view. In this way, the elements that each agent can see may be different, and the interaction scenarios that the user ends up viewing are dynamically determined depending on the agent class that represents the interactive user at run-time.

Example.   *The second example in the previous section (Section 10.4) shows that node 4 groups together two population interaction units, one for class "User" and one for class "Administrator". A business rule determines that regular users cannot access the details of system administrators and, therefore, the class "User" in the conceptual schema does not have visibility over the "PIU_Admins" interaction unit, which is referenced by node 4.2. In the windows-based implementation of the action hierarchy tree described in the previous section, this would be reflected by disabling or hiding the appropriate menu item.*

10.5 Constructing a Presentation Model

We have described the Presentation Model and the three levels that incorporate the corresponding elements (as seen in Fig. 10.1), from the basic elements in level 3 to the more complex interaction units in level 2, and ending in the action hierarchy tree of level 1.

This does not mean that the construction of a Presentation Model must be performed following this sequence. In fact, the development of a Presentation Model can be approached in either a top-down or bottom-up fashion.

In the latter case, the engineer would start by defining the basic elements (actions, navigations, Display Sets, order criteria, filters, etc.), and then continue by assembling these into Interaction Units. Finally, the Interaction Units would be composed into the Action Hierarchy Tree.

Still, it is often more natural to develop the Presentation Model in a top-down fashion, by which the engineer would first outline the Action Hierarchy Tree. Each time a new leaf node is added, the necessary Interaction Unit would be defined. Basic elements would be incrementally created as necessary to flesh out the interaction units so added.

In any case, the OO-Method Presentation Model makes a clear distinction between an abstract user-interface specification and one that is done by using the presentation patterns provided by the method. These focus on what type of user interaction is desired, and not on how this interaction will be implemented in the resulting software product. Different concrete implementations are potentially valid when moving from the abstract to the concrete. From a precise Abstract Presentation Model, a Concrete User Interface is obtained. An open challenge for this type of method is how to provide the required expressiveness in order to enable adapting the user interaction wishes and constrains to the final, concrete user interface.

Having finished the description of the Presentation Model, we can state that the four basic components of the Conceptual Model have been presented: the object model, the dynamic model, the functional model and the presentation model. This provides the necessary infrastructure to represent an Information System in the context of the Problem Space, using the collection of conceptual primitives introduced so far. We must emphasize that these conceptual primitives have precise semantics and, when necessary, a precise textual specification.

Before proceeding to the description of the implementation of the Model Compiler, which can transform the abovementioned conceptual primitives into a final software product, we must introduce a new concept that augments OO-Method's expressiveness with regard to conceptual modelling; this is the concept of Legacy View, which tackles the issue of modelling legacy systems and is described in the next section.

11

Conceptual Modelling of Legacy Systems

The conceptual modelling primitives presented so far allow us to fully specify an organizational information system. The methodological objective of any software production process is to build a software product that is equivalent to the conceptual schema, assuming that the abstractions constituting the modelled system belong in the problem space, and the solution space contains the equivalent software abstractions.

However, it is too often that the abstractions that we visualise as part of the problem space need to interoperate with already existing software systems, which we call *Legacy Systems*. This poses a new problem: how can we manage, from a conceptual modelling perspective, those problem-space abstractions that already exist as software components?

In reality, neither the conceptual modelling approach so far presented, nor the conventional approaches allow us to include pre-existing software systems into the specification of a conceptual schema. It is evident, however, that any pre-existing software component is part of the universe of discourse being modelled.

All this suggests the need of augmenting the expressiveness of the modelling environment, extending it so that those pre-existing software components can be directly involved in the modelling process. This extension is a good answer to the problem outlined, and introduces a new conceptual primitive, namely the *Legacy View*.

11.1 Introduction to the Concept of Legacy View

Extending OO-Method to include the Legacy Systems forces us to consider preexisting software systems (or parts of them) as essential *components* of the Problem Domain.

Pre-existent software systems impose a filter on certain classes onto the engineer; these classes correspond to the abstraction that is used to represent the pre-existing software components. Each of these classes is characterized by the collection of accessible properties (attributes and services). The concept of *Legacy*

View is introduced at the Problem Space level in order to adequately represent this new modelling element.

A Legacy View is defined as the abstraction of a software component that represents a class (which is identifiable by the engineer). Through this concept, the *software component* on which the Legacy View is based can be considered part of the Problem Domain. Here lies the originality and expressive power of this concept: the components of the legacy system become a fundamental part of the specification in the world being modelled. This corresponds with reality, since the abstractions based on existing software components are as *real* as conventional object-oriented abstractions representing the relevant concepts being modelled.

Being an OO-Method object-oriented method, *Legacy Views* must be seen as classes, the instances of which have static properties in terms of attributes, offer certain services, and support queries. Evidently, all this will be possible only if the *Legacy System* exposes the necessary characteristics, since, by definition, the *Legacy System* cannot be modified to implement new functionality.

The introduction of legacy views has an immediate consequence for the model compilation process inherent to OO-Method. The specification of the attributes and services of a legacy view requires, as explained in detail in sections below, the characterization of the functions or procedures (in this case, in the Problem Space) that effectively carry out the corresponding function (such as a query on an attribute or the execution of a service). In other words, rather than specifying the behaviour that generates the code for the services of a class, the model compiler uses the information supplied by a legacy view to associate calls to the legacy system to services in the legacy view class.

In order to flesh out the concept of legacy view in OO-Method, the relevant conceptual constructors are introduced and discussed following the usual structure given by the Object, Dynamic, Functional and Presentation models.

11.2 Object Model

The major contribution of legacy systems in the context of the Object Model is the introduction of the concept of Legacy View itself.

11.2.1 Legacy Views

The legacy view is the basic object-oriented modelling concept that represents pre-existing or legacy systems. Its definition is similar to that of class, since it also denotes a structural and behavioural abstraction realised by a collection of objects; in this case, the abstraction exists as a representation of a software component in the problem domain.

Therefore, and as in the case of the notion of class, the properties of a legacy view can be organized into three groups: attributes, services and integrity constraints.

Graphically, a legacy view is represented as a box divided into three areas: Heading, Attributes and Services. This coincides with the notation used by UML to depict classes. In our case, however, the stereotype "legacy" is used to differentiate legacy views from regular classes.

Example.   *Figure 11.1 shows an example of the graphical representation used to depict a legacy view named "Class" with two attributes, "Attribute1" and "Attribute2", and two services, "Service1" and "Service2".*

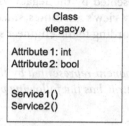

Fig. 11.1 Graphical notation for a legacy view.

The attributes and services shown inside the box are defined when the internal structure of the legacy view is specified. The heading is the topmost area in the box, and contains the name of the class together with the "legacy" stereotype. The name must be unique within the conceptual model, and it cannot coincide with that of another class or legacy view.

The relationships of a legacy view with other classes or legacy views, as we explain later, are graphically represented in the same way as if they were relationships between two regular classes. Being relationships that involve legacy views, however, they are subject to some specific restrictions that are described in this section.

Example.   *In order to introduce an example of a legacy view, let us imagine that our rent-a-car business is a branch of a larger company, which dictates the rental tariffs depending on the class and level of each vehicle. In this way, "Tariff" becomes an entity that is external to the system modelled so far, maintained externally by another software system. Our system can only benefit from its functionality.*

Example.   *The graphical representation of the "Tariff" legacy view is shown in Fig 11.2.*

Fig. 11.2 Graphical notation of the "Tariff" legacy view.

The properties associated to attributes, services and integrity constraints are discussed now.

Attributes

Attributes represent the characteristic properties of a legacy view. The legacy software component being represented by the legacy view may have properties that are not captured by the legacy view's attributes, since the legacy view needs to incorporate only those that, according to the engineer's criterion, are relevant for the problem domain.

Example.   *The legacy component represented by the "Tariff" legacy view, maintained by the reservations central, has the following properties:*

- *TariffId*
- *Description*
- *LastModificationDate*
- *ExpiryDate*
- *RentalRate*
- *InsuranceRate*
- *VehicleClass*
- *VehicleLevel*

However, the view of this entity that is relevant for our rent-a-car system restricts this set to "TariffId", "Description", "RentalRate", "InsuranceRate", "VehicleClass" and "VehicleLevel". These are the properties of interest for our system; the tariff's last modification date or its expiry date are not considered relevant.

The specification of an attribute in a legacy view involves an observation of a part of the state of the underlying Legacy System. For this reason, we need to assume that the Legacy System can provide a service in which one of the output arguments corresponds to the attribute being defined. If this is not the case, then the value of the attribute cannot be possibly obtained from the Legacy System.

According to this, an attribute of a legacy view is defined by associating it to the appropriate output argument of the appropriate legacy service. These links between attributes and output arguments are implemented by using *legacy attribute value expressions*, which are described in the next section.

Example.   *The rent-a-car system often needs to query the rental rate of a given tariff. This is implemented via a service offered by the legacy system (the one at the reservations central).*

From a syntactic point of view, this attribute can be used in the usual way by the legacy view and other classes related to this through associations (including aggregations and compositions). The usual dot notation is employed to specify inter-class navigation paths.

The specification of a legacy view attribute is done through the following properties:

- A name.
- A data type.
- A size, for attributes of type "string".
- A default value.
- A flag indicating whether the attribute value is required when an object of the class is created.
- A flag indicating whether null values are accepted.

Example.   *Table 11.1 lists the attributes of the "Tariff" legacy view.*

Table 11.1 Attributes of the "Tariff" legacy view.

Name	Type	Identifier	Data type	Size	Default value	Require on creation	Nulls allowed
TariffId	Constant	Yes	Autonumeric			Yes	No
Description	Variable	No	String	30		Yes	No
RentalRate	Variable	No	Real			Yes	No
InsuranceRate	Variable	No	Real			Yes	No
VehicleClass	Constant	No	String	1		Yes	No
VehicleLevel	Constant	No	String	1		Yes	No

Other additional and optional properties of attributes are:

- An alias.
- Comments.
- A help message.

The three types of attributes that were described for regular classes (constant, variable and derived) can be also found in legacy views. Unlike in regular classes, the constant/variable characteristic has no effect on code generation, since the software components that represent these attributes are part of the Problem Space. An attribute is constant or variable depending on whether or not it can be modified in the existing implementation.

- *Constant.* The value of constant attributes does not change during the object's lifetime. This type of attribute is necessary, since the definition of legacy view identification function (defined later) is based on these. Even though these are legacy views, this information can be obtained by the engineer.

Value expressions on legacy arguments are used to obtain the attribute's value, as we have mentioned before. Details of these are given in the next section.

Evidently, the specification of the constant characteristic for an attribute is something that the engineer provides, but does not guarantee, by itself, that the attribute being defined is really constant in the underlying legacy component. The constant/variable characterization must be determined from the nature of the legacy system, with which the engineer must be familiar enough.

Example.   *The attributes "TariffId", "VehicleClass" and "VehicleLevel" of the "Tariff" legacy view are defined as constant. This means that the underlying legacy system will not change the values of these attributes at any point.*

- *Variable.* The value of variable attributes can change during the object's lifetime. The values of these attributes are always changed by the legacy system: either internally or through calls from the Legacy View, which are made via legacy events (defined later).

Value expressions on legacy arguments are used to obtain the attribute's value, as we have mentioned before. Details of these are given in the next section.

In this case, as in that of constant attributes, there is no way to guarantee that an attribute defined as variable is actually variable; this specification reflects the ability of the Legacy System to modify the attribute's value. It must be noted that an attribute marked as variable cannot be part of the identification function.

Example.   *The attributes "Description", "RentalRate" and "InsuranceRate" of the "Tariff" legacy view are defined as variable, which means that the underlying legacy system has the capability of modifying their values.*

- *Derived.* The value of derived attributes is computed from the values of other attributes in the legacy view. Therefore, and as in the case of regular classes, derived attributes have one or more derivations associated to them. It is worth noting that the possibility to define derived attributes on legacy views provides an interesting mechanism for the extension of the static part of the legacy system.

Example.   *The information stored by the legacy system for the attributes "VehicleClass" and "VehicleLevel" of the "Tariff" legacy view is a string of size 1.*

Table 11.2 Derivations for the "VehicleInfo" attribute.

Condition	Effect
VehicleClass = "R" AND VehicleLevel = "T"	"Regular top-level"
VehicleClass = "R" AND VehicleLevel="M"	"Regular mid-level"
VehicleClass = "R" AND VehicleLevel = "E"	"Regular entry-level"
VehicleClass = "V" AND VehicleLevel = "T"	"Van top-level"
VehicleClass = "V" AND VehicleLevel = "M"	"Van mid-level"
VehicleClass = "V" AND VehicleLevel = "E"	"Van entry-level"
VehicleClass = "I" AND VehicleLevel = "T"	"Industrial top-level"
VehicleClass = "I" AND VehicleLevel = "M"	"Industrial mid-level"
VehicleClass = "I" AND VehicleLevel = "E"	"Industrial entry-level"
	"No information"

This encoding of information may prove to be inappropriate for our rent-a-car system. To solve the problem, a derived "VehicleInfo" attribute (a string of size 40) can be added to "Tariff" that derives a more significant description of the vehicle's class and level from the "VehicleClass" and "VehicleLevel" attributes, as shown in Table 11.2.

Attribute Value Expressions

Attribute value expressions can be defined for each constant or variable attribute in a legacy view and a service defined within the same legacy view. By considering the legacy system as an interface, the values of the attributes defined in the legacy view can be obtained by calling one or more services. Attribute value expressions are responsible of determining how the value of an attribute can be obtained from the arguments of the services that the legacy system provides.

An attribute value expression is a pair <Condition, Effect>. The Condition component is optional, and consists of a well-formed Boolean formula that allows us to specify a condition that must be satisfied in order for the attribute value to be retrieved.

The Effect component is also a well-formed required formula that establishes the value of the attribute (if the associated condition, if any, evaluates to true) in terms of the output arguments of the associated service.

Example.   *The values of attributes "Description", "RentalRate", "InsuranceRate", "VehicleClass" and "VehicleLevel" must be determined within our system. The legacy system represented by the "Tariff" legacy view provides a "GetData" service that returns this information for a given tariff. Therefore, the "Tariff" legacy view needs a "GetData" service with a "p_thisTariff" input argument and the following output arguments:*

- *ps_Description (the tariff's description)*
- *ps_RentalRate (the tariff's rental rate)*
- *ps InsuranceRate (the tariff's insurance rate)*
- *ps_VehicleClass (the tariff's vehicle class)*
- *ps_VehicleLevel (the tariff's vehicle level)*

A single value expression is defined for each attribute on the "GetData" event and with no condition. The effect is set to the name of the appropriate output argument: "ps_Description" for "Description", "ps_RentalRate" for "RentalRate", and so on.

Similarly to what happens with derivations, when a single value expression exists for any given attribute, no condition must be attached to it because, being unique, its effect is always evaluated.

Also, if multiple value expressions exist for a given attribute, then all of them but one must have a condition. The value expression with no condition becomes the default one, and is evaluated when none of the specified conditions are satisfied.

Example.   *Let us imagine that, under some circumstances, the description of the tariff can be retrieved from the legacy system as an empty string. In this case, a better value is desirable, such as "No description", rather than an empty text. This can be accomplished by modifying the value expressions of the "Description" attribute as shown in Table 11.3.*

Services

Service specification is a crucial aspect of Legacy Views, since it determines how the services of the underlying legacy component can be accessed. Services are used to

Table 11.3 Value expressions for the "Description" attribute.

Condition	Effect
ps_Description <> ""	ps_Description "No description"

modify the state of the objects in the legacy system and, consequently, of the legacy system itself.

The services of a legacy system share some basic properties with regular classes, such as name, input and output arguments, which cannot be modified since they are fixed by the implementation provided by the legacy system. In fact, and although legacy software components can be used in OO-Method as part of the problem domain, they have to be used as they are provided by their very nature. Nonetheless, the concept of legacy view provides some mechanisms that allow engineers to enrich the functionality given by the legacy system.

It must be noted that the functional specification that takes place for regular classes (including, for example, evaluations) is not relevant in the context of legacy views, because the functionality is given by the legacy system.

Graphically, services are depicted in the bottom area of the box of their owner legacy view. Each service is represented by its name, which must be unique within the legacy view.

Example. *Figure 11.3 shows the graphical notation for the "Tariff" legacy view, which includes services "GetData", "UpdateRentalRates" and "UpdateDescription".*

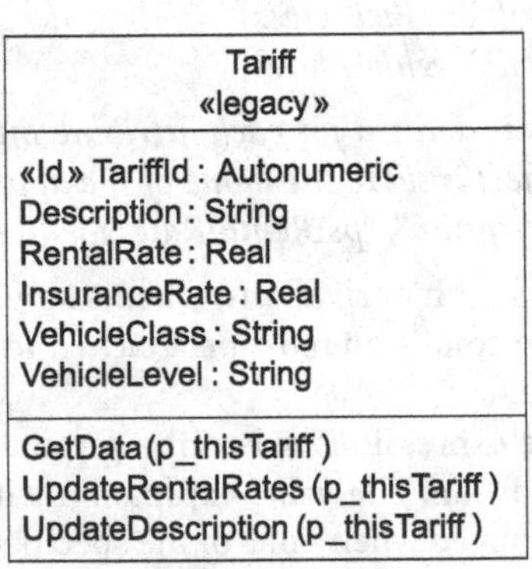

```
┌─────────────────────────────────────┐
│              Tariff                  │
│             «legacy»                 │
├─────────────────────────────────────┤
│ «Id» TariffId : Autonumeric          │
│ Description : String                 │
│ RentalRate : Real                    │
│ InsuranceRate : Real                 │
│ VehicleClass : String                │
│ VehicleLevel : String                │
├─────────────────────────────────────┤
│ GetData (p_thisTariff )              │
│ UpdateRentalRates (p_thisTariff )    │
│ UpdateDescription (p_thisTariff )    │
└─────────────────────────────────────┘
```

Fig. 11.3 Graphical notation of the "Tariff" legacy view, including attributes and services.

In addition to its name, a service also has an alias, some comments and a help message.

Events

Events represent the atomic actions that are exposed by the legacy interface, which determine the basic available actions in the problem domain.

In order for a Legacy View to invoke a legacy service, an event is defined with the appropriate arguments. Functionality, as we have already indicated, is not specified, since it is fully determined by the legacy system.

Similarly, value expressions on output arguments are also irrelevant, since the values of the arguments are determined by the legacy system and cannot be controlled by the legacy view.

Example. *The previous example shows the "Tariff" legacy view with three events: "GetData", "UpdateRentalRates" and "UpdateDescription".*

The first one, which was already described in the section on Attribute Value Expressions, is a query service that can be used to retrieve the values of the legacy view attributes "Description", "RentalRate" and "InsuranceRate".

The second one can be used to update the rental and insurance rates, and the third one to update the tariff description. Since the necessary logic to perform these operations is already implemented by the legacy system, we only need to take care to request the appropriate calls.

In addition to events – which change attribute values and, consequently, produce a change of state – in legacy views, query services can be specified that are used only to retrieve the values of the legacy view attributes but do not cause a change of state.

Example. *The "GetData" event has the "p_thisTariff" input argument, which identifies the tariff in the legacy system, plus five output arguments:*

"ps_Description", "ps_RentalRate", "ps_InsuranceRate",
"ps_VehicleClass" and "ps_VehicleLevel".

These output arguments return the values of, respectively, the tariff description, the rental rate, the insurance rate, the vehicle class and the vehicle level for the given tariff.

Transactions

Transactions are molecular execution units, defined by composition from other already existing services (events and/or transactions). The specification of transactions in legacy views is very interesting because it allows the engineer to extend the functionality provided by the underlying legacy system through the composition of already existing functionality.

Example. *It is possible to compose events "UpdateRentalRates" and "UpdateDescription" of legacy view "Tariff" into a single execution unit that would become a new service present in the system being modelled but not in the legacy system.*

This new service would be of the form "UpdateData(pt_thisTariff)", and would be defined by the formula:

UpdateRentalRates(pt_thisTariff) . UpdateDescription(pt_thisTariff)

In this formula, the events "UpdateRentalRates" and "UpdateDescription" (existing in the legacy system) are sequentially executed, taking as input argument the value of "pt_thisTariff" defined for the transaction.

By doing this, the functionality in the legacy system is not being modified, since only existing services are being invoked. However, its functionality is being augmented by composition, in the legacy view, of already existing functionality.

It must be noted, furthermore, that transactions can be defined on a legacy view only if the encapsulated legacy calls are also of a transactional nature. This introduces a very interesting issue where some characteristics in the solution space (involving the technology used to implement transactions in the legacy system) determine characteristics in the problem space. This is not surprising if we take into account that the introduction of the concept of Legacy View is justified by the fact that existing software components are part of the problem domain. The potential transactional nature of the existing Legacy System becomes in this way an important aspect to be taken into account in the modelled system.

Example.   *Returning to the previous example, and in the case that the services provided by the legacy system were not of a transactional nature, four different execution traces would be possible:*

- *Both services are successful*
- *Both services fail*
- *The first service is successful, but the second one fails*
- *The first service fails, but the second one is successful*

In the two top cases, the resulting behaviour is identical to that obtained in a transactional situation. In the two bottom cases, however, this premise is not satisfied, which can be a serious problem if the execution of the second service is dependent on the effects caused by the successful execution of the first one (fourth case) or if the effects of the second service are to be kept only if the first service succeeds (third case).

Therefore, the specification of transactions on legacy views is under the responsibility of the engineer, and will depend on whether or not the legacy system offers transactional services.

Operations

As we have explained elsewhere, operations are very similar to transactions, the only difference being that operations are not of transactional nature. When defining operations, the global success or failure of the operation is not conditioned to the success or failure of its individual component services. Operations are simply sequences of actions, equivalent to the user manually executing the corresponding services.

Since no transaction-related issues exist and the observability of intermediary states is not relevant, there are no specific issues with the specification of operations on legacy views, and they can be defined without any particular constraint. In fact, they constitute an alternative way to enrich the functionality of the existing Legacy Systems, when it has no transactional properties.

Preconditions

There are two different types of services that can be specified within a legacy view:

- Events, which are *atomic* services implemented directly by the legacy system.
- Transactions and operations, which are *molecular* services defined by composition of other services. They do not necessarily exist in the legacy system, and allow engineers to augment its functionality by composing existing services into new ones.

In general, the precondition associated to a service establishes what conditions must be satisfied before the service can be executed. Preconditions can be defined for events, transactions and operations of legacy views.

The effect of preconditions on legacy views is the same as that for regular classes, i.e. restricting the execution of a service to those cases where the precondition is met. Note that this does not modify the functionality of the legacy system; it only restricts access to it. Therefore, associating preconditions to services of legacy views is perfectly valid, and the same conditions and charactcristics as those explained for regular classes apply.

Example.   *Let us imagine that the reservations central allows rate updates for any tariff, via the "UpdateRentalRates" service.*

In our system, we wish to restrict the possibility of rate updates to those tariffs that are applicable to regular vehicles (as opposed to vans or industrial vehicles); this is modelled by the "VehicleClass" attribute having a value of "R". A precondition to guarantee this can be defined in the "UpdateRentalRates" service with the following formula:

VehicleClass = "R"

This does not modify the service in the legacy system, but limits access to it to those situations that satisfy the stated precondition.

Integrity Constraints

Integrity constraints establish conditions that must be satisfied by objects of a class at any point in time, guaranteeing that the objects represent valid states. Since the responsibility for modifying objects belongs to the legacy system, and not to the legacy view, the responsibility of maintaining this object integrity also belongs to it.

Consequently, it is not possible to specify integrity constraints on legacy views. Doing this would imply the modification of the legacy system in order to guarantee the integrity constraints, which is not possible by the very nature of legacy systems.

11.2.2 Relationships

The object-oriented model in which OO-Method is based involves three types of semantically relevant relationships that can occur between classes in a conceptual model:

- Agent relationships.
- Association, aggregation or composition relationships.
- Specialisation relationships.

This section describes these types of relationships when they involve legacy views, rather than regular classes. Whenever it is necessary, the distinction will be made between scenarios in which a regular class is related to a legacy view and those in which two legacy views are related to each other.

Agents and Agent Relationships

Any class in the conceptual schema can be an agent of any service, regardless of whether the services are provided by regular classes or legacy views.

Therefore, the server role in an agent relationship (i.e. the entity that provides the services) can be played by either regular classes or legacy views.

Example.   *Tables 11.4 and 11.5 show the visibility of class "Administrator" over the attributes and services of the legacy view "Tariff", which acts as server class in the agent relationship.*

Table 11.4 Visibility of class "Administrator" over the attributes of legacy view "Tariff".

Tariff	Administrator
TariffId	Yes
Description	Yes
RentalRate	Yes
InsuranceRate	Yes
VehicleClass	No
VehicleLevel	No
VehicleInfo	Yes

Table 11.5 Visibility of class "Administrator" over the services of legacy view "Tariff".

Tariff	Administrator
GetData	Yes
UpdateRentalRate	No
UpdateDescription	No
UpdateData	Yes

Similarly, the inverse case is also possible: in an agent relationship, the agent role can be played by either a regular class or a legacy view.

Nothing stops a legacy view from participating in an agent relationship, either as service consumer (agent) or as service provider (server), very much like any other class.

Associations, Aggregations and Compositions

Legacy views can be involved in association, aggregation and composition relationships. However, some constraints need to be taken into account. Firstly, the legacy system is, by definition, not modifiable, which restricts the expressiveness of these relationships. Secondly, the relationships are different if they occur between two legacy views or between a legacy view and a regular class. In the former case, it is necessary to distinguish between those relationships that are implemented by the legacy system and those that are implemented only by the system being modelled.

Let us recall that association relationships[1] in OO-Method's object model are binary relationships that allow objects to bidirectionally share their states. This implies that some restrictions must be imposed on the specification of associations between legacy views, since the states of objects in the legacy system are managed exclusively by the legacy system. In other words, modification and deletion of legacy objects is performed by legacy system services, depending on the functionality exposed through the software components that make up its implementation.

The different kinds of association relationships that can involve legacy views are described in this section. These kinds include:

- Relationship between a regular class and a legacy view.
- Relationship between two legacy views that represents an association relationship implemented by the legacy system.
- Relationship between two legacy views that represents an association relationship that is not implemented by the legacy system.

Each of these cases is analysed in the next sections.

Relationships Between a Regular Class and a Legacy View

A relationship between a regular class and a legacy view has specific properties regarding temporality, shared events, identification dependency and valid cardinality ranges.

Temporality

The static property of a relationship indicates that the relationship is established when the composite class is created, and it cannot be altered afterwards. Since instances of a legacy view can be deleted by the legacy system, it is not possible to guarantee that the relationship will not be altered. Therefore, the relationship must be dynamic.

---

[1] Unless otherwise stated, in this context of Legacy Views we will refer to associations, aggregations and compositions whenever we use the word "associations".

Shared Events

As a consequence of the dynamic nature of the relationships between regular classes and legacy views, the associated insertion and deletion events will exist as explained for regular classes.

Identification Dependency

The establishment of identification dependencies is not possible, since the relationship must be static to do this.

Cardinalities

Minimum cardinalities above zero present the problem that objects can be deleted by the legacy system without any previous notification or check, and consequently minimum cardinality requirements might be violated.

Two examples illustrate this.

Example.   *Figure 11.4 shows a situation in which legacy objects (instances of "Client") can "appear" into the system at any time (created by the legacy system), and there is no way in which the corresponding instances of "Country" can be obtained in order to satisfy the relationship minimum cardinality. A "Client" object just created would immediately violate the cardinality constraints, since it would have no associated country. For this reason, no minimum cardinality above zero can be specified.*

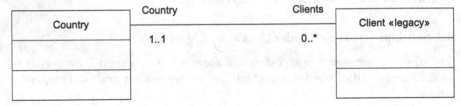

Fig. 11.4 Minimum cardinality of 1 from the legacy view towards the regular class.

Example.   *Figure 11.5 shows a situation in which "Destination" objects are created by the system being modelled, so they can be appropriately linked to "Client" legacy*

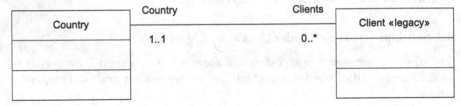

Fig. 11.5 Minimum cardinality of 1 from the regular class towards the legacy view.

*objects. The creation problem described in the previous example does not appear.
However, it is possible that "Client" objects are deleted by the legacy system, thereby
violating the minimum cardinality requirement from "Destination" towards "Client".*

Neither of these two situations can be allowed, so the minimum cardinalities at the
association ends can only be zero.

Relationships Between Legacy Views that Exist in the Legacy System

These are relationships that are modelled in order to represent relationships that
already exist within the legacy system through the appropriate mechanisms.

Example.   *Figure 11.6 shows an example relationship between two legacy views.*

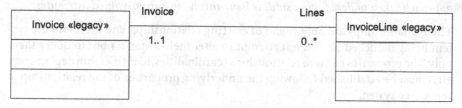

Fig. 11.6 Relationship between two legacy views.

Evidently, this kind of relationship can exist only if the legacy system provides a
mechanism to access the objects related to any object of either class. The services
used to achieve this must be associated to the relationship between legacy views.

Example.   *These population query services can be approached from two different
perspectives, which we illustrate here using the previous example as a reference.*

Alternative 1

*Each population query service is modelled as a query service in the corresponding
legacy view, having an output argument that returns the associated collection of
objects.*

In the case of Fig. 11.6, the following services would be created:
  On "Invoice":
  InvoiceLines(p_Invoice: Invoice, p_InvoiceLineCol: CollectionOf(InvoiceLine))

  On "InvoiceLine":
  InvoiceOfLine(p_InvoiceLine: InvoiceLine, p_Invoice: Invoice)

Alternative 2

*Each population query service is modelled as a filter that returns the corresponding
population.*

In the case of Fig. 11.6, the following filters would be created:
   On "Invoice":
   F_InvoiceOfLine(vo_Line: InvoiceLine)
        Formula: EXIST(Lines) WHERE (Lines = vo_Line)

   On "InvoiceLine":
   F_InvoiceLines(vo_Invoice: Invoice)
        Formula: vo_Invoice = Invoice

In alternative 1, the output argument would be of a collection type, whereas in alternative 2 the filters must be seen as query services.
   Regardless of the chosen alternative, query services should be associated to the legacy aggregation.
   The proposed selected option is alternative 1, since it is more coherent with the approach taken to deal with a similar issue involving datum-valued attributes.

These relationships are only *copies* of existing relationships, and therefore the system being modelled should not attempt to alter their instances but to query them only. The properties of these relationships (cardinalities, identification dependency, etc.) must be established following the underlying properties of the relationship in the legacy system.

Relationships Between Legacy Views that Do Not Exist in the Legacy System

New relationships between legacy views can be introduced as a way to extend the query services of the legacy system. These relationships would actually reside in the system being modelled, and would serve to establish links between objects that are not really linked in the underlying legacy system.

   These relationships must not be too restrictive. Constraints to be fulfilled include the following:

- No minimum cardinalities above zero are permitted.
- The relationships are always dynamic and therefore cannot involve identification dependencies.

Specialisation

Specialisation relationships are those that allow a child class to inherit properties from its parent class. Let us consider the three possible cases that involve legacy views:

- A legacy view is a child of a regular class.
- A regular class is a child of a legacy view.
- A legacy view is a child of another legacy view.

In the next sections, we explain why two of these three cases are not permitted, and another is allowed but uncommon.

A Legacy View as a Child of a Regular Class

Since a legacy system is, by definition, not modifiable, a legacy view cannot be specialised from a regular class, since the implied inheritance that would occur would require the modification of the legacy system.

A Regular Class as a Child of a Legacy View

It could seem that a regular class can be specified as a child of a legacy view. In this case, the properties of the legacy view would be inherited by the class, which would exhibit the usual behaviour associated to the specialisation condition described elsewhere.

   However, there are two reasons that discourage us from modelling such situations:

- Determining whether a specialisation condition is satisfied or not, or whether a carrier event has been triggered in the legacy system, is usually impossible, since the legacy system does not necessarily notify about its changes of state.
- It is impossible to exert any control over the deletion of legacy objects, and therefore any object of a class that is specialised from a legacy view is subject to partially "disappearing" at any time.

For these reasons, we conclude that this kind of specialisation relationship is not permitted.

A Legacy View as a Child of Another Legacy View

As with association relationships, representing the existence of a specialisation relationship within the legacy system might be interesting in some cases.

   Following the same argument, query services that allow accessing the parent class from the child class, and vice versa, would be necessary. This is a possible case, although, as we have said, it is not common. A possible use of this scenario is defining associations with elements of the specified specialisation hierarchy.

11.3 Dynamic Model

We now examine the treatment of State Transition Diagrams and Object Interaction Diagrams of the Dynamic Model of OO-Method as far as Legacy Views are concerned.

11.3.1 State Transition Diagrams

State Transition Diagrams are used to determine and control an object's valid lifetime, that is, which are the valid sequences of services.

   Given the characteristics of legacy views, it is evident that the lifetimes of objects (in terms of state changes) cannot be controlled by them, and therefore it is not possible to monitor an object's current state or whether the sequences of services that are carried out make up valid lifetimes or not. For these reasons, State Transition Diagrams do not make sense within Legacy Views.

As a consequence, no State Transition Diagram can be specified on legacy views, and the transactions and operations defined for these are to be considered always available for execution, independently of the state of the legacy object.

11.3.2 Object Interaction Diagrams

Triggers

We have said that triggers enable us to define the internal activity in the system, that is, the mechanisms that automatically and systematically perform certain services whenever certain conditions are met. The question now is whether it is possible to define a trigger on a legacy view.

A trigger must be activated whenever the corresponding condition is satisfied. For this reason:

- The class that defines the trigger cannot be a legacy view.
- No legacy view can participate in the trigger condition.

As the implementation of a legacy view is assumed to be fixed and provided by the system, the reason behind this is that it is impossible to control state changes within the legacy system and, therefore, it is impossible to determine when the trigger condition is met.

Other scenarios involving legacy views are permitted. For example, it is possible to trigger services for a legacy view as a consequence of satisfying a condition for a regular class.

Global Transactions and Operations

Global transactions and operations can make reference to services defined for legacy view as if they were defined for regular classes.

The only restriction to take into account refers to global transactions, and is the same as the one we have already mentioned in the context of local transactions of legacy views: the transactional or non-transactional nature of the underlying legacy system determines whether transactional semantics can be attained in the system being modelled. It is the responsibility of the engineer to know and take this into account, and model the system in consequence.

11.4 Functional Model

As we have repeatedly said in the context of services (events, transactions and operations), changing the state of the legacy system is under the control of the legacy system itself. The system being modelled cannot exert control on the state of the legacy system, being limited to using the services exposed by it. For this reason, defining evaluations of a legacy view is meaningless.

Intuitively, this is a logic consequence of the definition of legacy system. The software components of a legacy system become elements in the modelling of the new system, and their functionality is dictated by the existing implementation. It makes no sense, therefore, to consider what the functionality should be, since it is fixed beforehand. The Model Compiler will not generate any code for the implementation of the legacy system; it has only to generate the code necessary to make the appropriate calls to the legacy services.

11.5 Presentation Model

The Presentation Model describes how the interaction between the users and the system will take place and, for this purpose, it introduces a series of modelling elements that serve to specify how different interaction units are organized to expose data and functionality in an optimal way.

Most elements in the Presentation Model build upon elements that have been previously defined in the object model: classes, attributes, services and relationships. In this context, whether a regular class or a legacy view is being considered does not make any significant difference, since well-defined collections of attributes and services are equally available in both cases. Data entry formats, valid value selection mechanisms, grouping criteria and other entities are equally defined regardless of whether the underlying element is a regular class or a legacy view.

If, in addition, the legacy system provides (as is expected from a correct and complete specification) the appropriate access mechanisms to these attributes and services, then most of the basic elements in the presentation model can be used for legacy views without any special considerations.

The following sections explain the relationship between the Presentation Model and Legacy Views in the three different areas that were used for the Presentation Model: basic elements, interaction units and action hierarchy tree, as the three levels that structure the Presentation Model in the OO-Method.

11.5.1 Basic Elements

Let us see how presentation characteristics can be specified in the context of the 3-level, basic conceptual presentation patterns when dealing with legacy views.

Entry

Let us recall that the Entry basic element is defined for a particular data type and can be assigned to:

- Attributes.
- Service input arguments.
- Datum-valued filter variables.

There is nothing that stops an entry basic element from being associated to any of these element kinds when defined for a legacy view.

Defined Selection

Like the Entry basic element, the Defined Selection basic element is defined for a particular data type and can be assigned to:

- Attributes.
- Service input arguments.
- Datum-valued filter variables.

Like in the previous case, there is nothing against assigning a defined selection basic element to any of these element kinds when defined for a legacy view, rather than a regular class.

Argument Grouping

The Argument Grouping basic element is defined for a service. It is possible to define argument grouping basic elements for services that are defined for a legacy view.

Argument Dependency

The Argument Dependency basic element is defined for the input arguments of a service. It is possible to define argument dependency basic elements for the services of a legacy view.

Filter

For practical purposes, a filter can be seen as a service that returns the instances of a class that meet a given condition.

Defining a filter for a legacy view is similar to defining a filter for a regular class. Two cases are to be taken into account:

- The filter mechanism also exists in the legacy system.
- The filter mechanism does not exist in the legacy system.

The first case corresponds to those scenarios in which the legacy system exposes a service that can return a collection of objects that meet a given condition. In this case, the filter formula must not be specified: only the name of the legacy service must be specified, together with the filter variables, if any, which correspond to the input arguments of the legacy service.

Example.   *The legacy system in the reservations central exposes a service "GetTar-iffsOfClass" that takes a vehicle class as input argument and returns a collection of all the tariffs that exist for that particular vehicle class.*

In the system being modelled, a filter "GetTariffsOfClass" could be defined for the "Tariff" legacy view with a single filter variable, "v_VehicleClass", corresponding to the input argument for the abovementioned legacy service.

In the second case, the legacy system does not provide any service implementing the filter operation. Therefore, a filter formula must be specified so that the system being modelled can perform the filtering as a step after the complete population is retrieved from the legacy system.

Example. *The legacy system in the reservations central does not have any service that can return the collection of tariffs applicable to a particular combination of vehicle class and level. To achieve this, it is necessary to define, in the system being modelled, a "GetTariffsOfClassAndLevel" filter with two filter variables, "v_VehicleClass" and "v_VehicleLevel", and the following formula:*

VehicleClass = v_VehicleClass AND VehicleLevel = v_VehicleLevel

Order Criterion

Order criteria are defined for the attributes of a class or classes related to it through deterministic role name sequences. As for regular classes, order criteria can be also defined for attributes of a legacy view or other legacy views related to it through deterministic role name sequences.

Example. *Let us imagine that the retrieved tariffs are to be sorted by ascending rental rate and then insurance rate. An order criterion can be defined for the "Tariff" legacy view with the following properties:*

- *Name: OC_Rates*
- *Alias: By rental and insurance rates*
- *Help message: Tariffs sorted by ascending rental and insurance rates*
- *Comments: This allows ordering tariffs by ascending rental and insurance rates*
- *Elements:*
  - *Element1:*
    - *Attribute: RentalRate*
    - *Direction: Ascending*
  - *Element2:*
    - *Attribute: InsuranceRate*
    - *Direction: Ascending*

Display Set

As in the previous case, Display Sets are also defined for the attributes of a class or classes related to it through deterministic role name sequences. As for regular classes, Display Sets can also be defined for attributes of a legacy view or other legacy views related to it through deterministic role name sequences.

Example.   *A Display Set for the "Tariff" legacy view can be defined with the following properties:*

- *Name: VS_Tariff*
- *Comments: Tariff details*
- *Elements:*
  - *Element1:*
    - o   *Attribute: Description*
    - o   *Alias: Tariff description*
  - *Element2:*
    - o   *Attribute: RentalRate*
    - o   *Alias: Rental rate*
  - *Element3:*
    - o   *Attribute: InsuranceRate*
    - o   *Alias: Insurance rate*
  - *Element4:*
    - o   *Attribute: VehicleInfo*
    - o   *Alias: Vehicle information*

Navigation

Navigation basic elements can be defined for the association, aggregation and composition relationships between classes. Likewise, they can be defined for similar relationships between legacy views, as long as the appropriate legacy query services make the corresponding object-valued attributes available.

Example.   *A navigation basic element can be defined for the "Tariff" legacy view with a single element (since "Tariff" is related only to class "VehicleType") and the following properties:*

- *Name: N_Tariff*
- *Help message: Access to vehicle types*
- *Comments: Gives access to information associated to a tariff, showing the vehicle types it is associated to*
- *Elements:*
  - *Element1:*
    - o   *Interaction unit: PIU_VehicleType*
    - o   *Path: VehicleTypes*
    - o   *Alias: Vehicle types*

Actions

Action basic elements can be defined for the services of classes; similarly, they can be defined for services of legacy views, defining the collection of services that are available to be executed for an instance of the corresponding legacy view.

Example.   *An action basic element can be defined for the "Tariff" legacy view to specify which services are available at any time. The actions basic element would have the following properties:*

- *Name: A_Tariff*
- *Help message: Options to update rates and tariff description*
- *Comments: Gives access to services to update tariff rates and tariff description*
- *Elements:*
  - *Element1:*
    - ○ *Interaction unit: SIU_UpdateRates*
    - ○ *Alias: Update rates*
  - *Element2:*
    - ○ *Interaction unit: SIU_UpdateDescription*
    - ○ *Alias: Update description*

11.5.2 Interaction Units

The specification of interaction units for legacy views is not different from that for regular classes, as a consequence of that discussed in previous sections.

11.5.3 Action Hierarchy Tree

The specification of the Action Hierarchy Tree is not affected by whether the interaction units that it involves are based on regular classes or legacy views. This is logical, because the Action Hierarchy Tree is a high-level abstraction of system functionality, for which regular classes and legacy views are modelling primitives at the same level.

Up to this point, we have characterized the collection of primitives provided by OO-Method and organized into four major views: Object Model, Dynamic Model, Functional Model and Presentation Model. All these together provide the basic building blocks needed to construct a Conceptual Schema that constitutes the system representation from which a corresponding Software Product has to be obtained.

In addition, we have introduced an original conceptual extension that enables us to include the modelling of Legacy Systems within the software production process of OO-Method. The concept of Legacy View has thus been introduced and conveniently characterized in terms of the abovementioned four major models.

As a result, we have a rigorous software production method that is supported by a precise Conceptual Modelling process. This provides a solid foundation on which tools can be based so that Information Systems can be easily specified and represented in the form of Conceptual Schemas. We can now say that the characterization at the Problem Space level is complete. The next step involves considering how a Conceptual Schema can be transformed into a Solution Space software representation, which is achieved by the OO-Method Model Compiler.

Before getting into this matter, we will close this chapter with a last section devoted to the conceptual model validation mechanisms that are available in OO-Method.

Conceptual Model Validation

12.1 Introduction

A rigorous conceptual modelling method must precisely define the conceptual primitives or constructors that it uses. The best strategy to ensure that such a precise definition exists is to use the appropriate formalism to fit the modelling language with the appropriate syntax and semantics, so that the specifications developed with it can be made correct and complete. This concept of correctness and completeness is analysed in this section.

In OO-Method, the necessary formalism is given by the object-oriented OA-SIS formal specification language (Pastor 1992; Pastor and Ramos 1995). OASIS provides the necessary set of formally and precisely defined conceptual primitives.

In addition, OASIS provides the formal support that is needed to approach the formal validation of Conceptual Schemas with the objective of ensuring their correctness and completeness.

In this context, it is necessary to clarify what we understand by a correct and complete specification. These terms are often used in the context of information systems modelling, but rarely in an appropriate way. This may be due to the notion that correctness and completeness can exist in two different realms: formal and informal. In the case of OO-Method and OASIS, the interpretation that must be made of the terms "correct" and "complete" is rigorous in both senses, unlike in many other approaches that may be similar on the surface but plagued with serious problems when a precise semantic specification is attempted.

From a formal point of view, a logic inference system associated to a formal specification language is *correct* if all that can be demonstrated using the appropriate inference rules is true according to the semantics of the language, and is *complete* if we can also argue the other way: all that is true – semantic view – can be demonstrated – syntactic view. The justification that we present now may appear convoluted and long-winded due to its formal contents; however, we believe that it is necessary to introduce the appropriate basic principles and refer to the appropriate sources.

Correctness and completeness proof in OO-Method is based on previous work done in the field of Dynamic Logics, by which the syntax, inference rules and semantics of multi-modal first-order logics with equality are characterized. To achieve this, a signature for a dynamic logic is defined as being composed of two sub-signatures that are linked, one to the static properties of the system, the other to the process specification. The next step consists of introducing a language for the defined dynamic logic as well as an interpretation structure. Finally, the semantic definition of truth is characterized and the inference relationship is introduced, proving that it is correct and complete according to the previously described formal context. The details of this kind of approach can be found in Wieringa (1990).

The relationship of this with OASIS comes from the fact that an OASIS specification (i.e. the formal representation of an OO-Method Conceptual Schema) is equivalent to the specification of a first-order dynamic logic constructed by following the steps outlined in the previous paragraph. Therefore, the outcomes and properties of the associated logic framework can be used, especially those regarding the correctness and completeness of the set of inference rules that is introduced for the said dynamic logic with equality. The fact that an OASIS specification can be represented as a dynamic logic specification allows us to consider correctness and completeness from a formal and rigorous viewpoint, and likewise transfer this formality to OO-Method Conceptual Schemas.

Validating that an OO-Method Conceptual Schema is formally correct and complete is not everything that can be done. An informal validation is also possible, although, in this case, the concepts of correctness and completeness are based on linguistic acceptations often used in software engineering contexts that are not based on formally defined logic frameworks.

In this kind of context, we say that an element is completely specified when all its required properties have been specified, and we say that an element is correctly specified when all its properties (either required or optional) are valid. From this point of view, specification correctness and completeness are a way to ensure consistency.

In order to evaluate an OO-Method Conceptual Model in terms of correctness and completeness from this perspective, points must be fixed: which are the required properties, and what kind of validations must be performed on each element of a specification. The four usual viewpoints (object model, dynamic model, functional model and presentation model) are to be considered.

The following sections deal with this pragmatic, informal characterization of correctness and completeness, approaching each of the four models in turn. Basically, each section describes the characteristics that an OO-Method Conceptual Schema must exhibit for it to be considered correct and complete. These collections of characteristics come as direct consequence of the definitions of the conceptual primitives presented so far. They show the direction to be followed by any tool that implements OO-Method in order to provide correctness and completeness check, using either a more formal, logic-based approach or a more informal perspective associated to the linguistic acceptation of the terms correct and complete.

12.2 Object Model

12.2.1 Classes

Required properties:

- Name
- Every class must have at least one identifier attribute and a creation event.

Validations:

- The class name must be a valid identifier[1].
- The class name must be unique in the context of the conceptual model (i.e. it cannot coincide with the name of another class or legacy view).
- If the class is not involved in a specialisation hierarchy or is the root of a specialisation hierarchy, then it must have at least one associated creation event.
- If the class is involved in a specialisation hierarchy and is not the root class, then it cannot have explicit creation or destruction events. These services are to be placed only in the root class. Carrier and freeing events, which play the roles of creators and destructors of non-root classes, can exist in other classes.
- If the class is not involved in a specialisation hierarchy or is the root of a specialisation hierarchy, then it must have an identification function.

Attributes

Required properties:

- Owner class.
- Name.
- Data type.
- Attribute type (constant, variable or derived).

Generic validations:

- The attribute name must be a valid identifier.
- The attribute name must be unique within the context of the owner class and its specialisation hierarchy.
- The attribute name cannot coincide with any role name that is visible[2] from the class.
- The attribute name cannot coincide with that of any service argument defined for the class or any of its predecessors in the specialisation hierarchy.
- If the attribute has a default value, then its formula must be valid[3].

---

[1] An identifier is valid if it does not contain blanks and it does not coincide with an OASIS reserved word.

[2] By visible role we mean, in this context, any association, aggregation or composition relationship that is defined for the class.

[3] The notion of valid formula is extensively used in this section. The detailed syntactic definition of valid formulas can be found in Pastor and Molina (2006), where are explained in detail those formulae that are considered correct in OO-Method (depending on their context) as well as the associated formula construction mechanisms.

- If the attribute data type so requires, a size must be specified.

Additional validations for constant attributes:

- If the attribute is not required on creation, it must have a default value or admit null values.
- If the attribute belongs to a legacy view, then at least one value expression must be defined.
- All the value expressions associated to attributes of a legacy view must have valid condition and effect formulae.
- If the attribute has a single associated value expression, then this must not have a condition.
- If the attribute has multiple associated value expressions, then all, except for one, must have conditions.

Additional validations for variable attributes:

- If the attribute is not required on creation, then it must have a default value or admit null values.
- A variable attribute cannot be an identifier attribute.
- If the attribute belongs to a legacy view, then at least one value expression must be defined.
- All the value expressions associated to attributes of a legacy view must have valid condition and effect formulae.
- If the attribute has a single associated value expression, then this must not have a condition.
- If the attribute has multiple associated value expressions, then all, except for one, must have conditions.

Additional validations for derived attributes:

- A derived attribute cannot be required on creation.
- A derived attribute cannot be an identifier attribute.
- All the derivations associated to the attribute must have valid condition and effect formulae.
- If the attribute belongs to a class that is not involved in a specialisation hierarchy, then it must have at least one associated derivation.
- If the attribute belongs to a class that is involved in a specialisation hierarchy, then it must have at least one associated derivation either in its owner class or in any of the specialised classes.
- If the attribute has a single associated derivation, then this must not have a condition.
- If the attribute has multiple associated derivations, then all, except for one, must have conditions.

Services

Required properties:

- Owner class.
- Name.
- Service type (event, transaction or operation).

Generic validations:

- The service name must be a valid identifier.
- The service name must be unique within the context of the owner class and its specialisation hierarchy.
- The service name cannot coincide with any role name that is visible from the class.

Events

Required properties:

- Owner class.
- Event type (creation, destruction or own).

Validations:

- If the event is a creation or destruction event, then it cannot have associated evaluations.
- If the event is a creation event, then it cannot have an object-valued argument that represents the object on which the event is executed.
- If the event is not a creation event, then it must have an object-valued argument that represents the object on which the event is executed.
- If the event is shared, then it must have an object-valued argument for each class that shares the event.
- If the event is marked as an internal service, then its arguments cannot be linked by dependency relationships. This is because internal services are not exposed to users, and dependency relationships are closely linked to user interaction.

Arguments

Required properties:

- Owner service.
- Name.
- Data type.

Validations:

- The argument name must be a valid identifier
- The argument name must be unique within the context of the owner service
- The argument name cannot coincide with that of any attribute of the owner class or any of its predecessor classes in the specialisation hierarchy.

- The argument name cannot coincide with that of any visible role name.
- If the argument has a default value, then its formula must be valid.
- If the argument data type so requires, a size must be specified.

Additional validations for output arguments:

- The argument must have at least one associated value expression.
- If the argument has a single associated value expression, then this must not have a condition.
- If the argument has multiple associated value expressions, then all, except for one, must have conditions.

Transactions

Required properties:

- Owner class.
- Transaction type (creation, destruction, other).
- Formula.

Validations:

- The transaction formula must be valid.
- If the transaction is a creation transaction, then the first service in it must be a creation service (a creation event or transaction).
- If the transaction is a destruction transaction, then the last service in it must be a destruction service (a destruction event or transaction).
- If the transaction is a creation transaction, then it cannot have an object-valued argument that represents the object on which the transaction is executed.
- If the transaction is not a creation transaction, then it must have an object-valued argument that represents the object on which the transaction is executed.
- If the transaction is marked as an internal service, then its arguments cannot be linked by dependency relationships. This is because internal services are not exposed to users, and dependency relationships are closely linked to user interaction.

Operations

Required properties:

- Owner class.
- Operation type (creation, destruction, other).
- Formula.

Validations:

- The operation formula must be valid.
- If the operation is a creation operation, then the first service in it must be a creation service (a creation event or operation).

- If the operation is a destruction operation, then the last service in it must be a destruction service (a destruction event or operation).
- If the operation is a creation operation, then it cannot have an object-valued argument that represents the object on which the operation is executed.
- If the operation is not a creation operation, then it must have an object-valued argument that represents the object on which the operation is executed.
- If the operation is marked as an internal service, then its arguments cannot be linked by dependency relationships. This is because internal services are not exposed to users, and dependency relationships are closely linked to user interaction.

Preconditions

Required properties:

- Owner service.
- Formula.

Validations:

- The precondition formula must be valid.

Integrity Constraints

Required properties:

- Owner class.
- Formula.

Validations:

- The integrity constraint formula must be valid.
- Integrity constraints cannot be defined for legacy views.

12.2.2 Relationships Between Classes

Agent Relationships

Required properties:

- Agent class.
- Server class.

Validations for the agent relationship:

- An agent class must have visibility over at least one attribute, role or service of its server class.
- If a horizontal visibility formula exists, then it must be valid.

Validations for the model:

- At least one agent relationship must exist in the model.

Associations, Aggregations and Compositions

Required properties:

- Class or pair of classes that are connected by the relationship.
- Minimum and maximum cardinalities at both ends of the relationship.
- Role names at both ends of the relationship.
- Relationship name.

Validations:

- The relationship name must be a valid identifier.
- The minimum cardinality cannot be greater than the maximum cardinality for both ends of the relationship.
- The role name must be a valid identifier for both ends of the relationship.
- The role name cannot coincide with that of any attribute of the related class or any of its predecessor classes in the specialisation hierarchy, for both ends of the relationship.
- The role name must be unique within the context of its owner class, for both ends of the relationship. This means that the role name cannot coincide with that of any other role that is visible from the other end of the relationship.
- If a class is marked as having identification dependency, then its end of the relationship must be static, and the minimum and maximum cardinalities must be 1.
- If the maximum cardinalities at both ends of the relationship are greater than 1, then the relationship name must be unique within the context of the conceptual model.
- If the minimum and maximum cardinalities at either end of the relationship are both 1, then the relationship cannot have deletion events.
- If the relationship is reflexive, then the role names at both ends must be different.

Specialisation

Required properties:

- Parent class.
- Child class.
- Specialisation conditions (if the specialisation is permanent or temporary by condition).
- Carrier event (if the specialisation is temporary by event).

Validations:

- The parent and child classes must be different.
- If the specialisation is by condition (either permanent or temporary), then the formula must be valid.
- The condition formula of a permanent specialisation can involve only constant elements (constants, constant attributes or role names that label static relationship ends).

- The condition formula of a temporary specialisation must involve at least one variable element (variable attributes or role names that label dynamic relationship ends).
- No cycles can exist in a specialisation hierarchy.

12.3 Dynamic Model

12.3.1 State Transition Diagram

Required properties:

- Defining class.
- Pre-creation state.
- Intermediate state.
- Creation transitions.

Validations:

- Every class must have exactly one associated state transition diagram.
- Legacy views cannot have associated state transition diagrams.
- The state transition diagram must have at least one pre-creation state and an intermediate state.
- The state transition diagram cannot have multiple pre-creation states.
- In a state transition diagram associated to a class not involved in a specialisation hierarchy or to a class that is the root of a specialisation hierarchy, transitions leaving the pre-creation state can be labelled only with actions that correspond to creation events.
- In a state transition diagram associated to a class specialised by event, transitions leaving the pre-creation state can be only labelled with actions that correspond to carrier events.
- In a state transition diagram associated to a class not involved in a specialisation hierarchy or to a class that is the root of a specialisation hierarchy, transitions ending in the destruction state can be labelled only with actions that correspond to destruction events.
- In a state transition diagram associated to a class specialised by event, transitions labelled with actions that correspond to freeing events must end in states that exist in the state transition diagram associated to the parent class.
- No transitions can flow directly from the pre-creation state into the destruction state.
- No transitions can be labelled with actions corresponding to operations.
- The name of an intermediate state must be a valid identifier.
- The name of an intermediate state must be unique within the context of the state transition diagram of the class and those of the predecessor classes in the specialisation hierarchy.

12.3.2 Object Interaction Diagram

Triggers

Required properties:

- Owner class.
- Destination class.
- Trigger condition.
- Destination type (SELF, OBJECT, CLASS or FOR ALL).
- Service.

Validations:

- The trigger condition formula must be valid.
- If the trigger is of the "self" type, then the destination and owner classes must coincide.
- If the trigger is of the "for all" type, then a role name sequence must be supplied that allows reaching the destination class from the owner class.
- The service to be triggered must exist in the destination class or in any of its predecessors in the specialisation hierarchy.
- The arguments of the service to be triggered (except for the one representing the object on which the trigger is executed) must be initialized.

Global Transactions and Operations

Required properties:

- Name.
- Formula.

Validations:

- The transaction or operation name must be a valid identifier.
- The transaction or operation name must be unique within the conceptual model.
- The formula must be valid.

12.4 Functional Model

12.4.1 Evaluations

Required properties:

- Defining class.
- Attribute.
- Event.
- Effect formula.

Validations:

- No evaluations can be defined for creation events.
- No evaluations can be defined for destruction events.
- No evaluations can be defined on legacy views.
- No evaluations can be defined for constant or derived attributes.
- Condition and effect formulae must be valid.
- At least one evaluation with no condition must exist for each pair <*attribute, event*> where *attribute* is a variable attribute and *event* is an event that can modify that attribute.
- For each pair <*attribute, event*> with multiple associated evaluations, all except one must have conditions.

12.5 Presentation Model

12.5.1 Basic Elements

Entry

Required properties:

- Name.
- Data type.

Validations:

- The name must be a valid identifier.
- The name must be unique within the presentation model.
- If a default value is specified, then the formula must be valid.
- If a range is specified, then the maximum value must be greater than the minimum value, and both values must conform to the stated data type.

Defined Selection

Required properties:

- Name.
- Data type.
- Elements.

Validations:

- The name must be a valid identifier.
- The name must be unique within the presentation model.
- At least two elements must be specified.
- For each element, the code must be a value that conforms to the stated data type, and the label cannot be empty.

Argument Grouping

Required properties:

- Service.

Validations:

- All the arguments of the service must belong to exactly one argument grouping basic element.

Argument Dependency

Required properties:

- Argument.
- Agent.
- Event.
- Condition.
- Associations (one at least).

Validations:

- Argument dependency basic elements can be defined for input arguments only.
- The "SetActive" event can be associated only to the "Internal" agent.
- The condition formula must be valid.

Filter

Filter required properties:

- Defining class.
- Name.
- Formula (except for legacy filters).

Filter validations:

- The name must be a valid identifier.
- The name must be unique within the defining class and its predecessor classes in the specialisation hierarchy.
- The filter formula must be valid.

Filter variable required properties:

- Name.
- Data type.

Filter variable validations:

- The name must be a valid identifier.
- The name must be unique within the filter.
- If a default value is specified, then the formula must be valid.

Additional validations for datum-valued filter variables:

- If an entry basic element is assigned, then its data type must be compatible with that of the filter variable.
- If a defined selection basic element is assigned, then its data type must be compatible with that of the filter variable.

Additional validations for object-valued filter variables:

- If a Display Set is assigned as additional information, then it must be associated to the same class as that of the filter variable, or to a predecessor class in the specialisation hierarchy.
- If a population interaction unit is assigned to help with object selection, then it must be associated to the same class as that of the filter variable, or to a predecessor class in the specialisation hierarchy.

Order Criterion

Required properties:

- Defining class.
- Name.
- Elements.

Validations:

- The name must be a valid identifier.
- The name must be unique within the defining class and its predecessor classes in the specialisation hierarchy.
- At least one element must be specified.
- Every defined element must refer to an attribute in the defining class or its predecessor classes in the specialisation hierarchy, or to an attribute reachable through a deterministic role name sequence.

Display Set

Required properties:

- Defining class.
- Name.
- Elements.

Validations:

- The name must be a valid identifier.
- The name must be unique within the defining class and its predecessor classes in the specialisation hierarchy.
- At least one element must be specified.
- Every defined element must refer to an attribute in the defining class or its predecessor classes in the specialisation hierarchy, or to an attribute reachable through a deterministic role name sequence.

Navigation

Required properties:

- Defining class.
- Name.
- Elements.

Validations:

- The name must be a valid identifier.
- The name must be unique within the defining class and its predecessor classes in the specialisation hierarchy.
- At least one element must be specified.
- Valid elements must refer to interaction units defined for a class (or one of its predecessor classes) related to the defining class (or one of its predecessor classes).

Validations on each element:

- The path, if specified, must be a role name visible from the defining class (or one of its predecessor classes) or a valid role name sequence starting on the defining class.
- If the path is not specified, then it is assumed that the element's interaction unit has been defined on a class specialised from the defining class.
- The referenced interaction unit must be defined for the class that is reached from the defining class through the role name sequence given as path, or in a predecessor class.
- The referenced interaction unit cannot be an instance interaction unit if the role name sequence specified as path reaches an object population with multiple members.

Actions

Required properties:

- Defining class.
- Name.
- Elements.

Validations:

- The name must be a valid identifier.
- The name must be unique within the defining class and its predecessor classes in the specialisation hierarchy.
- At least one element must be specified.

Validations on each element:

- The referenced service interaction unit must be defined for the same class as that for the action basic element.

12.5.2 Interaction Units

Service Interaction Units

Required properties:

- Service.
- Name.

Validations:

- The name must be a valid identifier.
- The name must be unique within the class owning the service and its predecessor classes in the specialisation hierarchy.

Instance Interaction Units

Required properties:

- Defining class.
- Name.
- Display Set.

Validations:

- The name must be a valid identifier.
- The name must be unique within the defining class and its predecessor classes in the specialisation hierarchy.
- The referenced Display Set must be defined for the same class as that for the interaction unit or one of its predecessors.
- If an actions basic element is specified, then it must be defined for the same class as that for the interaction unit or one of its predecessors.
- If a navigation basic element is specified, then it must be defined for the same class as that for the interaction unit or one of its predecessors.

Population Interaction Units

Required properties:

- Defining class.
- Name.
- Display Set.

Validations:

- The name must be a valid identifier.
- The name must be unique within the defining class and its predecessor classes in the specialisation hierarchy.
- The referenced Display Set must be defined for the same class as that for the interaction unit or one of its predecessors.

- If an actions basic element is specified, then it must be defined for the same class as that for the interaction unit or one of its predecessors.
- If a navigation basic element is specified, then it must be defined for the same class as that for the interaction unit or one of its predecessors.
- If filters are specified, then they must be defined for the same class as that for the interaction unit or one of its predecessors.
- If ordering criteria are specified, then they must be defined for the same class as that for the interaction unit or one of its predecessors.

Master/Detail Interaction Units

Required properties:

- Defining class.
- Name.
- Master interaction unit.
- Detail interaction units.

Validations:

- The name must be a valid identifier.
- The name must be unique within the defining class and its predecessor classes in the specialisation hierarchy.
- The master interaction unit must be defined for the same class as that for the master/detail interaction unit or a predecessor class.
- At least one detail interaction unit must be specified.

Validations on each detail interaction unit:

- The path[4], if specified, must have a role name visible from the defining class (or one of its predecessor classes) or a valid role name sequence starting from the defining class.
- If the path is not specified, then it is assumed that the detail interaction unit has been defined for a class specialised from the defining class.
- The detail interaction unit must be defined for the class that is reached from the defining class through the role name sequence given as path, or in a predecessor class.
- The detail interaction unit cannot be an instance interaction unit if the role name sequence specified as path reaches an object population with multiple members.

---

[4] Recall that every detail specified in a master/detail interaction unit is characterized by a list of <interaction_unit, path, alias>. The path to traverse in order to reach the associated class is specified by "path".

12.5.3 Action Hierarchy Tree

Required properties:

- View.
- Elements.

Validations:

- The view must have at least one agent relationship.
- Valid elements include nodes and leaves. Nodes are mere grouping devices. Leaves reference previously defined interaction units.
- The tree must have at least one valid leaf.
- Every interaction unit directly accessible through a leaf must be visible by at least one agent in the view.

The validations that can be performed on an OO-Method Conceptual Schema have been described. As we have said elsewhere, the collection of properties and validations described here is highly useful to ensure the correctness and completeness of a Conceptual Schema. Their definitions are a consequence of the precise semantic specification of the conceptual primitives that can be used in OO-Method, which allows us to determine the required properties of each element and those validations that can be performed on them.

In addition, this collection of validations can be easily implemented on any CASE tool that supports OO-Method, adding the necessary functionality so that the correctness and completeness of specifications can be automatically checked.

Once this information has been explained, we are now in the position of approaching the transformation process that the Conceptual Model Compiler applies to convert a Conceptual Schema into a Software Product. The next section is devoted to this.

Part III

Conceptual Model Compilation:
From the Problem Space to the Solution Space

13. Transforming Models into Applications
14. Requirements for the Compilation of Conceptual Models
15. Application Execution Strategy
16. Application Architecture
17. Transformation Strategy
18. Building a Conceptual Model Compiler
19. Issues with Other Approaches
20. Analogies Between OO-Method and MDA
21. The OO-Method Development Process
22. OO-Method Implementations

Conceptual Model Compilation:
From the Problem Space to the Solution Space

13

Transforming Models into Applications

We have described how OO-Method establishes a clear distinction between the Problem Space, where a Conceptual Schema models a given universe of discourse, and the Solution Space, where a software product that represents that Conceptual Schema through a given technology is obtained.

So far, we have explained how the structure and behaviour of an information system can be specified using the conceptual modelling approach proposed by OO-Method. We have introduced the appropriate conceptual primitives or constructors, their composition mechanisms, and the process by which an OO-Method conceptual schema can be validated in order to guarantee its coherence. This conceptual schema is what in MDA (MDA 2006) terms would be called a Platform-Independent Model (PIM).

The conceptual schema plays a crucial role but, logically, there is more to the software production process. Two additional aspects must be considered in particular:

- Describing the resultant software product forces us to describe the software architecture.
- The transformation process that translates the Conceptual Schema into a Software Product must be described.

The process of translating a conceptual schema into an application is called *Conceptual Modelling Compilation*. In fact, the development of conceptual schemas comprises the representation of the real world using an abstraction level higher than that of source code. Likewise, source code is a representation at a higher abstraction level that that for machine code, which is obtained through a conventional compilation process. It seems logical, therefore, to refer to the process of transforming a conceptual schema into a software product using the term "compilation". Furthermore, the model compiler is more powerful than a conventional source code compiler from the conceptual point of view, since it significantly raises the level of abstraction.

We can take this argument further; conventional source code programs remove all the details pertaining to the hardware platform on which the generated machine code will run. The compiler bridges this gap by taking into account the character-istics of the hardware platform, such as register usage or memory organizations. Similarly, a model compilation process operates on a conceptual schema, removing all the details about the software platform on which the application will run, such as execution control mechanisms, in-memory representation of data or data access strategies. The outcome is a program expressed in some conventional programming language that will address the specific requirements for the software platform.

In addition, and as we have already introduced, the architecture of the target software platform must be taken into account. By software architecture, we mean the collection of software components that constitute the final product, as well as the rules that regulate their interrelationships.

There are some widely known software architectures, such as three-tier archi-tectures in which different tiers address user interface, application logic and data ac-cess concerns, and intercommunicate through middleware services. In client/server architectures, on the other hand, client-side software components manage the inter-action between the user and the system and handle the necessary communications with server-side components, which implement the main application logic.

Since OO-Method conceptual schemas are totally independent of the details of the software platform, the same conceptual schema can be compiled targeting different software platforms.

Example.   *The Conceptual Schema of our rent-a-car system can be executed in a Microsoft Windows environment as a C# application that interacts with a Microsoft SQL Server database; or in a Linux environment as a Java application that interacts with an Oracle database server.*

In this way, different compilations of the same conceptual schema can produce different applications that target different software platforms. In any case, and re-gardless of the selected target software architecture, the transformation process is based on a single pattern: the technology-specific software representation of a collection of common conceptual primitives. Characterizing the Model Com-piler therefore means determining the mappings between conceptual primitives and software representations in a precise manner, and using the chosen software architecture as a parameter of the transformation.

The fact that a technological consensus exists with regard to how tiers or layers must be organized in a software product makes the task easier, since the potential variability of the software architecture domain is significantly reduced. It is true that every single technology available on the marketplace may propose a unique and different software architecture but, at a certain abstraction level, organizing an application in logical layers always makes sense. In fact, the traditional con-cept of monolithic application has been displaced in favour of the more flexible client/server, three-tier or, more generally, n-tier architectures.

This makes building a model compiler an easier task, since the problem is naturally partitioned and its complexity reduced; it is not necessary to generate a complete application from a conceptual schema but, rather, a collection of logical layers that, once conveniently connected, compose the final application. In this way, the model compilation process can be approached in different stages, each considering a subset of the model and generating a single logic layer.

Example.   *For a three-tier architecture, a staged approach to model compilation can be followed, in which different strategies are used to obtain the different tiers (persistence, business logic and presentation). This can be synchronized with a conceptual modelling strategy that, as is the case for OO-Method, enables us to model the structural, functional, dynamic and presentation aspects of the system separately. In this way, the correspondence between conceptual views (problem space) and architectural tiers (solution space) is direct.*

This staged compilation process means that the final software product is obtained as the union of the outcomes from applying three different sub-compilations on a single conceptual schema.

Example.   *Let us imagine that the rent-a-car system is to be compiled as a web-based, three-tier application that uses Oracle as a database, J2EE for the business logic and JSP for the user interface. This can be obtained by applying three different sub-compilations to the same conceptual model: the first one would generate an Oracle database, the second would create the J2EE application, and the third would generate a collection of JSP pages. These results, once conveniently assembled, would constitute the final rent-a-car software product.*

This approach also means that model compilers that generate different software architectures can be implemented. When a conceptual model is to be compiled, the optimal architecture (and compiler) can be chosen depending on non-functional application requirements, such as performance, latency or data persistence.

Example.   *The model compilers used in the previous example are appropriate for a system that is accessed by users through the Internet and by administrators through an intranet. Using a presentation tier compiler that generates a Java user interface would not be appropriate in this context, however, because this would clash with the need of user Internet access.*

We devote the last section of this introduction to the issue of whether the model compilation process must be automated. It is fundamental in OO-Method that the semantics of both conceptual model elements and their software representations are precisely defined. Automating this process results in highly convenient advantages, improving the software production process in a way that can be termed as revolutionary, compared to the usual software production mechanisms.

We must note, however, that the compilation of a conceptual model can also be done by hand, since the problem space specification expressed by the conceptual schema contains all the necessary information. The fact that the manner in which each conceptual primitive must be represented as software is precisely known makes this process certainly approachable by a programmer. Moreover, different programmers who implement a same conceptual model would construct different applications that are functionally equivalent, regardless of the selected technologies in each case.

Why are these observations relevant? We believe that using automatic tools, such as model compilers, to generate source code poses significant advantages over manual approaches; however, even without these tools, the general approach to software development described in this book provides a methodological framework that can be applied to real-world cases, with immediate benefits in terms of final product quality and productivity.

Still, the main interest of the approach is precisely the possibility of using tools that, firstly, help developers to create, maintain and validate models and, secondly, enable them to transform these models into a software product automatically by following some predefined transformation rules that are described in this chapter.

No matter what approach is taken, manual or automatic, to model compilation, some requirements must be taken into account and some guidelines need to be determined so that correct and complete compilations can be performed. This is our focus from this point on.

14

Requirements for the Compilation of Conceptual Models

The transformation process that translates a conceptual schema into a software product must be a systematic one. To achieve this goal, the conceptual modelling method proposed by OO-Method, as well as the associated Model Compiler, must address the following issues:

- The manner in which a conceptual schema can be represented as software in any development environment must be determined, considering static, dynamic and presentation concerns. This will enable us to establish a strategy for the transformation of conceptual model elements into an application architecture.
- As a direct consequence of the previous point, the architectural styles of the resulting applications must be determined, since this will dictate the types of different components that the compilation process needs to generate, as well as the relationships between these.
- An execution strategy that guarantees the functional equivalence between a specification and its implementation must be established.

Therefore, the model compilation process can be characterized by considering three aspects, which are dealt with in the following sections:

- Application execution strategy.
- Application architecture.
- Transformation strategy.

The *application execution strategy* characterizes the execution semantics of the different modelling elements, determining how they behave and interrelate at run-time. It can be seen as an Abstract Execution Model that determines how a Conceptual Schema is executed. To achieve this, it must describe the steps that compose the abstract execution of the program that represents a given conceptual schema.

The appropriate specification of this execution strategy is a key to guarantee the functional equivalence between the generated application and the conceptual schema, that is, to ensure that the functionality of the final product is a coherent representation of the functionality expressed by the conceptual schema.

The *application architecture* determines how the generated code is organized into components and component interrelationships. This architecture must reconcile the requirements dictated by the execution strategy and those imposed by the chosen software platform.

The *transformation strategy* establishes how an application that follows a given architectural style can be obtained from an initial conceptual model. This strategy must determine the mappings between conceptual modelling primitives and the appropriate software representations. These mappings, in turn, will guide the transformation process implemented by the Model Compiler. Consequently, the precise characterization of these transformation rules is essential to bridge the semantic gap that exists between Problem Space and Solution Space, and constitutes a crucial aspect for the automation of the entire process.

As we advanced before, the following chapters deal with each of these three issues. Chapter 15 describes the execution strategy for applications obtained from OO-Method Conceptual Schemas. Chapter 16 describes application architectures. Chapter 17 focuses on the definition of transformation strategies. Chapter 18 builds on the previous ones to establish the guidelines to follow when developing a model compiler. Chapter 19 analyses the current state of the art, examining alternative proposals and discussing why none of these fulfil the objective of providing a Model Compiler capable of generating functional applications from conceptual schemas. In addition, we will explain how OO-Method solves some issues that are found in other proposals. Chapter 20 explains the relationships between OO-Method and MDA (MDA 2006), the initiative from the Object Management Group (OMG http://www.omg.org) that attempts to establish a standard framework for this kind of approach, constituting an excellent referent for any discussion on Model Engineering as one of the most promising areas in Software Engineering in the near future. Chapter 21 presents an overview of the development process associated to OO-Method, describing the different roles and tools involved. Finally, Chapter 22 introduces an implementation of the OO-Method methodology that has been used successfully in an industrial context.

15

Application Execution Strategy

The first major aspect to take into account when implementing a conceptual model compilation process is the manner in which the generated applications will use the modelling primitives in the conceptual model. In other words, we need to determine how the final product, seen as a projection of the Problem Space specification, will work in the Solution Space. The strategy proposed by OO-Method is defined in terms of the modelling elements, rather than the software platforms on which applications can run. This *Abstract Execution Model* describes how users will access the system, which options will be available once a session has been started, what sequence of actions must be performed in order to execute a service, and so on.

The advantages of this approach are three. Firstly, the same strategy can be used regardless of the specific platform of any particular compilation process. Secondly, the semantics of modelling elements are augmented, extending the *what* (described in the previous chapter) with the *how*, i.e. how each modelling element is projected onto the chosen implementation technology. Thirdly, the approach ensures the functional equivalence between the input conceptual schemas and the corresponding output software representations.

This is, therefore, the first requirement to observe, and the one that we develop now. OO-Method's application execution strategy describes how to realise three different aspects that every application must implement:

- *System access*
- *System view*
- *System interaction* (i.e. activation and execution of services and/or queries)

By system access, we mean the manner in which users "connect" and start a session for the application. OO-Method's conceptual schema determines who the users are: those belonging to at least one agent class defined in the conceptual schema through the corresponding view[1]. This aspect of the application controls user access, taking into account identity and authentication issues.

---

[1] Let us recall that a view, in the conceptual model, is a collection of agent relationships seen as interfaces between an agent class and a server class; each of these interfaces indicates which attributes and services of the server class can be "seen" by the agent class.

The system view is the collection of possible interaction scenarios that are offered to the user. Each interaction scenario refers to the activation of a service or the execution of a query. Scenarios are obtained from the intersection of the information defined by the action hierarchy tree in the presentation model and the information contained in the view for which the action hierarchy tree has been defined, which determines what actions are available to users of a given agent class.

System interaction refers to the sequences of steps that characterize the behaviour of the system for each specific scenario in an abstract fashion, that is, without any reference to any particular implementation technologies.

These three aspects are described in detail in the following sections.

15.1 System Access

System access includes the basic security issues that determine who can start a session for the application, and which actions each user can perform once "connected". This section focuses on authenticating the user, and the next one describes authorisation, i.e. how the system guarantees that an interactive user has access to the appropriate actions only.

It is important to recall that agent classes have been defined in the conceptual model, and that model validation rules enforce that at least one agent class exists. Agent relationships are organized in views. The users who can start a session for the application are those who are represented by an agent class included in a view.

Example.   *The rent-a-car system contains two agent classes, Administrator and Client, the interfaces (i.e. agent relationships) of which have been included in a view.*

When a conceptual schema is compiled, the resulting application must incorporate a mechanism to grant access to the appropriate users, depending on the contents of the view. The requirement at this level expresses that the access mechanism must exist but does not dictate any particular implementation choice.

Example.   *When our system is implemented, an authentication system that requests a user name and a password from the user will be provided in order to authenticate administrators. An alternative implementation would be to leverage Microsoft Windows's security services and request only a password.*

The fact that an OO-Method conceptual model can be seen as an "interacting object society" in which agents are also objects does not restrict the possible implementation options for this mechanism. Although the most common alternatives with current-day technologies involve requesting a user name plus password pair, other alternatives such as thumbprint recognition or retinal scan are also possible.

15.2 System View

Once the system has granted access to a user, the scenarios that must be available have to be determined. The action hierarchy tree defines the logical organization of all the interaction scenarios; for any particular user, these must be restricted to only those over which the agent class that represents the user has visibility. Since the information describing which services and queries must be available for each agent class are specified in the Conceptual Schema, a customized view of the application can be produced for each agent class from the information contained in the Action Hierarchy Tree.

Consequently, the application that results from the compilation of a conceptual schema must provide the appropriate mechanisms to configure the set of available interaction scenarios, depending on the type of user authenticated, hiding the scenarios or scenario elements that must be non-available, and constraining the available options depending on the applicable permissions. Like in the previous section, the requirement is that these mechanisms must be provided but no specific implementation strategy is stated. Implementations will be determined, as we explain later, when the transformation strategy is chosen.

Example. *A compilation strategy that transforms the action hierarchy tree into a window with a menu can disable the menu items that correspond to options not available for the current user. A different compilation strategy would hide the menu items, rather than disabling them. More advanced compilation strategies would not rely on a window with a menu but on alternative interaction features such as virtual reality or speech recognition.*

In any case, and regardless of the chosen implementation, each agent class must have a precise representation of which scenarios are available and which are not; the required information is provided by the conceptual schema.

15.3 System Interaction

Once the user has been authenticated and the available scenarios (and scenario elements) have been determined, the manner in which the system must react to user actions needs to be established.

This can be approached by initially considering which are the valid kinds of interaction. OO-Method contemplates the following:

- Service execution (which modifies system state).
  - Class events, transactions and operations.
  - Legacy view events, transactions and operations.
  - Global transactions and operations.
- Query execution (which reads system state).
  - Class filters.
  - Legacy view filters.

The specific ways in which access is provided for service and query execution are characterized by the corresponding Interaction Units, which organize how access is achieved and provide the necessary context information.

The following Interaction Units are available:

- Interaction units (associated to service or query execution).
  - Service.
  - Instance.
  - Population.
  - Master/detail.

In summary, the canonical interaction scenarios are those that represent the execution of a service or a query, and the manner in which they can be conveniently organized is given by the corresponding Interaction Units, which provide structure and presentation-oriented information.

Each of these elements is described in detail in the following sections.

15.3.1 Service Execution

We will start by describing event execution, since events are the basic (atomic) execution units. Then, we will describe local transactions and operations, which are composite (molecular) execution units, at the class level. We will do the same for legacy views and, finally, we will describe the execution of global transactions and operations.

The following sections focus on the functional aspects of services. Presentation aspects are dealt with when the corresponding Interaction Units are discussed. In implementation terms, this will facilitate the generation of the system functionality-oriented and the system interaction-oriented software components.

Execution of Events

The execution of an event on a class is structured in two phases: the *construction of the message* and the proper *execution of the event*.

In the message construction phase, the server object (i.e. the object that the event will be executed on) must be first identified. This object will be referenced by the first service argument for any class-level event. Logically, if the event is a creation event, then no server object is identified, since the object is going to be created and does not exist yet.

Example.   *In the rent-a-car system, whenever a "Retire" event of class "Vehicle" is to be executed, the specific vehicle to be retired must be first identified.*

The second step in the message construction phase is giving values to the remaining event arguments, for which the software system must provide a mechanism. This mechanism is highly dependent on the specific interaction style determined by the Presentation Model, which we will describe later.

In the event execution phase, the following steps take place:

1. The existence of the server object is verified.
2. The state transition caused by the event is determined.
3. Event preconditions are checked.

4. Event evaluations are executed.
5. The integrity constraints of the modified object are checked.
6. Object modifications are made effective.
7. Trigger conditions on the modified object are checked, and the appropriate services are executed.
8. Execution result is reported.

These steps configure an abstract execution model that can be applied to any event of an OO-Method class. The execution model is said to be abstract because it describes what is to be done, leaving the specific implementation mechanisms to the underlying software technologies.

Each of the above-listed steps is now described in detail.

Verifying the *existence of the server object* is necessary before an event can be executed on it, unless this is a creation event, as we have said before. The system must include a mechanism to make this verification.

According to the state transition diagram of the class of the server object, a transition must exist from the current state of the server object into another state labelled with an action that involves the service that is about to be executed. The destination state of this transition becomes the final state that the object will assume once the event finishes executing. The system must provide a mechanism to find this state and to abort event execution at this point if it cannot be found.

Each *precondition* that exists for the event, and for which the user is an agent, must be satisfied. The system must perform these checks and abort event execution at this point if any of these are not met, in which case it reports on the precondition that failed.

For each *evaluation* of the event, two tasks must be performed:

1. Its evaluation condition, if any, must be checked.
2. The evaluation effect, if appropriate, must be applied to modify the associated attribute.

The software system must check the evaluation conditions and assign values to the appropriate attributes, depending on the specified effects. Evidently, creation and destruction events do not involve evaluations, since evaluations imply a change of state for an existing object.

In the case of creation events, the system must assign values to the object's attributes, using:

- The values of event arguments for those attributes marked to be required on creation. This can be seen as an implicit evaluation that assigns the appropriate argument value to each required attribute.
- The default values for those attributes that are not required on creation and for those attributes that are required but for which no values have been provided.

In addition, and for creation events, the appropriate links to other objects must be established according to the constraints imposed by the relevant association cardinalities. This can even imply the creation of additional objects, for example, when the minimum cardinality of a relevant relationship is 1 and the object to be linked does not exist.

In the case of destruction events, the system deletes links to other objects (deleting the objects if necessary) according to the cardinalities of the relevant relationships. A mechanism must be provided by the system to delete the server object.

In the case of association insertion events, the system must provide the mechanism to establish the appropriate link between the server object and the related object according to the dynamic relationship associated to the insertion event. As usual, cardinality restrictions must be enforced.

Similarly, in the case of association deletion events, the system must provide a mechanism to delete the link between the server and the related objects, again according to the associated dynamic relationship.

Once all the evaluations have been performed, *integrity constraints* must be checked in order to guarantee the integrity of the server object or, in the case of shared event, objects. The system must abort event execution at this point if any of the applicable integrity constraints are not satisfied. In this case, the modifications made to the server object so far must be undone.

Not every integrity constraint needs to be checked every time that an event is executed. Checking only those constraints that involve attributes that have been possibly modified by the event is sufficient. This kind of simplification can result in performance improvements.

Once integrity constraints have been checked, modifications to the server object must be *made effective*. The system must provide the necessary mechanisms to achieve this.

Once the modifications have been persisted, the server object is now in its final state, and any applicable *trigger condition* must be checked. The system must provide a mechanism to check these conditions and, in the appropriate cases, determine the object population on which the associated service is to be executed. Once the collection of services to trigger has been determined, these services must be called for the appropriate object populations, initializing service arguments in accordance with the specification of each trigger. Synchronous and asynchronous implementation strategies are possible.

If a synchronous strategy is used, then the execution of the event does not finish until all the triggered services finish successfully. If, on the contrary, an asynchronous strategy is chosen, then the execution of the event can be considered finished once the triggered services have been invoked. In any case, using a confluence synchronisation point before considering the event finished is considered to be a meaningful practice.

Finally, the software system must give some feedback about the *result of the execution* of the event, describing the context and type of any errors if the event is not completed successfully. Appropriate usability guidelines must be considered at this point.

Execution of Local Transactions

A local transaction, as a molecular execution unit, involves a collection of services that can be either events or transactions themselves; these, ultimately, are composed of events. The main issue with transactions is characterizing the correct execution of a collection of events that satisfies the two *transactional* conditions of "all or nothing" execution and non-observability of intermediate states.

As in the case of events, the execution of a transaction has two phases: message construction and transaction execution.

Also as in the previous case, message construction involves determining first the server object, i.e. the object on which the transaction is to be executed. If the transaction is a creation transaction, then no object must be identified.

The next step of message construction involves assigning values to the transaction arguments, which is accomplished through a mechanism that the software system must provide. The details of this process are described later in the context of Service Interaction Units.

Transaction execution is done by following these steps:

1. The existence of the server object is verified.
2. The state transition caused by the transaction is determined.
3. Transaction preconditions are checked.
4. For each service in the transaction:
   - The guard, if specified, is checked.
   - The target object population is determined.
   - For each object in the target population:
   - Arguments are initialized.
   - The service is executed.
5. The integrity constraints of the modified objects are checked.
6. Object modifications are made effective.
7. Trigger conditions on the modified objects are checked, and the appropriate services are executed.
8. Execution result is reported.

The major difference between event executions and transaction executions is that, in the latter case, integrity constraints and trigger conditions must be checked only after all the services in the transaction have been executed. Likewise, the effective modification of the objects is done at the end, once all the services have been successfully executed. The details are explained below.

Verifying the *existence of the server object*, unless this is a creation transaction, is necessary before a transaction can be executed on it, as in the case of events. The system must include a mechanism to make this verification.

According to the state transition diagram of the class of the server object, a transition must exist from the current state of the server object into another state labelled with an action that involves the transaction that is about to be executed. The destination state of this transition becomes the final state that the object will assume once the transaction finishes executing. The system must provide a mechanism to find this state and to abort transaction execution at this point if it cannot be found.

Each *precondition* that exists on the transaction, and for which the user is an agent, must be satisfied. The system must perform these checks and abort transaction execution at this point if any of these are not met, in which case it reports on the precondition that failed.

Since the transaction is a molecular execution unit, it is composed of services, which we call here transaction *components*. *For each component* in the transaction:

1. If a *guard* has been specified, then it must be checked. The software system must provide the appropriate mechanisms to do this and to cancel the execution of this component if the guard condition is not satisfied.
2. The *target objects population* is then determined, according to the part of the transaction formula that corresponds to this component.
3. For each target object, *arguments are initialized* and the *service is executed*. The software system must provide the necessary mechanisms to implement argument initialization as dictated by the transaction formula, and to execute the service. Note that determining the target object population and initializing the arguments constitute the first step of the execution of any service, namely the construction of the message.
   The system must provide the necessary mechanisms to check the result of the execution of each individual component service in the transaction, and to abort this if execution fails, rolling back any changes so far.
   In those cases where the transaction component is an event (rather than another transaction), its execution implies only the validation of the corresponding state transition, checking the preconditions and execution of evaluations. Integrity constraints and trigger conditions are addressed only at the end of the whole transaction, since this is the moment when integrity of all the objects involved must be verified.

So, once all the transaction components have been successfully executed, *integrity constraints* must be checked in order to guarantee the integrity of the server object and other objects modified by the transaction. The system must abort event execution at this point if any of the applicable integrity constraints are not satisfied. In this case, the modifications made so far to the server object and other affected objects must be undone.

Once integrity constraints have been checked, modifications to the server object and other objects affected by the transaction must be *made effective*. The system must provide the necessary mechanisms to achieve this.

Once the modifications have been persisted, the server object and other objects are now in their final states, and any applicable *trigger conditions* must be checked. The system must provide a mechanism to check these conditions and, in the appropriate cases, determine the object population on which the associated service is to be executed. Once the collection of services to trigger has been determined, these services must be called for the appropriate object populations, initializing service arguments in accordance with the specification of each trigger. All the comments made in the previous section about synchronous vs. asynchronous execution and confluence synchronization are valid also for transactions.

Finally, the software system must give some feedback about the *result of the execution* of the transaction, describing the context and type of any errors if the transaction is not completed successfully.

Execution of Local Operations

Local Operations differ from Local Transactions in their non-transactional behaviour. This explains the differences that will appear in their model execution description. As in the previous case, the execution of an operation has two phases: message construction and operation execution.

Message construction involves, first of all, determining the server object, i.e. the object on which the operation is to be executed. If the operation is a creation operation, then no object must be identified.

The next step of message construction involves assigning values to the operation arguments, which is accomplished through a mechanism that the software system must provide. The details of this process are described later in the context of Service Interaction Units.

Operation execution is done by following these steps:

- The existence of the server object is verified.
- Operation preconditions are checked.
- For each service in the operation:
  - The guard, if specified, is checked.
  - The target object population is determined.
  - For each object in the target population:
    - o   Arguments are initialized.
    - o   The service is executed.
- Trigger conditions on the modified objects are checked, and the appropriate services are executed.
- Execution result is reported.

Verifying the *existence of the server object*, as usual, and unless this is a creation operation, is necessary before an operation can be executed on it. The system must include a mechanism to make this verification.

Each *precondition* that exists on the operation, and for which the user is an agent, must be satisfied. The system must perform these checks and abort operation execution at this point if any of these are not met, in which case it reports on the precondition that failed.

Like transactions, operations are molecular execution units that are composed of component services. *For each component* in the operation:

1. If a *guard* has been specified, then it must be checked. The software system must provide the appropriate mechanisms to do this and to cancel the execution of this component if the guard condition is not satisfied.
2. The *target objects population* is then determined, according to the part of the operation formula that corresponds to this component.

3. For each target object, *arguments are initialized* and the *service is executed*. The software system must provide the necessary mechanisms to implement argument initialization as dictated by the operation formula, and to execute the service. Note that determining the target object population and initializing the arguments constitute the first step of the execution of any service, namely the construction of the message.

According to the abstract execution model associated to events, each of the events that ultimately compose the operation must check the integrity constraints, make changes effective and check trigger conditions. This is an important distinction with respect to the behaviour of local transactions. As operations can fail at any moment without generating a rollback, integrity constraints are checked after every correct execution of operation events.

Once the collection of *services to trigger* has been determined, these services must be called for the appropriate object populations, initializing service arguments in accordance with the server object in each case, and the corresponding trigger specification.

Finally, the software system must give some feedback about the *result of the execution* of the operation, describing the context and type of any errors if the operation is not completed successfully.

Execution of Events on Legacy Views

We have explained how the concept of legacy views allows us to incorporate legacy systems as part of the modelling process in OO-Method. Now, it is necessary to describe how legacy views are characterized in terms of the abstract execution model. We approach this following the same structure as that used for regular classes, addressing the execution of events, transactions and operations on legacy views.

The execution of an event on a legacy view (which corresponds to a service already implemented by the legacy system) is structured in two phases: the construction of the message and the proper execution of the event.

In the message construction phase, the server object (i.e. the object that the event will be executed on) must be first identified. If the event is a creation event, then no server object is identified, since the object is going to be created and does not exist yet.

The next step in the message construction phase is giving values to event arguments, for which the software system must provide a mechanism. This mechanism is highly dependent on the specific interaction style determined by the Presentation Model, which we will describe later.

Up to this point, the process is similar to that described for the execution of events on regular classes. The execution of the event on the legacy view, however, requires a different approach, which is based on the following steps:

1. The existence of the server object is verified.
2. Event preconditions are checked.

3. The legacy event is executed.
4. Trigger conditions on the modified object are checked, and the appropriate services are executed.
5. Execution result is reported.

It must be noted that evaluation execution and integrity constraint checking are not performed, since a legacy event involves calling an existing service implemented by the legacy system with fixed functionality. This is consistent with the description of legacy events given elsewhere.

The remaining steps have their usual meaning. Verifying the *existence of the server object* is necessary before an event can be executed on it, unless this is a creation event, as we have said before. The system must include a mechanism to make this verification.

Each *precondition* that exists on the event, and for which the user is an agent, must be satisfied. The system must perform these checks and abort event execution at this point if any of these are not met, in which case it reports on the precondition that failed.

The software system must also provide the mechanism to *invoke the legacy service* that implements the event, including locating the component that implements the service, initializing the necessary arguments and performing the call, doing, if necessary, the appropriate processing and formatting[2] tasks.

Example.   *Let us imagine that the legacy system exposes an interface based on web services. In this case, the system must be able to obtain the necessary information from the WSDL contract of the appropriate web service, construct the corresponding XML request with the input data and extract the output data from the XML response.*

Once the legacy service has been executed, the server object is now in its final state, and any applicable *trigger condition* must be checked. The system must provide a mechanism to check these conditions and, in the appropriate cases, determine the object population on which the associated service is to be executed. Once the collection of services to trigger has been determined, these services must be called for the appropriate object populations, initializing service arguments in accordance with the specification of each trigger.

Finally, the software system must give some feedback about the *result of the execution* of the event, describing the context and type of any errors if the event is not completed successfully.

Execution of Local Transactions on Legacy Views

As with local transactions on classes, the execution of transactions on legacy views has two phases: message construction and transaction execution.

---

[2] Processing and formatting tasks are usually necessary to pass information between heterogeneous systems. They typically include data type and representation format conversions, although they can also require the usage of specific communication protocols.

Message construction involves determining, first of all, the server object, i.e. the object on which the transaction is to be executed. If the transaction is a creation transaction, then no object must be identified.

The next step of message construction involves assigning values to the transaction arguments, which is accomplished through a mechanism that the software system must provide. The details of this process are described later in the context of Service Interaction Units.

Up to this point, the execution of transactions on legacy views is identical to the execution of transactions of regular classes. The differences can be found in the steps that are to be performed to execute the transaction:

1. The existence of the server object is verified.
2. Transaction preconditions are checked.
3. For each service in the transaction:
   a. The guard, if specified, is checked.
   b. The target object population is determined.
   c. For each object in the target population:
      i.   Arguments are initialized.
      ii. The service is executed.
4. Trigger conditions on the modified objects are checked, and the appropriate services are executed.
5. Execution result is reported.

Compared with regular classes, the first difference is that state transitions are not considered because no State Transition Diagram exists for legacy views. Similarly, modifications do not need to be made effective, and integrity constraints are not checked, since this is implemented by the underlying legacy system.

The remaining steps have their usual semantics. Verifying the *existence of the server object*, unless this is a creation transaction, is necessary before a transaction can be executed on it, as in the case of events. The system must include a mechanism to make this verification.

Each *precondition* that exists on the transaction, and for which the user is an agent, must be satisfied. The system must perform these checks and abort transaction execution at this point if any of these are not met, in which case it reports on the precondition that failed.

For each component in the transaction:

1. If a *guard* has been specified, then it must be checked. The software system must provide the appropriate mechanisms to do this and to cancel the execution of this component if the guard condition is not satisfied.
2. The *target object population* is then determined, according to the part of the transaction formula that corresponds to this component.
3. For each target object, *arguments are initialized* and the *service is executed*. The software system must provide the necessary mechanisms to implement argument initialization as dictated by the transaction formula, and to execute the service. Note that determining the target object population and initializing

the arguments constitute the first step of the execution of any service, namely the construction of the message.

4. The software system must also provide the mechanism to *invoke the legacy service* that implements the event. The system must also provide the necessary mechanisms to check the result of the execution of each individual component service in the transaction, and abort this if execution fails, rolling back any changes so far.

Once the modifications have been persisted, the server object and other objects are now in their final states, and any applicable *trigger conditions* must be checked. The system must provide a mechanism to check these conditions and, in the appropriate cases, determine the object population on which the associated service is to be executed. Once the collection of services to trigger has been determined, these services must be called for the appropriate object populations, initializing service arguments in accordance with the specification of each trigger.

Finally, the software system must give some feedback about the *result of the execution* of the transaction, describing the context and type of any errors if the transaction is not completed successfully.

Execution of Local Operations on Legacy Views

Given the semantics of the concept of operation, the execution of operations on legacy views is exactly the same as that for regular classes. This is so because operations are not included in the State Transition Diagram, and also because their non-transactional nature makes final integrity checks meaningless: these checks are done one by one as each operation component is executed.

In fact, the steps to follow in order to execute an operation on a legacy view are:

1. The existence of the server object is verified.
2. Operation preconditions are checked.
3. For each service in the operation:
   a. The guard, if specified, is checked.
   b. The target object population is determined.
   c. For each object in the target population:
      i.   Arguments are initialized.
      ii. The service is executed.
4. Trigger conditions on the modified objects are checked, and the appropriate services are executed.
5. Execution result is reported.

These are the same steps as those described in the context of regular classes, and everything said then also applies here.

Logically, executing a service in this case means invoking the appropriate legacy service exposed by the legacy system whereas, for regular classes, it involves performing a regular service execution. The overall pattern, however, is identical.

Execution of Global Transactions

Global transactions allow us to define "multi-class" services, making possible that a single transaction groups together services that belong to different classes. As with any other service, their execution involves two phases: message construction and transaction execution.

Message construction uniquely needs that the arguments be appropriately initialized, for which the software system needs to provide a mechanism. Since a global transaction is not associated to any particular class, no concept of server object exists. From a formal point of view, we can consider the server object as implicit, corresponding to an instance of the parallel composition of all the classes involved in the specification of the global transaction. From a more general point of view, we can also consider an implicit server object as an instance of the parallel composition of all the classes in the system.

The steps to follow to execute a global transaction are these:

1. Transaction preconditions are checked.
2. For each service in the transaction:
   a. The guard, if specified, is checked.
   b. The target object population is determined.
   c. For each object in the target population:
      i.   Arguments are initialized.
      ii. The service is executed.
3. Trigger conditions on the modified objects are checked, and the appropriate services are executed.
4. Execution result is reported.

Each *precondition* that exists on the global transaction, and for which the user is an agent, must be satisfied. The system must perform these checks and abort transaction execution at this point if any of these are not met, in which case it reports on the precondition that failed.

For each component in the global transaction:

1. If a *guard* has been specified, then it must be checked. The software system must provide the appropriate mechanisms to do this and to cancel the execution of this component if the guard condition is not satisfied.
2. The *target objects population* is then determined, according to the part of the global transaction formula that corresponds to this component.
3. For each target object, *arguments are initialized* and the *service is executed*. The software system must provide the necessary mechanisms to implement argument initialization as dictated by the transaction formula, and to execute the service. Note that determining the target object population and initializing the arguments constitute the first step of the execution of any service, namely the construction of the message.
   – The execution of the service is done according to the specification given for each type of service in OO-Method.

- The system must provide the necessary mechanisms to check the result of the execution of each individual component service in the transaction, and abort this if execution fails, rolling back any changes so far.

Each of the services that compose the global transaction must check integrity constraints, make modifications effective and check trigger conditions. Once all the component services have finished executing, *triggered services must be called* for the appropriate object populations, initializing service arguments in accordance with the specification of each trigger.

Finally, the software system must give some feedback about the *result of the execution* of the global transaction, describing the context and type of any errors if the global transaction is not completed successfully.

Execution of Global Operations

Global operations are different from global transactions only because they are non-transactional. A global operation is identical to a global transaction except for this characteristic and, consequently, its abstract execution behaviour has no significant differences. The flux of the abstract execution is the following:

1. Operation preconditions are checked.
2. For each service in the operation:
   a. The guard, if specified, is checked.
   b. The target object population is determined.
   c. For each object in the target population:
      i. Arguments are initialized.
      ii. The service is executed.
3. Trigger conditions on the modified objects are checked, and the appropriate services are executed.
4. Execution result is reported.

These are the same steps as those described for global transactions. The only difference lies in that, being operations non-transactional, no control mechanisms are necessary after each component service is executed. In the case of global operations, and unlike the case of global transactions, the global operation must not be aborted if the execution of a component service fails.

Now that the abstract execution model for service execution has been described, we focus on the description of another relevant type of interaction: query execution.

15.3.2 Query Execution

The execution of queries is carried out in the context of filters and their association to Population Interaction Units. A filter that is established on an object population provides a mechanism to retrieve only the information that is necessary, as expressed by the filter conditions. This section explains how the abstract execution model affects filters and query execution.

Execution of Filters on Classes

Executing a filter on a class has two phases: constructing the message and executing the query derived from the filter.

Message construction involves assigning values to three kinds of arguments:

- Filter variables.
- Order criterion.
- Display set.

Filter variables, strictly speaking, are the arguments of the filter. However, and since filters are executed in the context of population interaction units, which involve display sets and order criteria, these are considered filter arguments as long as message construction is concerned. The software system must provide the appropriate mechanisms to assign values to filter variables and specify the order criterion and display set to be used.

Executing the query derived from the filter involves obtaining those objects of the class on which the population interaction unit has been defined, sorting them using the order criterion and retrieving, for each object, the values of the properties indicated by the display set.

The mechanism provided by the system to execute queries must be able to work with query specifications that are dynamically given by the filter formula and the values of the associated variables.

Finally, the system must also provide the necessary mechanisms to display the results of the query.

Execution of Filters on Legacy Views

Executing a filter on a legacy view, as in the previous case, has two phases: constructing the message and executing the query derived from the filter.

Message construction involves assigning values to three kinds of arguments:

- Filter variables.
- Order criterion.
- Display set.

Filter variables, as in the case of regular classes, are the arguments of the filter. However, and since filters are executed in the context of population interaction units, which involve display sets and order criteria, these are considered filter arguments as long as message construction is concerned. The software system must provide the appropriate mechanisms to assign values to filter variables and to specify the order criterion and display set to be used.

The difference between executing filters on legacy views as opposed to classes is related to the execution of the derived queries. There are two cases to be considered:

- The filter exists in the legacy system.
- The filter does not exist in the legacy system.

If the filter exists in the legacy system, then the generated system must provide the appropriate mechanisms to invoke the necessary services so that the legacy system executes the filter.

If, on the contrary, the filter does not exist in the legacy system, the generated system must provide the necessary mechanisms to retrieve the complete population of the corresponding class, and then apply the necessary restrictions as given by the filter formula, sort the results and select the properties as specified by the display set.

Finally, the system must also provide the necessary mechanisms to display the results of the query.

15.3.3 Interaction Units

Interaction Units are the fundamental elements that the user perceives when the system is in operation; therefore, their appropriate characterization is key to complete the abstract execution strategy that we are describing.

Service Interaction Units

Service interaction units can be seen as collections of mechanisms that help the user to assemble a message to execute a service. These mechanisms perform the following actions:

- Identify the interaction unit by its alias.
- Display the associated help message.
- Identify each service argument by its alias.
- Display service arguments arranged in the appropriate order and groups as specified by the argument grouping basic element.
- Allow the user to give values to service arguments.
- Validate that user-specified argument values are appropriate, according to:
  - the associated data type,
  - the associated entry basic element (entry mask, valid value range).
- Display default values for service arguments.
- Access the object selection mechanisms given by population interaction units associated to object-valued service arguments.
- Display the help messages associated to each service argument.
- Enforce the dependency rules defined for each service argument, by:
  - checking for the occurrence of the *SetValue* and *SetActive* events,
  - checking the associated condition,
  - executing the necessary actions to assign values or activate/deactivate other service arguments.
- Display the complementary information given by the elements in the visualisation sets associated to object-valued service arguments whenever the values change.
- Cancel service execution interaction.
- Assemble the message that causes service execution.

Instance Interaction Units

Instance interaction units can be seen as collections of mechanisms that collaborate to display information about an object, enable the user to navigate to related information and execute applicable services. These mechanisms perform the following actions:

- Identify the interaction unit by its alias.
- Display the associated help message.
- Display the value of each element defined by the display set, in the appropriate order.
- Hide the elements in the display set for which the user does not have visibility.
- Provide access to the interaction units determined by each element in the actions basic element, identifying them by the appropriate alias, and hiding those for which the user does not have visibility.
- Display the help message associated to each element in the actions basic element.
- Provide access to the interaction units determined by each element in the navigation basic element, identifying them by the appropriate alias, and hiding those for which the user does not have visibility.
- Display the help message associated to each element in the navigation basic element.
- Cancel the interaction.

Population Interaction Units

Population interaction units can be seen as collections of mechanisms that collaborate to display information about a collection of objects obtained through some kind of selection process and sorted by the appropriate order criterion, enabling the user to select individual objects and navigate to their detail interaction units, which correspond to instance interaction units or service interaction units, already described. The mechanisms in population interaction units perform the following actions:

- Identify the interaction unit by its alias.
- Display the associated help message.
- Obtain the object collection:
  - by selecting one of the filters in the interaction unit and one of the order criteria;
  - by providing the necessary mechanisms to:
    - o identify each filter variable by its alias,
    - o display each filter variable in the appropriate order,
    - o allow the user to supply a value for each filter variable,
    - o validate filter variable user-supplied values according to:
      - ▪ the variable's data type,
      - ▪ the associated entry basic element (entry mask, valid value range);
    - o display the default value of each filter variable,

- o   access the object selection mechanisms given by population interaction units associated to object-valued filter variables,
- o   display the help message associated to each filter variable,
- o   display the complementary information given by the elements in the display sets associated to object-valued filter variables whenever the values change.
- Display the values of the properties specified by the display set for each object in the query result collection, identifying these by the corresponding alias and sorting them as dictated by the display set.
- Hide the elements for which the user has no visibility.
- Allow the user to select one object from within the collection. Two options exist, depending on the purpose:
  - if a query on the object is to be performed, then an instance interaction unit must be displayed;
  - if a service is to be executed, then a service interaction unit must be shown, and the select object's identifier passed as the corresponding service's object-valued argument.
- Provide access to the interaction units determined by each element in the actions basic element, identifying them by the appropriate alias, and hiding those for which the user does not have visibility.
- Display the help message associated to each element in the actions basic element.
- Provide access to the interaction units determined by each element in the navigation basic element, identifying them by the appropriate alias, and hiding those for which the user does not have visibility.
- Display the help message associated to each element in the navigation basic element.
- Cancel the interaction.

Master/Detail Interaction Units

Master/detail interaction units can be seen as mechanisms that collaborate to display a collection of objects that acts as master plus an object or collection of objects that act as detail. These mechanisms perform the following actions:

- Identify the interaction unit by its alias.
- Display the associated help message.
- Display the master interaction unit.
- Display the different detail interaction units.
- Synchronise the information displayed as detail:
  - when the objects in the master interaction unit are modified,
  - when an object in the master interaction unit is selected.
- Cancel the interaction.

The mechanisms by which the master and detail interaction units are displayed are those already described, and depend on the specific type of interaction unit in each case.

Application Architecture

The specification of an abstract execution strategy, as we have done above, is the first requirement for model compilation. This strategy determines a common base on which model compilation can be developed, and helps guarantee the functional equivalence of the generated software system with regard to the conceptual schema.

The mechanisms given by the execution strategy are abstract because they specify what any application must implement, avoiding any implementation issues. An essential aspect is to determine which is going to be the adequate software architecture that will represent how the conceptual schema will be properly projected on the solution space.

We focus now on the second requirement, namely the architecture of the generated applications.

Firstly, it is evident that the architecture of an application must provide the appropriate mechanisms to represent every element in the conceptual schema, such as classes, attributes, relationships, derivations and so on.

Secondly, an application's architecture specifies how each mechanism defined by the abstract execution mechanism is implemented. These mechanisms must interact at run-time according to the abstract execution strategy, in order to guarantee the functional equivalence between the application and the conceptual schema.

Finally, auxiliary common mechanisms such as error handling, communication protocols and data access, which do not depend on the conceptual schema, must also be provided.

In summary, the mechanisms provided by the architecture of an application include:

- the correct representation of the elements in the Conceptual Model.
- the adequacy for the Application Execution Strategy.
- the normalization of the Application Basic Elements.

The specific implementation of each of these mechanisms depends on factors such as the choice of programming language and programming model. The choice of programming language can make the implementation of specific mechanisms easier or harder.

The fact that OO-Method's approach is object-oriented (OO) does not impose any restriction on the programming language; non-OO languages can be used, although certain mechanisms will be harder to implement.

The choice of programming model can also impose limitations or determine requirements that make the implementation of certain mechanisms easier or harder.

Example. *The J2EE programming model and the EJB specification impose that certain methods such as* ejbCreate, ejbActivate, ejbPassivate *and* ejbRemove *be implemented.*

The application architecture is defined by reconciling the requirements expressed by the conceptual model and the application execution strategy with those imposed by the programming language and model of choice.

This is perfectly applicable even in those cases where the model compilation process to be used generates a single logic layer of the application, as opposed to the whole application. The elements in the conceptual model and the execution strategy, however, would be restricted to a particular subset.

Example. *In order to define the architecture of the persistence layer of an application (such as a relational database), the set of elements in the conceptual model to be contemplated would be restricted to classes, attributes and relationships. The resulting architecture would include mechanisms such as tables, columns, primary keys, foreign keys and indexes.*

Example. *In order to define the architecture of the presentation layer of an application (such as a JSP application), the set of elements in the conceptual model to be contemplated would be restricted mostly to those in the presentation model. The resulting architecture could include mechanisms such as pages, forms, hyperlinks and buttons.*

The definition of an application architecture is the first differential stage in the definition of a conceptual model compilation process; from this point on, the specification diverges whereas, up to this point, the specification is generic and common to any possible compilation process.

In other words, the conceptual model compilation model is parameterized by the chosen software architecture. Once this is fixed, a specific process is given to project conceptual schemas (residing in the problem space) onto software representations adjusted to the architecture selected (in the solution space).

The selection of the software architecture is a critical step that strongly influences the quality of the resulting applications, since factors such as performance, productivity, robustness and fault tolerance are heavily dependent on it.

Not all these factors must be taken into account to define every architecture: depending on the application's usage context, for example, the required performance and latency values may change. This kind of requirements must be well known to successfully select an application architecture.

A well-defined application architecture will allow us to apply the model compilation process to different models systematically, thereby obtaining different applications that will share common characteristics and quality profiles.

If what is considered tolerable in terms of performance, latency or any other quality factor changes during the life of an application, the architecture definition can be revised and the system re-compiled, without the need to change the conceptual model.

The set of elements and properties that compose the application's architecture, together with the relationships among these, is called the *Application Model*.

17

Transformation Strategy

A conceptual model and an application model have been defined up to this point. The missing piece to complete the specification of the model compilation process is a transformation strategy that enables us to obtain the latter from the former.

The transformation strategy is based on the definition of two kinds of elements:

- *Mappings*, which determine relationships between elements in the Conceptual Model and elements in the Application Model.
- *Transformations*, which determine how the application is obtained from each element in the Application Model.

17.1 Mappings

Mappings establish relationships between elements in the Conceptual Model and elements in the Application Model. Their objective is to characterize how elements in the latter can be created from elements in the former.

The application architecture implicitly determines most mappings, since a mechanism must be implemented in the architecture for each element in the conceptual model. This determines a relationship between model elements and is, therefore, a mapping.

Example. *A mapping can be created that relates a class in the conceptual model to a Java class, and an attribute in the conceptual model to a member variable in the Java class.*

The remaining mappings are given by the requirements imposed by the programming language and model. Finding these mappings is not as immediate as in the previous case, and examining architecture elements that already have mappings can make the task easier.

Mappings are not a bijective function of the Conceptual Model to the Application Model, since a single element in the Conceptual Model can be mapped to multiple elements in the Application Model. In practice, this reflects the fact that conceptual primitives admit different implementations, all of them potentially valid.

Example.   *An attribute in the conceptual model can be mapped to:*

- *A private member variable of a Java class.*
- *A public method of the Java class that returns the value of the private member variable.*
- *A public method of the Java class that modifies the value of the private member variable.*

An important objective for the model compiler is to select the best alternative among the available ones. The selection will depend on the specific characteristics of the programming environment being used. This "fine tuning" work is basic for a model compiler, to assure not only that a final software product can be obtained from a Conceptual Schema but also that the product is satisfactory in terms of software quality criteria.

The reverse situation is also possible, viz. that a single element in the Application Model has mappings from multiple elements in the Conceptual Model.

Example.   *An event of a class in the conceptual model can be mapped to a method in a Java class, and a transaction of a class in the conceptual model can also be mapped to a method in a Java class.*

The concept of mapping can be enriched by adding conditions, so that a mapping would be effective only when the associated condition is satisfied. These mappings are called conditional mappings, and the associated conditions can be expressed in terms of elements in the Conceptual Model and elements in the architecture.

Example.   *Since the value of a derived attribute is computed (via the specified derivations) from the values of other attributes, we can opt for not mapping them to columns in a relational table. To capture this, the mapping that exists between "Attribute" (an element in the Conceptual Model) and "Column" (an element in the Application Model) is qualified with a condition over the type of attribute, and will be effective only when the attribute type is not "derived".*

The concept of mapping goes beyond the mere relationship between elements in the models; it must be capable of assigning values to the properties of Application Model elements by examining the values of the properties of the corresponding Conceptual Model elements.

Example.   *A mapping between a class in the conceptual model and a Java class in the application model assigns the value of the "Name" property of the conceptual model class to the property "Name" of the Java class.*

In this way, the concept of mapping enables us to create an instance of the Application Model from an instance of the Conceptual Model.

17.2 Transformations

In order to complete the specification of the conceptual model compilation process, an additional element must be defined: transformations.

Once the Conceptual Model, the Application Model, and the mappings between both are in place, it is possible to generate the latter model from the former by using the mappings. What remains to be done is to generate the application's source code from the elements in the application model.

To do this, each element in the application model must contain enough information so as to be translatable into source code.

Example.   *Let us assume that a class in the conceptual model is mapped to a Java class in the application model. If the Java class does not contain a "Name" property, then it will be impossible to generate code like this:*

public class ClassName
{

   ...

}

since "ClassName" cannot be substituted by anything.

This can be used to reveal deficiencies in the Application Model, which can be solved by adding the required properties and adjusting the necessary mappings. Each transformation must be able to obtain all the information necessary to generate the required source code from the Application Model.

A transformation can be seen as a function that has a chunk of source code as output and a collection of variables as input. These variables are the values of the properties of the associated application model element. The outcome of applying the function is a source code fragment that represents that application model element.

Transformations must be fully defined; in other words, they must be able to generate code for any possible combination of values in the associated model element. As stated before, if this is not the case, then the transformation must be adjusted, possibly requiring also adjustments to related elements.

Each application model element must have exactly one associated transformation. Changing the transformation associated to a model element means changing the conceptual model compilation process.

The specification of transformations completes the definition of the conceptual model compilation process. Multiple iterations may be necessary to fully define this, each one acting on the application model (modifying its elements and their properties) and the transformation strategy (modifying mappings and transformations). Once a conceptual model compilation process has been successfully defined, it can be repeatedly applied to different conceptual schemas to obtain fully fledged applications that are functionally equivalent to the corresponding conceptual schemas.

As a last point, it is worth mentioning that a balance must be struck between the application architecture and the associated transformations. The more detailed the architecture (more elements and properties), the simpler the transformations, but more mappings are needed. Less detailed architectures require fewer mappings but transformations are more complex. The perfect balance does not exist; in case of doubt, increasing the level of detail in the architecture is preferable, since the resulting software product would be closer to the original conceptual schema. Complex and long-winded transformations tend to produce higher numbers of defects associated to the transformation process.

18

Building a Conceptual Model Compiler

We have so far introduced the fundamental principles that support a precise conceptual model compilation process, which can be systematically applied by a team of people.

Having done this, a question immediately appears: can the process be automated? According to this book, it can, although a complete explanation of such a complex task would need another book. Basically, the core of the process is composed of two different steps. First, the mappings between conceptual elements and software elements must be specified and implemented. Second, the transformation that will generate the final application from the software model must be implemented.

We will avoid getting into the detailed explanation of how mappings and transformations must be implemented; however, we give here some advice on some basic aspects that must be taken into account for the development of a conceptual model compiler. There are four different major areas that need attention:

- The conceptual model repository
- The application model repository
- The specification and implementation of mappings
- The specification and implementation of transformations

First of all, a *Conceptual Model Repository* is necessary to store the model compiler input information. By repository, we do not necessarily mean a database; an XML file or XMI- or MOF-based tool can be perfectly adequate. In any case, the chosen representation of conceptual schemas must conform to some standard mechanism that can facilitate model interchange and interoperability between different work environments. The minimum requirements of this repository include the coherent storage of the information and the availability of the necessary mechanisms to access it.

Similarly, an *Application Model Repository* is also necessary. Application Models represent software architectures that are potentially valid as target development environments. This kind of repository stores the software components of the architecture, as well as the valid relationships that can occur between these to compose a product that is compatible with the chosen architectural style.

The same considerations as those we made for the Conceptual Schema Repository can be applied here. A database is not strictly necessary, although this is desirable, as long as the information is stored in a coherent and accessible way and the appropriate creation, modification and usage mechanisms are available. If the conceptual model compiler is to be implemented, for example, in Java, then the Application Model Repository can be seen as a collection of Java classes that expose an API composed of creation and query services.

Moreover, *mappings must be specified and implemented*. Let us recall that mappings are the rules that allow us to create elements in the Application Model by examining the elements in the Conceptual Model. The precise specification and correct implementation of this activity is crucial for the development of a model compiler.

Once an application model is given, the specification of a collection of mappings must determine precisely which software components are linked to each conceptual primitive. The particular manner in which this is made constitutes the essential information that the model compiler will use. Several options exist to approach this, from the informal description of mappings to the semi-formal algorithmic description, and even a formal specification based on graph transformation languages. Whichever option is chosen, the collection of mapping specifications becomes an essential component for the correct construction of a model compiler.

The implemented mappings read the information stored in the Conceptual Schema Repository and create information elements in the Application Model Repository. Each individual mapping can be seen in this context as the implementation of an algorithm that reads one or more elements in the Conceptual Schema Repository and, if the associated conditions are satisfied, creates an element in the Application Model Repository, assigning values to each of its properties.

Finally, *transformations must be specified and implemented*. This phase performs the "fine tuning" that generates the final software product. Taking as input the Application Model created by the mappings, each individual element in this model is used to generate source code. The particular characteristics of the chosen development environment, as well as the specific properties of the programming language of choice, are taken into account to ensure that the resulting product is technologically appropriate. As we stated in the previous section, more detailed application architectures tend to require simpler transformations.

The specification of transformations must guarantee that perfect documentation is obtained. Its implementation can be approached from different perspectives, using programming language functions and procedures or templates and template engines.

Once these four essential components are combined, a conceptual model compiler is obtained, which can automate the application of the previously described conceptual model compilation process.

19

Issues with Other Approaches

The generation of applications from conceptual models is not a new idea. In the last few years, numerous proposals and technologies have appeared, with mixed degrees of success. Most of these have conveyed the false impression that the source code of a complete application can be magically generated with a simple click. The term "code generation" has been abused in the context of CASE tools, fostering unsupported expectations and damaging the few rigorous attempts to demonstrate that the implementation of model compilers is possible and that the generation of correct and complete software products from conceptual models can be accomplished within today's Software Engineering state of the art.

None of the proposals of the last few years have achieved the goal of systematically producing complete applications from conceptual models, making of the conceptual model the "new program" and raising abstraction to levels higher than traditional programming. This section discusses some of the possible causes of such a failure and explains how OO-Method addresses these issues.

Firstly, a modelling language capable of capturing the necessary information is essential in order to create applications from models; therefore, we discuss some issues with existing modelling languages.

Secondly, model compilation is also a crucial part in the automatic generation of applications from models, and so we also describe some of the issues that appear when addressing model compilation.

19.1 Issues with Modelling Languages

19.1.1 Lack of Adequacy

The first and foremost problem that can appear associated to a modelling language is its lack of adequacy for the specific application domain that is to be modelled. If this happens, then obtaining a complete application from a partial model becomes impossible. The model may be valid during the earlier stages of development but, as iteration proceeds and the specification is fleshed out, the model loses value and the source code becomes the most valuable asset in the process.

As development progresses, the modelling language reveals certain character-istics of the application that are unable to be represented, and that can be described only by using source code, so that the model is abandoned and the development process focuses on the source code.

The lack of expressive adequacy of modelling languages appears fundamentally in two areas: the functional and presentation aspects of the application.

Functional aspects are inadequately addressed by most current modelling lan-guages. Frequently, it is possible to specify the service interface of a class but spec-ifying the inner workings of each service is not possible. Development tools based on languages such as these usually choose one of two possible options:

- Integrate service implementation in the model.
- Synchronise model and code.

None of these solutions are valid because they cannot avoid making the definition of the problem dependent on its implementation, which violates basic conceptual modelling principles. If service implementation is integrated as part of the model, then:

- source code (at a lower level of abstraction) is being mixed in with model-level information,
- the model is rendered possible to compile for a given architecture and program-ming language only (the one used to implement the integrated services),
- model validation is hampered (or even made impossible), since two different languages (specification and implementation) are being mixed, and
- the thorough understanding of the model requires knowledge of the two lan-guages.

If, on the contrary, the model and code are synchronized, then:

- the model is kept free from implementation details but is still linked to a specific implementation,
- synchronisation does not solve the validation problem; for example, changing the interface of a service may cause the appearance of a defect in the associated implementation, which will be noticed only when the source code is compiled, and
- the understanding of the model requires knowledge of only one language but a thorough comprehension of the complete problem cannot be attained, since many details are absent from the model and present only in the source code.

OO-Method addresses this issue by enabling engineers to fully specify the func-tional aspects of the application through:

- Evaluations in the Functional Model, which indicate how attribute values are modified as a response to events.
- Transaction or Operation formulae, which indicate how events are composed in order to create more complex services.

The consequence of this is that full service implementation can be automatically obtained through a rigorous transformation process from the declarative specification of the functionality. Service implementation, therefore, is a direct outcome of the specification given by the model. In addition, the synchronization between model and code is guaranteed by the compilation process that generates the source code from the model.

Presentation aspects are often neglected by modelling languages. Interaction with an application is not limited to its service interface but is much more complex and often organized in different scenarios that exhibit different characteristics. These aspects cannot be represented in an abstract manner using conventional modelling languages, although some abstract user-interface specification proposals exist. Often, the Human–Computer Interaction (HCI) community (rather than the software engineering community) is the source of these proposals, which makes them hard to relate to existing conceptual modelling approaches.

In this context, it is remarkable to realise that, even if the design and the implementation of User Interfaces (UIs) are recognized to be the most time-consuming step of any software production process, its modelling has rarely been considered at the same level of data and function modelling when specifying a system. As we have stated, a whole community emerged to face that problem: the HCI.

To face and solve this dichotomy, one challenging goal in the context of both Software Engineering (SE) and HCI is to provide proper bridges between their best-known software production methods and techniques. Starting from the idea that SE is considered to be strong in specifying data and functional requirements, while HCI is centred on defining user interaction at the appropriate level of abstraction, a sound software production process must provide ways for precisely specifying data, functionality and interaction, all together. If any of these aspects are not properly faced, then the whole software production process will fail, because the reality to be modelled is a mixture of data, functionality and interaction. Consequently, software production methods that combine the most data-oriented and functionally oriented, conventional requirements specification with the more interaction-oriented, UI modelling aspects are strongly required.

In this context, Model-Transformation technologies (i.e. MDA approaches) make it possible – as it is our intention to show in this book – to provide a global software process where all the relevant aspects of the analysed problem (structure, behaviour and user interaction) are specified. These resulting system views are initially projected onto a Conceptual Schema and subsequently onto the final software product. Based on the use of a Model-Transformation approach, it is necessary to provide the basis to build such a software production process, with two basic principles in mind:

1. Model Transformation is used as the basic software production paradigm, to automate the conversion of a source Requirements Model into its corresponding Conceptual Model, and then converting this conceptual model into the System Design and Implementation. A Model Compiler should be responsible for implementing the corresponding mappings.

2. Each modelling step provides appropriate methods to deal adequately with the specification of structural, functional and interaction properties. To do this, the conceptual primitives (conceptual constructs) that constitute the basic build-

ing blocks of the required models must be properly identified. The definition of Conceptual Patterns constitutes an appropriate strategy to define these conceptual primitives in detail.

This is precisely the goal behind the OO-Method proposal. OO-Method enables engineers to fully specify abstract interaction scenarios using the Presentation Model, which complements the information captured by the Object, Dynamic and Functional models. In fact, the Presentation Model is part of the global Conceptual Model. In this way, OO-Method provides an integrated approach that unifies experiences and research outcomes of the two aforementioned communities.

19.1.2 Imprecise Semantics

Another important issue is that of imprecise semantics usually associated to modelling languages. Most existing object-oriented modelling languages share only a small set of common elements with precise semantics, such as class, attribute and relationship.

Elements with precise semantics are usually limited to the static (data-oriented) view of the application, probably because data modelling methods have been studied and developed for quite a long time. Even in this area, however, it is not uncommon that ambiguities appear for elements seemingly as simple as associations, aggregations and specialisations. If we move out of the static realm and into the dynamic aspect of modelling, the situation worsens, and semantics cease being precise, the interpretation of model elements being highly variable from one developer to another.

OO-Method defines the semantics of each modelling element in a precise manner, avoiding ambiguities and contradictory interpretations from the very beginning. The fact that modelling elements are given by a formal specification language (OASIS; Pastor1992; Pastor and Ramos 1995) implies that their syntax and semantics are precisely determined.

19.1.3 Strong Versus Weak Formalisms

Some specification languages are based on solid formalisms, whereas other are based on weak formalisms or no formalism at all.

The former tend to be unpopular because of the complexity that is often associated to their formal character, and the consequent scarce commercial availability.

The latter are more popular and usually supported by available tools. This is especially true of graphical languages such as UML, which are supported by many modelling tools.

Using UML as a notational standard (i.e. in a syntactic context) is an important improvement, since this eliminates the need to invent new notations for well-known modelling elements.

When the semantics of model elements are taken into account, however, the imprecise semantics problem described in the previous section appears. Since no formal infrastructure exists that can characterize model elements unambiguously, defect-laden models can be constructed. For example, many tools that fully support UML do not perform type checking.

OO-Method addresses this problem by combining the advantages of formal methods and popular notations such as UML. The graphical notation used by OO-Method to depict conceptual primitives is the UML notation, using UML-provided extension mechanisms where necessary. From a semantic point of view, however, every model element is precisely defined by the underpinning formal specification, OASIS, on top of which a simple graphical and textual notation is used to hide its complexities.

19.1.4 Low Abstraction Level

Some specification languages (or language variants) elude the two first problems described above but introduce a new one: an abstraction level that is too low. This is the case for UML profiles such as the UML profile for EJB.

These specification languages represent the problem at a level of abstraction that is too low: in fact, they do not represent the problem as a collection of classes, attributes, services and relationships but rather as a solution to the problem that is composed of entity beans, session beans and Java classes.

The abstraction level of such a model is so low that it practically coincides with that of the source code. Transforming models of this kind into source code is usually straightforward, since no change of abstraction level is involved.

The development of an application using this approach requires almost as much effort as for its direct coding, and the contribution of the model compilation process is not significant.

In addition, most of the effort is devoted to the specification of a solution for a given low-level language and architecture, rather than the specification of the problem. As a consequence, porting the model to a different language or architecture becomes very difficult – if not impossible.

Once again, source code becomes the most valuable asset in the development process, relegating models to a second plane. Although sometimes it is presented differently, the truth is that the low abstraction level used makes the model become too close to the source code, both residing in the Solution Space and leaving the Problem Space out of all consideration.

This creates the additional problem that the knowledge embedded in the model can be understood only by someone who has experience with the specific programming language and architecture for which the profile has been defined.

The abstraction level of an OO-Method conceptual model is well above that of source code. OO-Method models are platform-independent, marking a clear distinction between the Problem Space model and the Solution Space source code. The conceptual models used in the Problem Space are those included in the Conceptual Schema, and their translation into software elements is the explicit step that the model compiler performs to exit the Problem Space and enter the Solution Space.

19.1.5 Action Semantics

This section deals with an issue that has already been introduced in previous sections: the lack of an appropriate mechanism to specify the functional aspects of a conceptual schema. Many proposals in this context are deficient in this respect.

Some modelling languages (or language variants) do offer mechanisms to specify functional aspects or, as they are sometimes called, action semantics. Some examples of such action semantics are those proposed by UML 2.0 (UML 2004), the *Action Specification Language* (Raistrick et al. 2004), Kennedy Carter's *xUML* (Kennedy Carter 2006), Kabira Technologies' *Kabira Action Semantics* (Kabira 2006) and Nucleus BridgePoint's *BridgePoint Action Language* (Mentor 2006). These initiatives are either at an early adoption stage or being effectively applied to the development of real-time embedded systems, a field where code generation techniques have been working for some time. From the point of view introduced in this book, they cannot be considered Conceptual Model Compilers that bring all the conventional programming complexity to the context of conceptual modelling. To have the final software program, different degrees of manual programming are always required and, too often, this manual low-level programming effort is as costly as usual.

UML's action semantics provide a collection of actions as fundamental units for the specification of behaviour. These actions permit tasks such as the creation and destruction of objects, the assignment of values to class properties, and the creation and destruction of links between objects. No standard notation exists to represent these actions, and some approaches such as those mentioned above have suggested different solutions. In addition, the semantics of these actions are not always precisely defined. Finally, these actions are applied to modelling elements for which semantics are not well defined either. In addition, the issue of weak semantics becomes more prominent for more complex behaviour modelling elements such as UML activities.

OO-Method's formula language, combined with its Functional Model and the definition of transactions and operations, provides a solution to this problem, permitting:

- data access according to the Object Model
- the definition of sequential logic
- the manipulation of classes and objects
- the manipulation of relationships
- the usage of arithmetic operators
- the usage of logical operators
- the usage of collection operators

Also, OO-Method's formula language is abstract and implementation independent, and is defined by a grammar that supports lexical, syntactic and semantic validations. All this makes it possible for OO-Method to behave as a true Model Compiler, where all the expressiveness provided by the Conceptual Schema constitutes the high-level program. The conceptual model (in the problem space) becomes the program (in the solution space), rather than the program being the model. This conceptual model is adequately converted into the associated set of software components through the corresponding conceptual modelling process.

19.1.6 Formulae

Some modelling languages try to avoid issues related to the imprecise or incomplete semantics of their modelling elements by associating formulae to model elements. This is the case for the Object Constraint Language (OCL) in the context of UML, for example.

Solutions of this kind introduce new problems. The kinds of modelling elements to which formulae can be associated are not always evident, and the semantics of a modelling element with a formula associated are not clearly stated. Sometimes, formulae are used for purposes other than those for which the formula language has been designed (such as using OCL to specify action semantics).

OO-Method clearly defines:

- which modelling elements can have associated formulae,
- what the semantics of an element with a formula are,
- what types of formulae there are, and which types can be used where.

19.1.7 Overspecification and Redundancy

A less serious but frequent issue with specification languages is that of overspecification and redundant specifications.

Overspecification and redundancy are not problems in themselves, as long as they do not extend beyond certain limits. A well-known example is SQL: this is a highly redundant language, because the same conceptual query admits several representations, with different performances. Nevertheless, it is a widely used, successful standard language in its context (databases). Overspecification and redundancy are harmful, however, when they have no use for the model compilation process. They also introduce important problems in terms of conceptual precision and clarity of the specification.

Example. *Most of the commercial tools that generate code from UML models use class diagrams as single source of information. UML defines 14 different types of diagrams. If a UML tool supports all of these, then what is the purpose of the time invested in creating diagrams for the remaining 13 types, if the code that is automatically obtained is derived from class diagrams only?*

This problem is particularly patent when certain types of information appear redundantly in multiple diagrams.

In OO-Method, each modelling element has a conceptual meaning in the formal infrastructure as well as an associated software representation in the chosen architecture. No conceptual primitive is superfluous, and no software component can exist that is not derived from a conceptual primitive.

In other words, every modelling element in OO-Method's views (Object, Dynamic, Functional and Presentation models) is necessary for the complete specification of an application domain, and consequently has an associated software representation in the resulting software product. Every single element in an OO-Method model is compiled and translated into source code, and all the effort spent in modelling has an effect on the final product, making models, rather than source code, the central assets in the development process.

19.2 Issues with Model Compilation

The proposed conceptual modelling framework is based on a specification language, which provides the necessary conceptual primitives. This language plays a central role in the development of applications but, no matter how good this language is, if the accompanying model compilation process is poor, then we have a problem.

The usage of modelling techniques that enable us to construct conceptual models based on this specification language is a convenient approach but must be supported by the ability to compile these models by systematically using a well-defined model compilation process. Most problems found in the context of model compilation are related to some or all of the requirements described in this section.

19.2.1 Lack of an Application Execution Strategy

The specification of an application execution strategy is a key first step in the definition of a model compilation process because it completes the execution semantics of models. Without an application execution, the functional equivalence between applications and models cannot be guaranteed.

This problem becomes more prominent when the specification language has imprecise semantics or, even worse, lacks action semantics. Model compilers based on languages with these deficiencies cannot generate logic for the complete application, especially if these compilers do not use a clear application execution strategy. In the best case, these tools can assist in the programming tasks by contributing some amount of source code, but large parts of the code must still be manually written using traditional methods. It is this characteristic that differentiates clearly between most CASE tools (capable of generating some source code) and a real model compiler.

A model compiler makes the conceptual model become the real program (at a higher level of abstraction than that of traditional programs), since the final software product is the outcome of model compilation, and conventional programming tasks have been eradicated.

As we explained elsewhere in this chapter, OO-Method incorporates an application execution strategy based on a platform-independent abstract execution model, which determines how an OO-Method conceptual model is to be executed. It characterizes the execution semantics of models, and guarantees the functional equivalence between applications and the models from which they are generated. This is a basic requirement of any model compiler.

19.2.2 Issues with Application Architectures

Incomplete or imprecisely defined application architecture cannot be used to compile a complete application from a model. If the software architecture is imprecise, then the compilation process will also be imprecise and will not be applicable in a systematic fashion. If the software architecture is incomplete, then the compilation process can be applied systematically but will produce only those parts of the application that are covered by the architecture.

This problem does not appear (or is less prominent) if the models to be compiled are expressed in a language that is very close to the source code, since these models implicitly define the application architecture. In this case, however, and as we have explained before, a real model compilation process does not exist.

OO-Method emphasizes that the complete and precise specification of software architectures is a basic requirement for a correct model compilation process. In fact, the link between the Problem Space (conceptual schema) and the Solution Space (resulting software product) characterizes the translation of each conceptual primitive into the corresponding software components according to the selected software architecture.

19.2.3 Insufficient Transformations

The third kind of issue that often appears associated to model compilation processes is that of insufficient transformations. This leads to two types of situations:

- no code is generated for some model elements,
- code for model elements is only partially generated.

The first case reveals that only a part of the model (that from which code is generated) is actually useful in the application development process.

Example.   *Most UML tools generate code only from the class diagrams. This covers the static aspects of the application but the declarative specification of dynamical aspects is omitted.*

The second case reveals that the model does not contain enough information to generate the complete source code (i.e. it is not computationally complete), or that the semantics of model elements are not perfectly defined.

In either case, the model compilation process is unable to generate the totality of the application's source code and, consequently, this is not a true model compilation process.

As we advanced in the previous section, the model compilation process proposed by OO-Method generates, by definition, source code for every element in the model, since this is computationally complete and the semantics of its elements are perfectly defined.

19.3 State of the Art

Given the issues presented so far, the current situation is that no alternative proposal fulfils the promise of obtaining complete applications from a model, guaranteeing functional equivalence between model and application.

Multiple manifestations of this can be easily observed in current technologies, including models that incorporate source code, model–code synchronization and reverse engineering.

Currently available tools provide a very low degree of automation; many of these can generate code, but how much code? What percentage of the final application code is automatically generated? An electronic survey carried out by the digital edition of the Application Development Trends magazine asked the question "How much code do you generate from tools?" (ADT 2006). Results were significant: at the time of writing, over 74% of the respondents stated that automatically generated code amounts to less than 20% of the total code in the final application. Only 7% of the respondents claimed to generate more than 80% of the code.

This shows that equating code generation and model compilation is misleading; code generation is a programming support technique that assumes that programming is still an essential task in every software production process. A model compiler introduces a fundamental shift: the conceptual model is automatically translated into the program and, consequently, it is assumed that modelling, rather than programming, is the essential task in the software production process. It is also assumed that models, rather than programs, become the main software development artefact.

Our conclusion is that the paradigm shift promised by MDA (viz. that models, and not code, are the key artefacts in software development) is not being fully addressed by any existing tool.

Analogies Between OO-Method and MDA

This section focuses on the relationships between OO-Method and MDA (Model-Driven Architecture), the best known initiative in the emergent area of Model Engineering.

The ultimate goal of MDA, promoted by the Object Management Group (OMG http://www.omg.org), is the separation of the application logic from the platform on which it is intended to execute. This separation permits decreasing the impact that technology evolution imposes on application development, by allowing the same specification to be reified on multiple software platforms. Besides, the knowledge and intellectual property usually associated to an application is moved out of the realm of the source code and into that of the specification.

MDA makes models the authentic protagonists of application development, at the expense of source code. Models are the most valuable assets because source code can be automatically obtained from them by applying some transformations.

The types of models and transformations involved in MDA are:

- a Platform-Independent Model (PIM), which describes the application without any implementation details.
- a Platform-Specific Model (PSM), which refines the aforementioned by including implementation details.
- an Implementation Model (or Code Model), i.e. source code, obtained from the previous model.

20.1 OO-Method and MDA

After having described OO-Method in this book, it is easy to verify that OO-Method incorporates the essential characteristics of MDA from its inception. This section analyses this relationship, to enforce the main argumentation of the book: OO-Method puts into practice the MDA proposal, providing a concrete, conceptual modelling-based software production process where model transformation is the key aspect to produce software of quality.

The first phase in OO-Method focuses on the construction of a Conceptual Model, which can be identified with an MDA Platform-Independent Model, since it describes the necessary aspects of the application independently of the platform on which it will be implemented and executed.

The second phase in OO-Method comprises the automatic translation of a Conceptual Model into the application's source code. This phase involves creating an Application Model, which can be seen as a Platform-Specific Model in MDA. Also, a collection of mappings is defined between elements in the Conceptual Model and elements in the Application Model; these mappings are formally equivalent to the PIM-to-PSM transformations in MDA. Finally, OO-Method associates a transformation to each element in the Application Model, so that the corresponding source code can be obtained; the collection of transformations is equivalent to the PSM-to-Code Model transformation in MDA.

Table 20.1 summarizes the analogies between MDA and OO-Method.

Table 20.1 Analogies between MDA and OO-Method.

MDA	OO-Method
Platform-Independent Model (PIM)	Conceptual Model
Platform-Specific Model (PSM)	Application Model
Implementation Model (IM)	Application Code
PIM-to-PSM transformation	Mappings
PSM-to-IM transformation	Transformations

20.2 Properties of OO-Method Absent from MDA

Some properties of OO-Method that we consider key for the implementation of a model compilation process cannot be related to MDA. The OMG (http://www.omg. org) acknowledges that, in some situations, a PIM can contain all the information necessary to generate an implementation and, consequently, no additional refinement or profile usage is required in order to generate the code. In relation to this, OO-Method provides a more precise solution, because the OASIS specification language that underpins OO-Method models is computationally complete. In other words, an OO-Method conceptual model (analogous to a PIM) always contains all the information that is necessary to generate the source code.

Also, and according to the OMG, a PSM is not necessary, and no information whatsoever is to be added to the PIM, in those cases for which the PIM contains all the necessary information. In these cases, engineers use tools that can interpret the PIM and translate it into code directly. OO-Method needs that an Application Model (analogous to a PSM) be defined. If an OO-Method compliant model compilation tool can be used, then the Application Model does not need to be explicitly known.

An approach where source code can be obtained directly from a PIM is valid as far as MDA is concerned. In OO-Method, however, we argue that an intermediate

PSM is always necessary to provide the characteristics of the chosen platform. This is so because OO-Method conceptual models (PIMs) are truly platform independent and, consequently, can be reified on any possible platform. The fact that MDA allows approaches in which PIMs can be directly translated into code reveals that MDA PIMs often contain enough detail to permit direct code generation. This is an implicit acknowledgment that either PIMs are not truly platform independent or that they are not computationally complete but can be translated into (incomplete) code directly.

Finally, the OMG claims that a development environment with these characteristics enables engineers to simply develop PIMs that can be directly translated into code. This is precisely one of the key aspects of OO-Method's approach: the application is obtained automatically from the conceptual model once this is manually constructed. OO-Method makes this possible in traditional scenarios based on component reuse, but also in those scenarios where 100% of the application code is generated from so-called scratch.

In other words, OO-Method conceptual models are computationally complete, and final applications can be obtained from them without the need of pre-existing components (such as source code libraries or controls) that would implement that functionality that cannot be obtained automatically from a conceptual model.

The OO-Method Development Process

OO-Method does not change the traditional software development phases, although it significantly modifies the meaning of analysis, design and coding. This section focuses on the description of this process, from the perspective of a non-automated environment in which analysis, design and coding are performed manually. Then, we explain how the adoption of a model compilation process introduces substantial improvements by permitting the automation of the design and coding phases. The overall outcomes include a spectacular reduction of development time and a large increment in the quality of the resulting product. The major roles involved in the software development process are also discussed.

During the *analysis* phase, modellers (we prefer the term "modeller", rather than "analyst") build a conceptual schema of the system being developed. Modellers need to know the desired functionality of the future system but do not need to concern themselves with *how* the functionality will be implemented. They focus on *what* the system is, rather than on *how* it is implemented.

During the *design* phase, the application model (i.e. the application software architecture) is defined, as well as the mappings between conceptual model elements and application model elements. In order to do this, knowledge of two areas is necessary:

- the semantics of the execution model elements and the application execution strategy,
- the software platform on which the system is to be implemented, plus service quality aspects.

These tasks are jointly performed by individuals with expertise in both areas. It is exceptional that a single set of individuals has all the required expertise.

During the *implementation* phase, transformations are defined for each element in the application model. This must be done by people with experience in the chosen software platform.

Figure 21.1 summarizes how OO-Method affects the overall application development process.

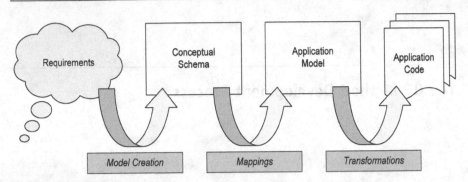

Fig. 21.1 Effects of OO-Method on the development process.

The roles that appear in an OO-Method development process include:

- Modellers, who create the Conceptual Schema of the application and know the semantics of the conceptual modelling elements,
- OO-Method experts, who provide knowledge about the semantics of Conceptual Schemas and the Application Execution Strategy targeted to the construction of the Application Model, guaranteeing the functional equivalence between specification and implementation,
- Software Platform experts, who contribute their expertise on the chosen software platform, and
- Programmers, who develop the transformations that will translate each element of the application model into code.

As have said earlier, the design and coding phases correspond to the definition and application of a conceptual model compilation process. If the same process can be used for the development of multiple systems, then it would suffice to define it once to then apply it repeatedly. The implementation of such a model compilation process in the form of a collection of model compilers (targeting different software architectures) dramatically improves the productivity of development teams. This is possible because the definition of the model compilation process is done independently of any particular conceptual model; it is done considering only the conceptual primitives that can be used to specify any system. Figure 21.2 shows the different roles and development phases in the OO-Method process.

The same model compiler (or collection of model compilers) can be used repeatedly during the successive iterations in the development lifecycle of an application. Each iteration incorporates new or changed requirements that are translated into changes of the conceptual model; also, changes to the model are possible deriving from observed malfunction of the compiled system. Defects found in the source code must be fixed by changing the model from which the code has been obtained.

It is also possible that the same compiler or compiler set be used for the development of multiple applications, which logically would share a large number of design, architecture and programming language characteristics.

If we assume the availability of conceptual model compilers that can generate the complete source code of the application, then the most prominent role in the software development process is that of the modeller, because the design and implementation phases are almost fully automated and performed by the model compiler once a conceptual model has been created.

Since model compilers target specific Application Models and collections of transformations, situations may appear in which the source code obtained is not perfectly adjusted to the service quality requirements of a particular application. In these cases, two options are available:

- The model compilation process can be redefined and the model compiler re-implemented.
- The source code generated by the model compiler can be manually tweaked.

The first option involves the roles of OO-Method expert, Software Platform expert and programmer. This is the most appropriate choice from a methodological point of view, although it can be the most costly to carry out and the least profitable if a single system is being developed. This option usually involves the modification of the transformations associated to the elements in the Application Model, or even changing the Application Model itself, in which case both transformations and mappings would be modified.

In any case, this is the correct option from a theoretical perspective, because any defect in the resulting product is seen as a consequence of a deficient mapping or transformation. Whatever the reason is, the correct approach is to detect the problem and to adjust the model compilation process accordingly.

However, we must admit that some issues with the generated code, especially during the first experiences in a model compilation environment, are easily solvable at the programming language level. This is the second possible option, which involves only the programmer role and is not as recommendable as the previous one because it violates the fundamental notion of model compilation, although it may be quick and efficient in very specific situations. As stated before, acting in this way has a justification based on the current industrial environment, in which the first implementations of model compilers are starting to be presented, although these are not mature enough yet.

When a development process based on model compilation is being adopted, the development team must strive to reach a balance between:

- The definition of model compilation processes for software platforms that produce applications that satisfy most of their requirements, so that they can be systematically applied to as many cases as possible.
- The manual tweaking of generated code, which in any case would affect only a tiny fraction of the total code obtained.

A correct balance permits the application of a single model compilation process to the development of multiple applications that only rarely require manual adjustments by the programmers. In some cases, it is even possible that no manual tweaking is necessary at all.

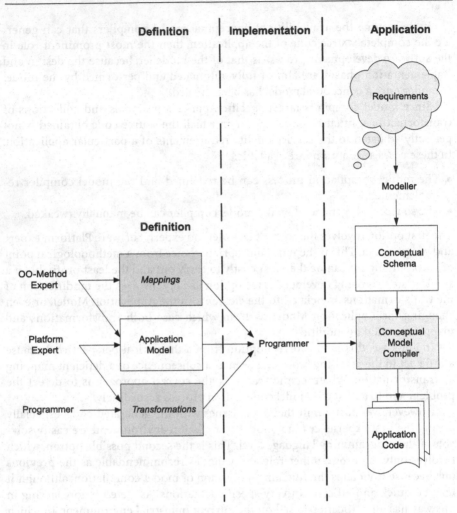

Fig. 21.2 Roles and phases in the OO-Method software development process.

We must emphasize that manual modifications of code are not intended to supply functionality not provided by the conceptual model, but to cater for aspects not contemplated by the model compilation process. If missing or incorrect functionality is detected in the generated code, then the design of the Application Model, mappings and transformations must be revised and fixed appropriately, since OO-Method is assumed to be capable of expressing any required functionality at the conceptual model level.

00-Method Implementations

The document "MDA Guide version 1.0.1" of the OMG (Miller and Mujerki 2003) states that a technological proposal needs to include a PIM and at least one PSM in order to be adopted. In addition, an implementation, or the commitment to produce a working implementation within one year, must exist.

It is evident that the ideas presented in this book can be used in practice only if they are implemented in tools. This is why we wish to close this book by providing concrete working references where all the discussed technology can be put into practice and can be properly proved. Currently, the OO-Method approach is commercially implemented by the OLIVANOVA Model Execution technology (CARE 2006), which basically includes:

- the OLIVANOVA Modeler
- the OLIVANOVA Transformation Engines

This makes it possible to check in practice the validity of the software process defended in this book. The OLIVANOVA software production environment goes beyond traditional and partial code generation (such as offered by CASE tools), providing a full-fledged operational method based on a model compilation process. From this point of view, OLIVANOVA is a fundamental tool in the emerging field of Model Engineering (i.e. Conceptual Model-Based Software Engineering).

The most relevant aspects of OLIVANOVA are now briefly discussed.

22.1 OLIVANOVA Modeler

OLIVANOVA Modeler is an OO-Method conceptual model editing and validation tool. Its features include:

- Support for the four models: objects, dynamic, functional and presentation.
- Support for legacy view modelling.
- Formula creation wizards.
- Automatic model validation.

- Creation of models from:
  - other existing OLIVANOVA Modeler models,
  - models created by third-party tools, using the XMI format,
  - database schemas.
- Support for cooperative modelling.
- Automatic generation of documentation for any model.
- Automatic generation of model metrics.

Since the four types of models as well as legacy views are supported, modellers can effectively specify the necessary functionality, plus relations to legacy systems, in a conceptual model.

Different kinds of formulae, which play a central role in the specification of certain conceptual primitives, can be easily created by using a full range of wizards and assistance tools.

OLIVANOVA Modeler is not a mere drawing tool or a conventional modelling tool. Since it is based on a formal specification language supported by precise semantics, it can formally validate models. These validations can be partial, each time a model element is created or altered, or they can be global, as a step preceding model compilation. In either case, the model validation feature highlights the parts of the model containing the errors and indicates the possible causes, so that modellers can quickly solve the problems.

Any conceptual model created with OLIVANOVA Modeler includes, in addition to the model itself, additional information about the properties of the model, so that the tool can automatically generate a number of metrics (such as statistics and functional size metrics) and documentation in different formats.

In MDA parlance, we can say that OLIVANOVA Modeler is a PIM editing and validation tool that implements a model repository that can be exported into XML format for interchange with other tools.

22.2 OLIVANOVA Transformation Engines

The OLIVANOVA Transformation Engines are implementations of different OO-Method model compilation processes.

Each transformation engine implements a conceptual schema repository, an application model repository, a collection of mappings and a collection of transformations.

The conceptual schema repository is common to all the transformation engines, and can load a conceptual model from an interchange XML file produced by OLIVANOVA Modeler. Its hierarchical structure reflects the XML layout, and a simple API is provided to query and compute derived information necessary for the transformation process.

Mappings are implemented as operations that read data from the conceptual model repository and create data into the application mode repository, assigning values to the appropriate properties. The application model repository contains elements associated to each conceptual model element, as well as additional information necessary to implement the application execution strategy for the specific software platform in each transformation engine.

Transformations read data from the application model repository and create the corresponding chunks of source code. They are also implemented as operations that read the properties of each element in the application model (the variable part in the transformation), and combine these with the fixed parts provided by the transformations to produce a code chunk. The combination of all the code chunks thus generated comprises the complete source code of the final application.

In MDA parlance, we can say that each OLIVANOVA Transformation Engine is a PIM-to-PSM and PSM-to-IM transformation tool.

Conclusions

The software development process presented in this book defends a concrete premise that can be summarized in the following statement of Prof. Antoni Olivé (Olivé 2005):

"To develop an information system it is necessary and sufficient to define its conceptual schema".

This idea appears in the work and proposals of some prestigious researchers. Toni Morgan defines his idea of using "Extreme Non-Programming" (Morgan 2002) as an operative alternative to failures obtained through years and years of using programming techniques in the area of the solution space as a software development method. Like us, Prof. Morgan argues that the basic activity in software development should be the modelling, and not the programming. The final objective is to make true the statement "the Model is the Code", rather than "the Code is the Model".

Following the same line of thought, Prof. Antoni Olivé introduced, in his keynote speech at the International Conference on Advanced Information Systems Engineering (CAISE) in 2005 (Olivé 2005), that the great challenge faced by the computer science community is to make it possible to achieve Conceptual Schema-Centred Development.

In "Model Driven Architecture: Principles and Practice", Alan Brown also emphasizes the role that modelling has, and has had, in software engineering, considered this critical in the successful development of business solutions.

Although for years this objective has been referenced by different authors in different ways, the reality is that automation in the software development has never been achieved until now. In the most advanced software processes based on model transformation, design, programming and testing continue requiring a substantial manual effort. The reality is that at the moment, in the most widely used developing methods, the true automation of building systems does not play a significant role.

In that context, this book accurately documents a method that makes real the appearance of a new programming paradigm centred in the execution of conceptual models, insisting that what allows us to reach promises of development based on models is not the transformation technology of models itself but rather the fact that models can describe the functionality of a system in a complete and precise manner, independently of considerations of design and implementation. At a time when standards such as MDA generalise types of strategies based on *models transformation*, the moment has finally arrived for software processes that really automate the production of software from conceptual schemas. OO-Method provides such a method, offering a precise set of conceptual primitives, all of them semantically characterized in a precise form in the context of an OO conceptual model.

Technological and conceptual bases of the method are justified in the book, linking with the philosophical tradition related to all thinkers who, during history, have tackled the problem of recognizing world components from different points of view, that is, have tried to explain how to model this.

Conceptual patterns from which system models can be created are introduced. In the book, it is shown how to associate each one of those conceptual patterns (problem space) with their related software representation (solution space). On this point, we reach a logical conclusion: the implementation of these mappings between conceptual patterns and software representations makes a solid base on which to develop a Conceptual Schema Compiler.

With this, three fundamentals aspects of the software development process centred in conceptual schemas are achieved: explicit, executable and timing evolutive.

- It is *explicit*, because it allows us to specify the functionality of the modelled system in a correct and complete manner. The schema is specified in a domain-independent language with formal and declarative support – which makes it possible to validate correctness and completeness – avoiding design and implementation considerations. All these reasons lead to the construction of tools that enable validating and executing the system specification represented by the Conceptual Schema.
- The schema is *executable* by definition: the unique description that must be done is the conceptual schema by itself. Whichever other description is internal to the system. The person who models focuses his/her efforts on *what* (*what* the system is), and not on *how* (*how* the system is going to be implemented in a particular software technology). The model-transformation process provided is automatic and complete. This is the only way of being at the front of a Conceptual Schema Compiler, as the OO-Method case is, compared with other existing advanced tools.
- Finally, the conceptual schema must be adaptable to the habitual changes in any system (evolution of schema). This means that if the system functions change, then it will be necessary to change only the corresponding conceptual schema. These changes will propagate in an automatic form to the software components that are affected.

In conclusion, the book explains the fundaments of the OO-Method, a method of conceptual schemas software production that becomes a significant tool for all professional software developers who wish to enter into the fascinating world of the Model Transformation supported by Conceptual Models Compilers.

References

ADT (2006) Application Development Trends
    (http://www.adtmag.com/poll.asp?pollId=134)

Astesiano E, Reggio G (2004) Tight structuring for precise UML-based requirement specifications, radical innovations of software and systems engineering in the future. Proc 9th Int Worksh RISSEF 2002. Springer, Berlin Heidelberg New York, Lecture Notes in Computer Science vol 2941, pp. 16–34

Bjorner D, Hoare CAR, Langmaack H (eds) (1990) Vdm '90: Vdm and Z-formal methods in software development. Springer, Berlin Heidelberg New York, Lecture Notes in Computer Science vol 428

Booch G (1994) OO Analysis and design with applications. Addison-Wesley, Reading, MS

Booch G, Rumbaugh J, Jacobson I (1997) UML, version 1. Rational Software, Rational Software Corporation, Santa Clara, CA, USA

Brown A (2004) Model driven architecture: Principles and practice. In: Journal on Software and Systems Modelling. Springer, Berlin Heidelberg. Volume 3, Number 4, December, 2004, pp 314–327

CARE (2006) OlivaNova. The Programming Machine. CARE Technologies
    (www.care-t.com)

Ceri S, Fraternali P (1996) Designing database applications with objects and rules (the IDEA methodology). Addison-Wesley, Reading, MS

Ceri S, Fraternali P, Matera M (2001) Conceptual modeling of data-intensive web applications. IEEE Internet Computing 6(4):20–30

Chen PP (1976) Entity-relationship model: towards a unified view of data. ACM Trans Database Systems 1(1):9–36

Clyde SW, Embley DW, Woodfield SN (1992) Tunable formalism in object-oriented system analysis: meeting the needs of both theoreticians and practitioners. In: Paepke A. SIGPLAN Notices 27(10), Vancouver, British Columbia, Canada Proc OOPSLA'92, Vancouver, pp 452–465

Coad P, Yourdon E (1990) Object-oriented analysis. Yourdon Press, Upper Saddle River, NJ

Coleman D, Arnold P, Bodoff S, Dollin S, Gilchrist H, Hayes F, Jeremes P (1994) Object-oriented development. The fusion method. Prentice-Hall, Englewood Cliffs, NJ

CREWS (1996) CREWS (Cooperative Requirements Engineering with Scenarios) Tech rep, ESPRIT Project Programme 21.903, CRI, University Paris 1 - Sorbonne

DeMarco T (1979) Structured analysis and system specification, Prentice-Hall PTR, Upper Saddle River, NJ

Douglas P, Alliger G, Goldberg R (1996) Client-server and object-oriented training. Computer 9(6):80–84

Dubois E (1995) The Albert II language: on the design and the use of a formal specification language for requirements analysis. PhD Thesis, Computer Science Department, University of Namur, Namur

Esdi (1993) ESDI S.A. OBLOG CASE V1.0. User's Guide. ESDI, Lisbon

Estrada H, Martínez A, Pastor O (2003) Goal-based business modeling oriented towards late requirements generation. In: Il-Yeol Song, Liddle S, Tok Wang Ling, Scheuermann P (eds) Conceptual modeling – ER 2003. Proc 22nd Int Conf Conceptual Modeling, October 2003, Chicago, IL. Springer, Berlin Heidelberg New York, LNCS 2813, pp 277–291

Falkenberg ED, Hesse W, Lindgreen P, Nilsson BE, Han Oei JL, Rolland C, Stamper RK, Van Assche FJM, Verrijn-Stuart AA, Voss K (1998) A framework of information system concepts: the FRISCO Report. IFIP

France RB, Ghosh S, Dinh-Trong T, Solberg A (2006) Model-driven development using UML 2.0: promises and pitfalls. IEEE Computer 39(2), Los Alamitos,CA February 2006, pp 59–66

Gane C, Sarson T (1979) Structured systems analysis: tools and techniques. Prentice-Hall, Englewood Cliffs, NJ, Professional Technical Reference

Gery E, Harel D, Palachi E (2002) Rhapsody: a complete life-cycle model-based development system. IFM 2002, Turku, Finland, May 15-18, 2002. Springer, Berlin Heidelberg, Lecture Notes in Computer Science 2335, pp 1–10

Griethuysen J (ed) (1982) Concepts and terminology for the conceptual schema and the information base. ANSI, New York, publ no ISO/TC97/SC5-N695

Harel D (1984) Dynamic logic. In: Gabbay DM, Guenthner F (eds) Handbook of Philosophical Logic II. Reidel, Dordrecht, pp 497–694

Harel D (1987) Statecharts: a visual formalism for complex systems. Sci Computer Programming 8(3):231–274

Harel D, Gery E (1997) Executable object modeling with statecharts. Computer 30(7):31–42

Harel D, Naamad A (1996) The STATEMATE semantics of statecharts. ACM Trans Software Eng Methodol (TOSEM) 5(4):293–333

Harel D, Pnueli A, Schmidt J, Sherman R (1987) On the formal semantics of statecharts. In: Proc Symp Logic in Computer Science. Computer Science Press, New York, pp 54–64

Hartmann T, Saake G, Jungclaus R, Hartel P, Kusch J (1994) Revised version of the modeling language Troll (Troll version 2.0). Technische Universität Braunschweig Informatik-Berichte 94-03

Hatley DJ, Pirbhai IA (1987) Strategies for real-time system specification. Dorset House, New York

Hoare CAR (1985) Communicating sequential processes. Prentice-Hall, Englewood Cliffs, NJ, International Series in Computer Science

Insfran E (2003) A requirements engineering approach for object-oriented conceptual modeling. PhD Thesis, DSIC, Universidad Politécnica de Valencia, Valencia

Jackson RB, Embley DW, Woodfield SN (1994) Automated support for the development of formal object-oriented requirements specification. In: Proc CAISE'94, Utrecht, 1994. Springer, Berlin Heidelberg New York, LNCS 811, pp 135–148

Jacobson I, Christerson M, Jonsson P, Overgaard G (1992) OO Software engineering. A use case driven approach. Addison-Wesley, Reading, MS

Jungclaus R, Hartmann T, Saake G, Sernadas C (1991) Introduction to Troll. A language for object oriented specification of information system. Proc 2nd Int IS-CORE Worksh, 1991, Imperial College, London

Kabira (2006) http://www.kabira.com

Kennedy Carter (2006) http://www.kc.com

Lauesen S (1998) Real-life object-oriented systems. IEEE Software, Los Alamitos, CA, USA

Letelier P, Sánchez P, Ramos I, Pastor O (1998) OASIS 3.0. Un enfoque formal para el modelado conceptual orientado a objetos. Servicio de Publicaciones Universidad Politécnica de Valencia, Valencia, SPUPV 98.4011

Liddle SW, Embley DW, Woodfield SN (1995) Unifying modeling and programming through an active, object-oriented model-equivalent programming language. In: Proc 14th Int Conf Object-Oriented and Entity-Relationship Modeling OOER'95, 13–15 December 1995, Gold Coast, Australia. Springer, Berlin Heidelberg New York, LNCS 1021, pp 55–64

Liu S, Offutt AJ, Ho-Stuart C, Sun Y, Ohba M (1998) SOFL: a formal engineering methodology for industrial applications. IEEE Trans Software Eng 24(1):24–45

Martínez A, Pastor O, Estrada H (2004) A pattern language to join early and late requirements. In: Anais WER04 Worksh Engenharia de Requisitos, 9–10 Dezembro 2004, Tandil, Argentina, pp 51–64 (accessible from WER Papers)

MDA (2006) Model Driven Arquitecture (http://www.omg.org/mda)

Mentor (2006)
http://www.acceleratedtechnology.com/embedded/nuc_modeling.html

Messeguer J (1990) A logical theory of concurrent objects.
In: Proc OOPSLA/ECOOP'90, ACM Press, New York, NY, USA, pp 101–115

Miller J, Mujerki J (eds) (2003) MDA Guide version 1.0.1. 12th June 2003,
http://www.omg.org/docs/omg/03-06-01.pdf

Milner R (1980) A calculus of communicating systems. Springer, Berlin Heidelberg New York

Morgan T (2002) Business rules and information systems – aligning IT with business goals. Addison-Wesley, Reading, MS

OlivaNova (2006) Care Technologies, Denia, Spain (http://www.care-t.com)

Olivé A (2004) On the role of conceptual schemas in information systems development. Ada-Europe 2004:16–34

Olivé A (2005) Conceptual schema-centric development: a grand challenge for information systems research. In: Proc Advanced Information Systems Engineering 17th Int Conf, CAISE 2005, 13–17 June 2005, Porto. Springer, Berlin Heidelberg New York, Lecture Notes in Computer Science vol 3520, pp 1–15

OMG (Object Management Group) http://www.omg.org

Parnas DL (1972) A technique for software module specification with examples. CACM 15(5):330–336

Pastor O (1992) Diseño y desarrollo de un entorno de producción automática de software basado en el modelo orientado a objetos. PhD Thesis, DSIC, Universidad Politécnica de Valencia, Valencia

Pastor O, Molina JC (2006) Well-formed formulas for the OO-Method. Care Technologies Tech Rep December 2005 (www.care-t.com)

Pastor O, Ramos, I (1995) OASIS 2.1.1: a class-definition language to model information systems using an object-oriented approach. Servicio de Publicaciones Universidad Politécnica de Valencia, Valencia, SPUPV 95-788, Depósito legal V-1285-1995

Pastor O, Hayes F, Bear S (1992) OASIS: an OO specification language. In: Proc CAISE-92 Conf, Springer, Berlin Heidelberg New York, LNCS 593, pp 348–363

Pastor O, Fons J, Pelechano V, Abrahão SM (2006) Conceptual modelling of web applications: the OOWS approach. In: Mendes E, Mosley N (eds) Web engineering: theory and practice of metrics and measurement for web development. Springer, Berlin Heidelberg New York, pp 277–302

pUML (2004) The precise UML Group (http://www.cs.york.ac.uk/puml/)

Raistrick C, Francis P, Wright J, Carter C, Wilkie I (2004) Model driven architecture with executable UML. Cambridge University Press, Cambridge

Rational (2006) http://www.rational.com/modelingcd/

Rossi G, Schwabe D (2001) Object-oriented web applications modeling. In: Information modeling in the new millennium. IGI Publishing, Hershley, PA, USA, pp 463–484

Rumbaugh J, Blaha M, Permerlani W, Eddy F, Lorensen W (1991) Object oriented modeling and design. Prentice-Hall, Englewood Cliffs, NJ

Selic B, Gullekson G, Ward PT (1994) Real-time object-oriented modeling. Wiley, New York

Sernadas A, Sernadas C, Ehrich HD (1987) OO Specification of databases: an algebraic approach. In: Stocker PM, Kent W (eds) Proc VLDB87. Morgan Kauffmann, San Francisco, CA, USA, pp 107–116

Spivey M (1992) The Z-notation: a Reference Manual. Prentice-Hall, Englewood Cliffs, NJ

UML (2004) The Object Management Group, Unified Modeling Language: Superstructure, version 2.0. OMG doc formal/05-07-04

Ward PT, Mellor SJ (1991) Structured development for real-time systems. Prentice-Hall, Englewood Cliffs, NJ, Professional Technical Reference

Wegner P, Zdonik SB (1988) Inheritance as an incremental modification mechanism or what like is and isn't like. In: Proc ECOOP'88 European Conf Object-Oriented

Programming, Oslo, 15–17 August, 1988. Springer, Berlin Heidelberg New York, Lecture Notes in Computer Science vol 322, pp 55–77

Wieringa RJ (1990) Algebraic foundations for dynamic conceptual models. PhD Thesis, Department of Mathematics and Computer Science, Vrije Universiteit, Amsterdam

Wieringa RJ (1991) Steps towards a method for the formal modeling of dynamic objects. Data Knowledge Eng 6:509–540

Wieringa RJ, Feenstra RB (eds) (1994) Information systems: correctness and reusability. Selected Papers IS-CORE Worksh, Esprit IS-CORE Work Group, Vrije Universiteit, Amsterdam

Wieringa RJ, Jungclaus R, Hartel P, Hartmann T, Saake G (1993) OMTROLL object modeling in TROLL. In: Lipeck UW, Koschorrek G (eds) Abstr Vol Int Worksh Information Systems – Correctness and Reusability, IS-CORE'93. September 1993, Hanover

Wirfs-Brock R, Wilkerson B, Wiener L (1990) Designing object oriented software. Prentice-Hall, Englewood Cliffs, NJ

Yourdon E, Constantine LL (1979) Structured design: fundamentals of a discipline of computer program and systems design. Prentice-Hall, Upper Saddle River, NJ

Index

Action   77, 118
Action Hierarchy Tree   184
Agent Relationships   76
Aggregation   76, 84
Application Model Repository   269
Argument Dependency Presentation
    Pattern   157
Argument Grouping Presentation Pattern
    155
Association   76, 81
Association Relationships
    Legacy View   203
Attribute Value Expressions
    Legacy View   197
Attributes   56, 58

Behavioural compatibility
    Specialisation   95

Cardinal Evaluations   141
Carrier Event   97
Change events
    Association   92
Class   55
Clusters   112
Completeness   22, 31, 36, 215, 216, 231, 294
Composition   76, 87
Conceptual Model Repository   269
Conceptual Modelling Compilation   235
Constant
    Attribute   61
Control Condition   120
Correctness   22, 31, 36, 215, 216
Creation Events
    Associations   90

Defined Selection Presentation Pattern
    153
Deletion events
    Association   92
Derivations in Associations   89
Derived
    Attribute   61
Destroy
    Events   64
Destruction Events
    Association   91
Display Set Presentation Pattern   165
Dynamic Model   116, 223

Effective Visibility   79
Entry Presentation Pattern   151
Evaluation   139
Event Execution
    Execution Model   244
Events   63
Execution Model   36, 42, 43, 50, 239, 241,
    245, 250, 255, 278, 285
Execution of Global Operations
    Execution Model   255
Execution of Global Transactions
    Execution Model   254
Execution of Legacy Events
    Execution Model   250
Execution of Legacy Local Operations
    Execution Model   253
Execution of Legacy Local Transactions
    Execution Model   251

Filter Execution   256
Filter Presentation Pattern   159

Freeing Events
   Specialisation   97
FRISCO   49
Functional Model   64, 137, 224

Generalisation   99
Global Operations   124
Global Transactions   124, 131

Human–Computer Interaction (HCI)   35,
   147, 273

Insertion events
   Association   92
Instance Interaction Unit   172, 175
Integrity Constraints   56, 73
Interface   79
Internal Action   118

Legacy View   192
Liberator Events
   Specialisation   97

Mappings   265
Master/Detail Interaction Unit   172, 181
Model-Based   XIII, 22, 41, 43, 289
Model-Driven   41
Moderate realism   4

Navigation Presentation Pattern   167
New
   Events   63
Nominalism   4

OASIS   29, 42, 43, 45, 49, 50, 59, 87, 124, 138,
   215, 216, 274, 282
Object Model   55, 83, 115, 148, 182, 192,
   203, 213, 217
Object model   209
Operation Execution
   Execution Model   249
Operations   71
Order Criterion Presentation Pattern   164
Own
   Events   64

Packages   112
Parallel Composition   104
Particulars   3
Permanent
   Specialisation   97
PIM (Platform-Independent Model)   131,
   147

PIM (Platform-Independent Model)   49
Population Interaction Unit   172, 178
Preconditions   71
Presentation Model   35, 147, 225
PSM (Platform-Specific Model)   131, 147
PSM (Platform-Specific Model)   49

Query Execution
   Execution Model   255

Realism   4
Role
   Association   82
   Specialisation   96

Service Interaction Unit   172
Services   56
Shared
   Events   64
Shared Events
   Association   93
Signature compatibility
   Specialisation   95
Situation Evaluations   141
Specialisation   76, 95
Specialisation Relationships
   Legacy View   206
State Evaluations   141
State Transition Diagrams   116
States
   State Transition Diagram   116
Subsystems   112

Temporality
   Association   82
Temporary
   Specialisation   96
Transaction Execution
   Execution Model   247
Transactions   69
Transformations   266
Transitions
   State Transition Diagram   116
Triggers   124, 125

Universal
   Specialisation   97
Universals   3

Variable
   Attribute   61
View   80